Durham
My Hometown

11-29-90

Best wishes to Gray
murdock, son of my
good friends elizabeth
and Henry murdock.

—George E. Lougee Jr.

Durham
My Hometown

George E. Lougee, Jr.

Carolina Academic Press
Durham, North Carolina

International Standard Book Number: 0-89089-435-3
Library of Congress Number: 90-84231
Printed in the United States of America

Carolina Academic Press
700 Kent Street
Durham, North Carolina 27701
(919) 489-7486

Dedication

Dedicated to those early day pioneers who, with enterprise and forethought, made Durham a tobacco empire and a textile giant; all reinforced with a deep sense of religious guidance.

The author wishes to thank the Durham Morning Herald for their permission to use his articles in this collection, and is grateful and appreciative for the generosity of George Watts Hill and Central Carolina Bank. He thanks Terry Sanford for his assistance in making this publication possible. Finally, he thanks Mayapriya Long and John Hughes of Carolina Academic Press for their careful attention to the production of this book.

Many of the photographs, and all of the articles in this collection were originally published in the Durham Morning Herald, and are reprinted with permission of the Durham Morning Herald Co., Inc. of Durham, N.C.

There was no attempt by the author to cover all of the important events, dates and pioneers of Durham through its some 136 years. Rather, the author has tried to relate personalities, places, and events which excited his pen, typewriter, and computer, and reflected more on the twentieth century. Should there be errors in his endeavors, he is most apologetic.

Contents

1

Origins and Comparisons

When Dr. Bartlett Snipes Durham, a bachelor, gave four acres of land for a depot of the North Carolina Railroad in 1852, the station was named in his honor. Dr. Durham was named its agent.

William Pratt, landowner and operator of a general store in the little town, refused to donate land for a depot because he feared trains would frighten the horses of his store customers and he would lose their trade. His refusal saved our town from being called Prattsville. Imagine our town baseball team being called "The Prattsville Bulls."

The little doctor never dreamed that Durham would become the largest of the nation's 10 Durhams.

Dr. Durham Gambled on Future and Won Enduring Fame in City

Dr. Bartlett Snipes Durham, Orange County country physician, unknowingly traded four acres of land for enduring fame and two burials.

After leaving his home some 12 miles west of Chapel Hill, Dr. Durham moved 24 miles east to set up an office-residence on a plot of ground now occupied by the Durham Hosiery Mill on Corcoran Street. The year was about 1848.

The handsome bachelor, calling his new quarters "Pandora's Box," had purposely and geographically situated himself 30 miles from Graham, 30 miles from Pittsboro, 30 miles from Roxboro, 30 miles from Oxford, and 30 miles (then) from Raleigh.

The North Carolina Railroad Co. expressed a desire to set up a railroad station in the little settlement which was without true name. Gambling on the future, Dr. Durham offered the railroad four acres of land. The offer was accepted. The community honored the generous physician by naming the settlement after him. Four years later, in 1854, the railroad was completed.

Thus was born the city of Durham through the benevolence of a man of few worldly goods.

Dr. Durham's skill as a medical practitioner was still in demand in the older village of Chapel Hill where he was highly esteemed, and when he died of pneumonia in 1858 at the age of 35, his body was laid in state in that hamlet's little hotel. A severe freeze and snowstorm had hit the area and when the physician's body was placed in a sealed iron coffin and buried deep in the frozen soil of the Snipes burial ground at Antioch Church, Orange County, the corpse too was frozen.

Seventy-five years later, in 1933, The Durham chapter of the American Business Club, through the cooperation of the Durham-Orange Historical Society, and Hampton Rich, official of the Boone Trail Association, announced that the remains of Dr. Durham would be exhumed and brought to Durham for ceremony and reburial. The body was exhumed on June 27 of that year, and hundreds of persons crowded into little Antioch Church for memorial services. In the crowd were at least three persons who had attended his funeral in 1858.

Dr. S. B. Turrentine, president of Greensboro College, made the principal address for the occasion. 87-year-old "Uncle" Mebane Edwards, 10 at the time of the first funeral, related its details in a brief speech.

When brought to Durham in the same iron casket and placed in the rear of the Hall-Wynne Funeral Chapel, Dr. Durham's body was found to be in a state of perfect preservation. The features of the face were easily distinguishable, and the collar, tie, and spectacles were all in place.

According to Durham Attorney R. O. Everett, who with Durham newsman Wyatt Dixon and Duke Prof. W. K. Boyd were members of the historical society, the body was "still frozen and the face was identical to his picture until the warm air caused disintegration."

Thousands of people, including residents of neighboring towns, came here to view through the coffin's glass pane the remains and remark about the miracle of preservation by freeze during the three-quarters of a century it remained under the red soil of Orange County. It was not until Jan. 1, 1934 that the casket was reburied in a beautiful spot of new Maplewood Cemetery donated by a grateful City of Durham.

The ceremony was simple and brief but hundreds of people, including Dr. Durham's relatives, were on hand for the services. Shortly afterwards a monument was erected at the gravesite with an epitaph which concluded with the Egyptian adage: "The merit belongs to the beginner should his successor do even better." This line was suggested by Lawyer Everett.

Later a relative of Dr. Durham's through marriage, Mrs. J. Ed Stagg, who was the niece of tobacco magnate Ben Duke, gave to Durham County a por-

This metal plaque of Dr. Bartlett Snipes Durham, for whom the town is named, is located at the old county courthouse.

trait of the illustrious physician. The picture was placed on the wall of Superior Courtroom just above the judge's bench. Four other prominent persons, all attorneys, occupied similar places of honor on the wall. On the extreme left side was the picture of the late Victor S. Bryant, father of Durham Attorney Victor S. Bryant Sr.

Bryant, a native of Mecklenburg County, had first moved to Roxboro before making his home and setting up practice in Durham. He was considered the outstanding trial lawyer of the area.

Between the pictures of Bryant and Dr. Durham was the portrait of Judge Robert W. Winston. Winston was first judge of Granville County and then judge of the old 10th Judicial District. He resigned the judgeship to come to Durham to join W. W. Fuller in the practice of law. Judge Winston also was to become a partner of Bryant.

The picture of Fuller was next to that of Dr. Durham. Fuller, a native of Raleigh, is credited with the legal organization of Durham County in 1881. He moved to Durham the following year and legally organized the American Tobacco Co.

The picture of Judge Howard A. Foushee, a native of Person County, was placed next to that of Fuller. Foushee came to Durham to practice law with J. S. Manning who was to become the campaign manager of Gov. W. W. Kitchen. As Manning's assistant in that venture Foushee was rewarded with a judgeship. He died while serving on the bench.

When Durham County remodeled the courthouse several years ago and made three courtrooms from the old large single courtroom, the pictures were removed and placed in storage at the County Home. The pictures have been available to members of the family who desired to claim them.

There have been several explanations why the pictures did not again occupy conspicuous public places of prominence in the courtroom. Some say that the new courtrooms have low ceilings and small wall space and that the pictures would not appear at their best. Others contend that there is a feeling of jealousy as to whose pictures would be placed in the courtrooms. And even others say there have been recommendations that the pictures of President Franklin D. Roosevelt, Judge A. R. Wilson, old county commissioners, and the North Carolina chief justice of the Supreme Court should be included, along with others.

"There was just no end in sight, so rather than incur ill feelings the pictures went from public view," was the way one county spokesman put it.

Of the Nation's 10 Durhams, the Largest is in N.C.

Tobacco, a weed whose pungent odors are repulsive to many but whose fragrance reminds countless others of money, changed Durham, N.C. from a dusty crossroads railway station to a center of industry, education, and medicine.

With its population of 100,831, according to the *1982 Rand-McNally Commercial Atlas & Marketing Guide,* this one-time boom town has nearly five times the population of all the nation's nine other Durhams put together. The Tar Heel city is not only the only Durham in the south, but it is also the only Durham in the nation to be called a city.

Durham, N.C., founded 130 years ago, is not the oldest Durham in these United States. In fact, it is 171 years younger than Durham, Conn., which was founded in 1708. It is likewise younger than the Durhams of New Hampshire, New York, California, and Pennsylvania. Durham, Okla. is the newest Durham, having been founded just 83 years ago. Other Durhams are in Missouri, Arkansas, and Kansas.

Durham, Okla. was founded with a post office and a general store. Wheat and cattle are the mainstays, but a considerable amount of cotton and broom corn and combine maize are also grown there. That Durham is situated seven miles south of the Antelope Hills near the Texas border.

Durham, Ark., a vacation spot, was named after early settlers. Its total citizenry is only 25. It is a scenic village in the foothills of the Ozark Mountains. The Frisco Railroad built a road through Arkansas's Durham soon after the Civil War, and timber became the leading business.

Durham, N.H., whose 12,200 University of New Hampshire students better the town's permanent population of 10,652, derived its name from Durham, England. The town has little agriculture, no industry, and is not a resort area. It is situated on the Oyster River and borders on Great Bay. The university was founded in 1866 as the New Hampshire College of Agriculture and the Mechanics Arts of Hanover, N.H. In 1893 the school was moved to Durham and in 1923 became a university.

Durham, Calif., located in the almond country, is within five miles of the rugged Sierra, Nev., mountains. Its population is 950. The town was named after Robert Durham, one of the first settlers. It was founded in 1848 by farmers raising wheat, barley, and cattle.

Durham, Conn., a town of 7,500, has the Old New England Town Meeting form of government. It was named in 1704 and incorporated in 1708. There is an excellent school system and firefighting program, and it has an active Little

League baseball program that provides trips to major league games in New York and Boston's Fenway Park. The town is holiday-conscious.

Durham, N.Y., named after Durham Conn., is in agriculture and dairy country at the foothills of the Catskill Mountains. The census shows 2,283 persons. It was founded in 1784 by pioneers who came across the country from Durham, Conn., and there up the Hudson River to the Catskills, and thence inland.

Durham, Mo., is a suburb of Quincy, Ill. It is 17 miles west of the Mississippi River and has a population of 200. The town hasn't grown and has been called a wide place in the middle of the road.

Durham, Kan. is typical of the predominantly rural areas of the Midwest. It was named after Bull Durham cattle, and its population is 130. The town celebrated its 60th anniversary in May 1947 with a historical pageant and games, a parade, a grand lottery, and the sporting of oldtime beards. The famous Santa Fe Trail of frontier days ran just one-half mile west of where Durham now stands. The nationally known figure of a "Durham Bull" is the town's office letterhead. The largest nearby city in Wichita.

Benjamin Franklin and Gen. George Taylor, another signer of the Declaration of Independence, are part of the history of Durham, Pa. It is a paradise for city farmers from New York City, Philadelphia, and New Jersey. Its population is 150. The town was established as an outpost of Philadelphia around 1720. In Colonial times, the Indians periodically raided Durham, Pa. The original furnace was built at Durham, and the town made the first stoves in the United States. During the Revolutionary War, they made cannon balls for George Washington's army. The original homes were mostly built of stone, and Bucks County is partly noted for its antiques and its old stone houses and stone barns.

Durham, N.C., was named after Dr. Bartlett L. Durham, a genial country gentleman who donated 130 acres valued at $90, on which the North Carolina Railroad built a train station. The depot was established in 1852, with Dr. Durham as agent. Prattsburg was the name originally intended for the station site, but Mr. Pratt, the owner, refused to grant the land.

Durham can date the beginning of its prosperity to 1865, when Gen. Joseph T. Johnston of the Confederacy and Gen. William T. Sherman of the Union army came together at the old Bennett house a few miles west of town. Here they shook hands, shared a bottle of whisky and arranged the terms of surrender that ended the Civil War.

The Yankee soldiers, so the story goes, raided Durham's lone tobacco factory, taking some of the tasty leaf back to their homes. Not long afterwards they wrote for more, and a thriving business resulted.

2

Leaf's Legacy

Tobacco, next to a letter from home, has long been the prime morale booster in the military.

Until recent years Liggett & Myers and the American Tobacco Company together had paid more than 45 percent of Durham County's taxes.

But for the so-called evil habit of smoking, chewing, or dipping the product of the golden weed, there would be no Duke University, Duke Hospital, and Duke Power Company. Think upon it.

'Tobacco Row' Scene Alive with Durham's No. 1 Event

Durham's No. 1 show, its tobacco sales market, opened another season this week with millions of pounds of the golden weed being swapped for green currency.

Rigsbee Avenue, appropriately and affectionately known as "Tobacco Row," is buzzing with activity and excitement as trucks and carloads of leaf roll onto the floors of warehouses that line midtown street.

Barkers, coaxing and waving tobacco sticks, point to the doors of their warehouses for patronage from the visitors, many of whom drive here from distant points.

Tobacco market sales breathe life into the Durham economy. Everyone benefits. This is Durham's game.

The fever pitch of the tobacco market was even more noticeable in the days when tobacco was hauled in by wagon, and its owners, helpers, and horse and mule all bedded down here for the night.

Special stalls were available for the animals and sleeping quarters for the men and boys.

The streets along "Tobacco Row" were not paved and in wet and icy weather, sand and gravel and hay were scattered about for surer footing. Rigsbee Avenue seemed to be much steeper then because of the difficulty experienced by the wagons in pulling their loads in wet and slippery weather.

Medicine shows were plentiful and entertaining, and the topic of many conversations when the farmers returned home after a visit here. Con men and prostitutes too were always on hand to finagle cash out of the newly rich tobacco farmers.

Many a farmer, hungry for excitement and thrills after a long, rugged period of monotonous work, fell easy prey to the wiles of the crooks. "Knockout drops" in drinks of whisky were a favorite method the swindlers used to get the farmer under control so his wallet or money pouch could be stolen.

Those who were duped woke up sick and with sore heads, and with an even deeper pain, the knowledge that they had to return home penniless and face the wife and children and field hands.

Of course tobacco warehousemen and police constantly warned the farmers against mingling with strangers, particularly after selling their tobacco. But many did not heed the advice.

Farmers long since have been wary of glib-tongued strangers and its becoming almost rare for police to receive a complaint that a farmer has been hoodwinked out of his cash. Besides, most farmers either return almost directly home after receiving their checks, deposit the checks in a bank, or make store purchases with watched-over cash.

And when women accompany the farmers to the sales market they usually keep an eagle-eye on the scene.

Durham was a most interesting place back in the days of feather beds, outhouses, flypaper, and water wings. Town kids could visit or peer into livery stables, some of which were located in the downtown area, getting closehand views of horses, mules, and cows, and sometimes goats, sheep, pigs, and guinea.

Downtown offered such amusements as vaudeville, street cars, watering trees used by drunks to sober up, frequent trains, fire horses with steam wagons, street ice cream venders, and firework stands.

Sometimes there were such features as "human spiders," daredevil acrobats who climbed up the sides of buildings, drawing gasps and feints when they pretended to lose their footing; the "man who does not smile," a robot-like fellow who gyrated mechanically, never showing emotion in the furniture store windows in which he operated; moving picture show hypnotists, bootleggers operating around "courthouse square," homebrew smuggled into poolrooms, pressing clubs where a fellow could get a sprucing up in a hurry, barbershops with showers, boxing on the stage at the Carolina Theater, and wrestling matches in the same room in which the city council now operates. On Parrish Street square dances were held.

At El Toro (the bull) baseball park, the home orchard of the Durham Bulls baseball team, there were such attractions as donkey baseball, college and high school baseball and football, Bloomer Girls, carnivals, circuses, city schools' May Day maypole dances, professional football games, boxing matches, rodeos, visits by baseball czars Judge Kenesaw Mountain Landis and W. P. Bramham, (Babe) Didrickson pitching baseball against the immortal Babe Ruth, tugs of war between Durham firemen and policemen, songfests, and even a speech by Socialist Party leader Norman Thomas.

In tobacco warehouses there were college dances, with big fans blowing across 300-pound blocks of ice, chatauquas, expositions, dog shows, track meets and political gatherings.

There was an airplane landing field on Roxboro Road in an area between the overhead bridge and south of Club Boulevard on the west side.

There were circus parades and on Halloween nights the town turned out to march up and down Main Street from Roxboro Street to Five Points, with the climax of the occasion being the awarding of prizes on the courthouse steps to those with the best costumes, and the King and Queen. Street dancing followed on Manning Place alongside Durham Auditorium.

Former Tobacco Buyer Says Market Has Lost Excitement

Robert Henry "Bob" Johnson, 80, who turned down a singing career to follow the chant of the auctioneer, says the tobacco market now doesn't hold the excitment for him that it once did.

"Years ago they would preach quality, quality. Now they take the tobacco out of the barn, tie it up in a sheet and bring it in like it is."

"The lowest grade gets about as much money as good tobacco," he said.

Competition is now so keen that the auctioneer will usually ration out the tobacco to the buyers, Johnson said. "An unheard of thing back in the old days."

Johnson lives at 1709 Roxboro Road, a couple of miles north of "Tobacco Row" (Rigsbee Avenue) where he bought tobacco for Liggett Myers Tobacco Co., before his retirement a few years ago.

Johnson was born at Milton ("the world's largest tobacco market before the turn of the century"), one of the eight children of Robert Edward Johnson, a tobacco auctioneer.

The Johnsons moved to nearby Roxboro when Bob was one year old, and eight years afterwards came to Durham, living first on South Street and then nearby McMannen Street.

Johnson recalls the early days in Durham when there was a tobacco ware-house at the corner of Main and Corcoran Streets (now the site of the CCB Building), one on Parish Street at the spot now occupied by the Mechanics Farmers Bank and one at the foot of Church Street, where the Union Train Depot was built in 1905.

While a pupil in the public schools, Johnson's voice attracted notice. Word got around and soon he was receiving free voice lessons from Mrs. Gilmer Ward Bryant, who with her husband operated the Southern Conservatory of Music in Durham.

Johnson lived next door to a garage and in his early teens learned to drive an automobile. He obtained a job as chauffeur for tobacco magnate Ben Duke and his family. The car was a Thomas Flyer.

While not driving the car, he said he was singing or rehearsing with the Trinity College Glee Club. "I was the only member of the glee club who wasn't a student. I went on my tours with them, singing with the group and as a soloist. I was a tenor."

Johnson was also singing with a couple of quartets.

"Frank Barfield, a tobacco auctioneer here, put on a minstrel show every year and I was one of his soloists as well as singing in a quartet," he said.

Johnson joined the U.S. Army in 1917 and was stationed at Camp Lee, Petersburg, Va.

"I had been courting Lola Duke who lived near Grace Baptist Church on E. Trinity Avenue. She came to Petersburg and we were married. The minister was named Dr. Love. Lola always got a laugh out of that," he said. Mrs. Johnson died in 1968.

Upon his return to Durham in 1918, Johnson went to work for Liggett Myers' leaf department. He later was transferred to Danville to head the leaf department but returned to Durham and was placed on the tobacco market as a buyer.

A famous New York voice teacher came to Durham, heard Johnson sing and urged him to go to New York and train his voice for opera. Johnson said he already had offers from Honeyboy Evans and Al Fields minstrel shows, and Pink Lady, a national musical comedy.

"I weighed them over carefully, but decided I just didn't want to leave Durham. I was doing all right here and was among friends. Besides, show business wasn't thought too much of in those days."

But he continued to sing, performing at college football games, with quartets, local minstrels, and at beaches and hotels when his wife and daughters Marian and Laura had a yen to travel.

Johnson recalls that about 35 years ago Liggett Myers had a movie made showing the entire process of tobacco, from seeding plant beds to the manufactured product.

"The movie was appropriately called 'Tobaccoland, U.S.A.,' with most of the picture built around the tobacco-famous Ellis family in the Bahama area. The movie director and his crew would get up as early as 3:30 a.m. to get pictures of the Ellis' feeding their cattle, hogs, and horses and mules," Johnson said.

L&M later sponsored radio programs featuring well-known personalities and once a year these stars would appear in Durham to give a show, usually in Duke Indoor Stadium (now Cameron Stadium), Johnson said.

Johnson was selected by L&M to escort the stars around, but he was already something of a celebrity himself. His picture appeared in many publications as a top tobacco buyer in action at tobacco auctions.

Asked about changes in tobacco, Johnson grunted and shook his head. "We worked five days a week from 9 a.m. to 5 p.m. We'd buy by grades, selecting for both cigarettes and plug tobacco. The sorry tobacco was usually thrown into the stables or used as fertilizer."

He said that in 1931 the best of the tobacco drew few offers. "Real good tobacco brought only about two cents a pound. That same tobacco today would bring 92 to 94 cents."

Johnson chuckled again. "In the old days tobacco farmers — of course it was a bribe and you really couldn't do much for them because tobacco was strictly graded — would come to my door bringing country hams, cakes, and other things. They did the same thing to all buyers."

Long ago, Johnson said, auctioneers took 5-cent and 25-cent bids, but later the bids climbed to 50 cents and a dollar.

"The auctioneer would start off kind of easy like and then get into a chant, running the scale of prices and knock out the sale. Back then I would nod my head or raise a finger if I wanted the tobacco on my bid. The auctioneers soon learned the traits of all the buyers."

"Nowadays a buyer will hold up a finger or make a ring, the bids usually moving up by $1. The range is small now because the bidding usually starts in the 80-cent class and climbs. The auctioneer has the same chant but with a different scale," he said.

Although he has retired now, Johnson still sings in the choir at Grace Baptist Church. "It wouldn't be me if I didn't," he added.

A Durham Legend

Frank Barfield—Auctioneer with 'Heart of Gold, Voice of Silver'

Children loved him as Santa Claus, the Pied Piper, a combination of W. C. Fields and Captain Kangaroo. Their parents adored him as good Samaritan and friend.

Durham hasn't been the same since the death of J. Franklin Barfield, who frequently was introduced as "the man with a heart of gold and the voice of silver—the world's original singing auctioneer."

The stories told of Barfield's generosity and showmanship are legend. When he died in 1952 at 60 after a career as auctioneer, promoter, and city councilman (he was usually the top vote getter in winning six terms), no one has taken his place.

Barfield grew up poor in Carthage, where he completed but four years of schooling. At 11, he got his first paying job, mossing buggies for just 14 cents a day.

He was nearing manhood when he was drafted into the Army during World War I. He recalled spending 28 boring and restrained days under the heavy discipline at Camp Jackson in Columbia, S. C.

With the end of the war came job famine. Barfield, who knew something about tobacco, went to Dillon, S. C., where he persuaded a warehouseman to give him a job as an auctioneer, his first job at being the center of attraction.

He knew at once this was what he wanted to do the rest of his life. Then he was fired. The reason given by his boss was: "They can't understand you."

But Barfield was never one to worry or care much about what people thought of him. He hid his disappointment behind an air of braggadocio and set about getting new employment.

He landed in Spring Hope where he told a warehouseman he was an experienced auctioneer and was given a job.

Barfield once estimated that the tobacco he sold would reach from Durham to San Francisco. His biggest season, he said, was in Mullins, S. C., in 1937 when he sold 6.5 million pounds of tobacco in six weeks.

A large, impressive, ruddy-faced fellow with thick, bushy hair, a hearty laugh and handshake, Barfield was working the Mebane market when he came to Durham at 27 to seek real business success.

Two people were responsible for his stay in Durham: capitalist John Sprunt Hill, who gave him a job as manager of the auction department of Durham Realty & Co., and Miss Ruby Day of Person County, a pretty blonde stenographer at First National Bank.

Barfield made good at his job and the two were married in 1920. Since that time he auctioned more real estate and tobacco than any two people combined.

A vibrant personality, Barfield usually wore tailored, checked suits, a carnation in his lapel, a stickpin, and sometimes, spats. He nearly always had a big cigar clamped in his teeth, but insisted that he liked the taste of the tobacco and rarely smoked.

In driving across his sales, Barfield sometimes waved a tobacco stick, like a wand, rapier, or swagger stick.

As a real estate auctioneer, he earned the title of "Barfield the Ballyhooist." Property was sold to the music of the large brass band of his Durham Auction Co.

But on occasion, sales were more subdued. Barfield then wore what he called his English walking suit of morning trousers, cutaway coat, and high silk hat.

Two of his largest auction sales were the Rigsbee estate, amounting to about $485,000, and the Northgate subdivision.

But it was his auctioneering of tobacco that first brought him major attention. Barfield was given a one-year contract with the American Tobacco Co. to do his tobacco auctioneering chant on its popular Lucky Strike *Hit Parade* radio show. This was before the days of Speed Riggs, who appeared on the same program.

Barfield and his wife commuted between Durham and New York for his appearances. It was on these programs that he was given such titles as "World's Original Singing Auctioneer," the "Caruso of Auctioneers," and "Triple-tongued as a cornet player making a cornet flutter."

He once chanted to the tune of *Shortenin' Bread*. The song was played by Carl Huff's 56-piece orchestra.

The famous and the near-famous usually wanted to see Barfield auction on trips to Durham.

Barfield was a partner in Planters and Banner warehouses in Durham, and auctioneer for Clark's Warehouse in Mullins.

Barfield helped those less fortunate than he in several ways. One of his favorites was providing a dinner and gifts on Christmas Eve for some 1,500 underprivileged children. At Eastertime he would hold a huge Easter egg hunt with hundreds of prizes.

He and the late O. B. Wagner donated Northgate Park on Club Boulevard to the city. The city in recognition of this named the park's youth center "Barfield Center." Part of the park became a bird sanctuary. It was said that Barfield never turned down anyone in need. He bought thousands of shoes and clothing for children.

Barfield promoted several merchants expositions in tobacco warehouses in Durham. Once he went into North Durham Drug Store at the time a young woman was selling tickets to the exposition. She asked him if he wanted to buy any. Barfield, noting the grins on the faces of several bystanders, asked: "Young lady, who is putting on this thing?"

"A Mr. Barfield. I don't know him but they say he is a good man even if he talks too much." Barfield bought all of her tickets.

He helped produce minstrel shows that generated money for the old American Legion Post 7 hut on Queen Street and a camp for Boy Scouts.

Barfield, who had played some baseball as a youth, organized the Durham Auction Co. baseball team. In 1924 the team was so good it attracted big league scouts. Alan "Dusty" Cooke of Durham was to play for the New York Yankees, and several other players also became professionals.

Something of a comic, Barfield would print and distribute cards that read: "If you're so damned smart, why aren't you rich?"

A left-handed golfer, he gave up the game because it was slow and he was restless.

Barfield would drive nothing but Cadillacs. He hunted quail and deer, but he loved best his brass band, his baseball club, children, and tobacco farmers.

Barfield lost some of his zeal when his wife died of pneumonia several days after Christmas in 1943, only a week after he gave a party for more than 500 of his friends at the National Guard Armory (now the Durham Civic Center).

When Barfield died in July 1952 at the beginning of his 22nd year on the City Council, City Attorney Claude Jones said: "Mr. Barfield did a lot of service for this city and the minute books will show it. He was always a man you could rely upon to foster the interests of the people. He was a champion of the people in fact as well as theory."

Bag Tagging

Bull Durham Pouches Meant Work for Many

They were called bag taggers, sack taggers, and people with patience and nothing else to do. But way back, from the administration of Theodore Roosevelt to Franklin D. Roosevelt, the drawstrings and the tags of famous Bull Durham smoking tobacco were attached by those Durham folks.

Pay was meager, but it was a means of earning a little money and working your own hours. And it was more than that. It carried respectability, and besides, it brought folks together, like a sewing circle, pea shelling, or a corn shucking. And it put to shame the idlers.

On warm days, mostly in Edgemont and East Durham, but also throughout town, you could see groups of women and children (and a few men) seated on cane-bottom chairs on front porches or in yards, inserting yellow drawstrings about the mouth of those little white cotton bags or sacks, turning the sacks wrongside out, and then looping the strings into a hole in the round white trademark tag of Bull Durham.

Simple, certainly; demeaning, no. It was a camaraderie without equal. Sometimes there would be pitchers of cold water or lemonade, and maybe a bowl of peanuts in the shell, but it added up to more than a hen party. The background music was conversation, seat shuffling and grunting, lots of it. Talking made the chore easier and faster.

Old folks with weak and bleary eyes and arthritic fingers worn with care, and nimble-fingered children who were excited to join their elders fit in comfortably with their more skilled companions.

In cold and wet weather and at night the scene shifted to inside the house. There was never any off-season because the sacks always needed attention. Bull Durham smoking tobacco was extremely popular throughout the smoking world, and it was a mark of distinction that a cowboy in a distant western state carried a bag of it in his shirt pocket, with the unique tag with the picture of a bull, dangling outside his pocket. And the tag read: "None genuine without the bull on each package."

The name Bull Durham was inspired by the bull's head on a jar of mustard made in England. Jules Kerner of Kernersville, who called himself Reuben Rink, painted the picture of a bull on billboards and signs throughout the world, even on the pyramids of Egypt.

At the very beginning a goodly number of prudish and indignant Durham women objected to the picture of a bull being portrayed with his testicles exposed. But Rink was adamant, insisting he didn't paint cows. He won the powerful backing of Julian S. Carr, Durham philanthropist and advertising genius. So the bull on the big sign atop Blackwell's tobacco factory and elsewhere was painted as endowed. Sometime afterwards the protests subsided, but few women here were ever seen pouring the makings from a sack of Bull Durham into the cigarette papers accompanying each sack.

It was said by old-timers that the baseball term "bull pen," designating the space where pitchers warmed up, was derived from a Bull Durham sign placed behind baseball dugouts where idle players sat during a game. And there is the jail term "Bull Pen," the area where prisoners are placed together temporarily after arrest.

Will Rogers once ran a syndicated little advertisement of Bull Durham smoking tobacco, using a few choice words of wit.

But back to bag tagging. In 1905 the *Morning Herald* newspaper of Durham ran an American Tobacco Co. story about Bull Durham.

The firm said that it afforded "home employment for widows and orphans" in the process of bag tagging and stringing. "The tobacco is put up in small linen sacks and each of these sacks has to be strung, that is, place the drawstrings in it by hand. These bags are delivered in quantities at the homes of those who desire them, and after they are fixed with the string, the company 's wagon calls for the goods. Money for this work is paid at the house, and thus hundreds of widows are kept from destitution through this light but profitable employment."

In addition to stringing the bags, the story said: "There is the occupation of tagging. Every package of genuine Bull Durham smoking tobacco is marked with a small tag about the size of a quarter. The obverse side of the tag contains the picture of a bull and the reverse side an inscription: 'None genuine without the bull on each package.'

"These tags are put on by women, the tags being taken to and from the homes by the company's wagons. A good price is paid for this work and adept can tag from 5,000 to 10,000 per day without exertion. Dozens of worthy people who cannot stand heavy employment make a livelihood in this manner . . . "

And, "there is not one person in the City of Durham who is dependent on charity, a good record for a city less than 50 years old. The prosperity and affluent circumstances in which citizens find themselves in large measure is due to the American Tobacco Company."

American Tobacco also manufactured in another building "the peerless Duke Mixture" smoking tobacco.

W. T. Blackwell & Co., the parent of the American Tobacco Co., also said in the article: "Remember this! Blackwell's Bull Durham smoking tobacco, under no circumstances, will ever be packaged in any other way than in white muslin bags, like this package, put up in such sizes as are authorized by law. Any offer of this standard brand in any other shape is fraudulent."

Then about 40 years ago a Durham man, Tom Dalton, who worked at Wright Machinery here, invented a machine that put the string as well as the tag on the bags of Bull Durham smoking tobacco. He also invented the machine for packaging tea for Lipton Tea Co. in England.

Thus came the end to bag tagging by hand, and to an era that some of the old folks recall with a moist blink of nostalgic eyes.

Times changed. And so did the price of a sack of Bull Durham smoking tobacco. From the nickel, it elevated handsomely to the stipend of 30 cents. And, Bull Durham was no longer manufactured in Durham. About 25 years ago the American Tobacco Co. moved the operation to Richmond, Va.

Long-Time Operator Liked the Work, People She Met

Miss Martha Halliburton Holloway was switchboard operator and receptionist for 45 years at Liggett & Myers Tobacco Co. before retiring 10 years ago. She once knew every employee of the firm, in and out of Durham.

Known by the personnel as "Miss Hallie," she remembers every president and the various executives of L & M, back to the horse and buggy days.

She was born in the Gorman section of Durham County to William G. Holloway, who ran a country store, and Henrietta Hicks Holloway. Miss Holloway recalls that the family, including four sisters and three brothers, moved to 219 Broadway St. in the city in 1915.

"The last two years I spent in Durham High School, then located in the building now used as the City Hall, I worked from 4 p.m. to 7 p.m. at Durham Telephone Co. —as an operator," Miss Holloway said.

Upon graduation in 1920 at the age of 18, she worked during the "green season" at Liggett & Myers for five months. Then she went back to the telephone company until she was employed full time at L & M.

"The switchboard was in the lobby and there were only four outside lines and about 20 extensions," she said. "The building was new, with private offices all around the lobby. Besides myself, there were two porters stationed in the lobby. I walked to and from work every day, and when lunchtime came, I would walk home and then back to work usually with my sister Thelma, Mrs. Reuben Johnson who was a stenographer."

Laughing, she said, "Everybody walked in those days and I think it did us good. There were very few automobiles."

About 15 years ago the office building was moved on giant rollers from the southwest corner of Main and Duke streets to near the northwest corner.

"We kept working during the moving process, even though there were four air hammers going full blast at each end of the building. I remember that when I went to lunch the office was sitting in the middle of Main Street. The building was one story but it was jacked up and another story added. We had to walk the 'gang-plank' to get to our stations," she said.

At the time she was hired by L & M, W. D. Carmichael was general manager, Charles H. Livengood was superintendent of the cigarette factory, H. E. White was office manager, Eugene Cole was superintendent of the stemmery, Perry Sloan was superintendent of the leaf department, W. L. Cole was superintendent of storage, and A. J. Bullington was head of all leaf buying. All of these men are dead.

"I remember the time James B. Duke, the top executive of the firm, who had his offices in New York, came to the company during his visit to Durham for the purpose of setting up the Duke Endowment for Duke University. With him was his young daughter Doris, who was about 12 at the time. Doris later was to be known as the richest woman in the world," Miss Holloway said.

"Mr. Duke had dropped by to see Mr. Carmichael. Young Doris was a cute little blonde and very quiet and polite. We had a porter named Frank Leathers, who was 5 feet tall and looked pretty sharp in his uniform. Mr. Duke led Doris to Frank and said, 'Frank, I want you to meet my daughter Doris (an only child). She shook hands and smiled. She was about as tall as he. The next time I saw Doris was the day of her father's funeral held at Duke Memorial Methodist Church. She was wearing a plain black Chesterfield coat, with velvet collar."

She said she was always fascinated by the long distance telephone calls she handled. "I placed a lot of overseas calls to Turkey, Greece, Mexico and England."

Miss Holloway said that during her early years at L & M the company paid off its personnel with silver dollars. "I can hear that counting machine now, rattling off the payroll and the merry, metallic clinking of the coins in the pockets of the employees as they headed home or down Main Street into town where the pocket music brought envy."

She said employees didn't wear uniforms then and the girls wore pleated skirts, middy blouses, and long dresses, "kind of like 'Buster Brown' suits."

Chuckling, Miss Holloway said, "Miss Blanche Ferrell, related to me by marriage, was C. W. Toms' secretary and helped me get my job. She worked for every L & M manager until she retired."

Miss Holloway never owned an automobile and never wanted one. It was walk, walk, except when she patronized a streetcar, taxi, or accepted a ride offered by a friend.

She said L & M gave the city space between two of the plant's buildings for a fire department, and the old station steamer was pulled by two husky horses.

"Of course there was no air-conditioning—except when windows were open—and no modern elevators. The stemmery employees had wonderful voices, and they sang most of the day. People would stop along the sidewalk to listen. We also had a park with pretty walks and benches right where the Research Building is located, and there was a beautiful tree which was decorated each Christmas."

Years ago Durham and Duke University got together annually to stage a big homecoming parade and L & M always supplied one of its long, flat body trucks upon which tobacco company employees handled the golden leaf and sang spirituals.

"The company also sponsored the entertainment for the Chamber of Commerce's annual dinner. The entertainers, who were on L & M's weekly radio program, included Paul Whiteman and his orchestra, Perry Como, Bob Hope, Barbara Hutton, Arthur Godfrey, Eddie Arnold, Frances Langford, Jerry Colona, and many others. I met them all when they toured the plant," Miss Holloway said.

Asked if she smokes, she grinned. "Well, I started smoking a little when cigarettes were passed among visitors when they entered the lobby, but I quit the habit a long time before I retired."

In the early days L & M featured Chesterfields, but also manufactured several other brands such as Fatima, Piedmont, and Picayune,

Miss Holloway said that on Oct. 15, 1954, when Hurricane Hazel struck, "the switchboard (we had progressed to five operators) lit up like a Christmas tree. It was the only time I ever saw every light alive. Everybody seemed to be calling in and calling out. We just didn't know when the switchboard would blow up."

She said the happiest news she ever received through the switchboard was when Chesterfield was the No. 1 cigarette in sales.

"The saddest time was when I learned of the assassination of President John Kennedy."

Asked if she ever considered marriage, Miss Holloway laughed. "I never had time to get married. Neither did my sister Agnes, who worked as a typist for L & M. We live together here at 1521 N. Duke St."

Conceding that she was enjoying her retirement, Miss Holloway said: "But

I can hardly believe that I am retired. I really enjoyed every day I worked for L & M. Each day was a happy day with new experiences, working with fine Southern gentlemen who had good manners and were always concerned about the employees. Can you believe I never heard a cross word as long as I worked there?"

'Bulljacks' Sacked Bull Durham

Retired Foreman At American Knows Machine Well

Lloyd Edwin Winn, "Mr. Bulljack" of the American Tobacco Company, recalls making salads and desserts in a millionaires' club in New York City when he was 18.

Now 68 and retired, he said, "the pay as a pantryman at the Montwak Club was good and the tips generous, until the stock market crash." Describing the great Depression of 1929–31 as "hell," he said, "people were jumping out of windows—mostly rich citizens who had gone instant broke."

Winn said things were vastly different two years earlier in 1927, when the big city turned out to welcome Charles "Lucky" Lindbergh, who had just made the solo flight across the Atlantic.

"It was a real thrill seeing the hero, hearing the cheers and screams and watching the confetti and ticker tape thrown from skyscraper windows. What a parade! Biggest crowd I ever saw."

Winn, a farm boy from Georgia, said his parents and three brothers were living in Florida when he received word that his father had died. "I had to go to West Palm Beach to help mother straighten out the estate, and I was struck hard by the depression when I got aboard a Greyhound bus. There were so many stores closed everywhere I looked. It was real frightening and disheartening. It made a young man like myself wake up to reality, seeing so many soup lines and beggars," he said.

Winn said it took 48 hours on the non-air-conditioned bus to travel to Florida from New York. It was hot weather. "After helping my mother in Florida I went by bus to Charlotte to visit a friend. He suggested that if I didn't want to return North I might be able to get a job in a Durham tobacco factory," he said.

Winn was a bit apprehensive. He had quit school in the eighth grade, left the farm and took a job at 16 in Atlanta installing a fire prevention sprinkler. Winn said he felt lucky when hired at the American Tobacco Co. "It was at 11 a.m. on Aug. 11, 1932. I won't forget it. People were all over the railroad tracks near the factory, looking for a job."

Winn said his first job at the plant was learning to run a "bulljack," a Rube Goldberg-looking machine used in processing sacks of Bull Durham smoking tobacco.

"The pay was 25 cents an hour and I was glad to get it," he said. "I thought about my job in Atlanta when I was two years younger, a squirt who had a good job while grown men were making only $1.25 for a 10- or 12-hour day in the same furniture factory where I was putting in a sprinkler system. I thought the men would run me out of town. Now I was working in another factory and men were seeking jobs."

Asked about the rum that was placed in Bull Durham tobacco, Winn said, "Yes, it was real rum all right because some of the employees were getting tanked up on it. The company then added a chemical to the rum which made the drinkers sick. This broke their habit."

He said the bulljack was officially a Patterson Packer, named after the man who invented the machine. That machine would pack 28 bags of smoking tobacco a minute. A sacker, the man who put the sack on the machine shapes, worked alongside the machine operator.

"We had 30 bulljack machines when I started at the factory. Later, the Fowler Building was added, about 1940, and the capacity was increased to 90 bull-jacks," Winn said.

He said Bull Durham tobacco was popular around the world, and that the famed humorist Will Rogers advertised the product. "If the bags or sacks were not being properly filled, the machine had to be cut off and adjusted. Later, Wright Machinery in Durham invented a better weighing machine which was installed on the bulljack. This was a great improvement because the machine no longer had to be stopped to adjust the amount of tobacco in the bags," Winn said.

He said that before he came to Durham the bags had to be strung by hand, turned wrong-side out and tagged. Men, women and children tagged the bags, sitting on their porches or in their yards, day and night. The pay was little but sure, and little effort was required in this work.

"Then a fellow named Tom Dalton, who worked at Wright's, invented a machine which put the string as well as the tag on the bag. He also invented the machine for packaging tea for Lipton Tea Co. in England," Winn said.

"I can see Mr. Dalton now, chewing tobacco. He was a great man, but evidently, as an inventor, he wasn't paid much."

Meanwhile, Winn said he had met Mary Vaughan in Durham, and they were married Nov. 11, Armistice Day, in 1932. The Winns have two sons, Loyd Jr., of Durham and Leon, of Atlanta. They have three grandchildren.

In 1957 the Bull Durham plant was moved to Richmond, and Winn was sent there for a two-week period which turned out to last nine months. "I was a foreman then and teaching people how to operate, adjust and repair the bull-jack machines," he said. "For quite some time before then, I had been transferred to the cigarette department. I later became machinery supervisor. The company gives a fellow an opportunity. The people are wonderful and generous."

About 1956, Winn said, American Tobacco Co. sponsored the Hit Parade, a nationally popular radio program. "It was a great advertisement for our cigarettes, but for years and years before then, our product were already known, especially Bull Durham."

Winn has worked on all types of tobacco and cigarette machines and worked in all of the company's departments except the plumbing and maintenance.

"When I started at the American, 800 cigarettes per minute were produced by each machine, and when I retired three years ago the machines were each turning out 3,500 cigarettes per minute," he said proudly.

Nodding his head, he said, "no doubt about it, people will always be smoking cigarettes." Winn gave up smoking about five years ago.

Recently he set up bulljack machine No. 77 at the historical Duke Homestead in Durham. The machine, which was donated by the American Tobacco Co., was made by American Foundry Co., in Brooklyn, in 1932, and cost $5,800.

"This bulljack did not have the weighing unit and the tie bag and bagger. It had been in use in the plant there and the parts added. The bulljacks were taken to Richmond by truck and this one was returned to Durham by truck," Winn said.

Still, Winn said, "I feel that it's an old friend returned home."

3

Durham's Chroniclers, the Herald-Sun Papers

Durham's chief chroniclers, the Durham Morning Herald and The Durham Sun, sister newspapers, once were such keen rivals for news as to incite reporters and desk people alike to chicanery, insults, finger pointing, and near fisticuffs. Of course the editors loved it; it promoted intensity and challenge.

Today, the competition is milder.

Six Decades Ago, as Paper Boy, Ink Got Into His Veins

Next to the Bible, a newspaper undisputably is the all-time favorite of the reader.

My romance with the printed news hearkens back to the 1920s. Then, as a boy, on downtown Durham streets I sold an "extra" edition of *The Durham Sun* about heavyweight boxing champion Jack Dempsey defeating France's Georges Carpentier. That $2.10 I earned seemed like a bonanza.

A few years later I was a carrier boy for the same paper at a time when collecting 15 cents for a week's output was far less than easy on my route.

I've stood by while the householder rolled dice or played "skin" poker. If he won, I'd collect. Otherwise I'd receive the typical excuse, "I'll catch up with you next week."

Bootleg joints, "blind tigers," and liquor houses, as they were wont to be called, usually paid me without quibble. If the operator was at home, that is.

Customers moved frequently without notice. Thus a loss never to be recovered. The carrier had to pay for his papers.

At times on Saturday afternoon collection days occupants of the house never answered a door knock at the front or back, even though you could hear him or her snoring or walking about.

In one such case I turned to a drastic ruse. I had heard all about some people being frightened about a hex at their door. I was ready. I placed several small bones and feathers together and poured a glob of catchup on the combination. And then I left.

Hours later I returned to the house to find the door ajar and a zombie-like, ashen-face man staring into space. I repeated to him for several minutes that I wanted 30 cents for two weeks. Never speaking he pulled a $1 bill from his shirt pocket and handed it to me. He waved away the change and said nothing. I removed the mess from the porch and left.

The next Saturday I returned to the house to find him gambling on the back porch. I told him I owed him a quarter. The man looked up and smiled. "You brought me good luck last week. I didn't find nothing on the porch on Sunday." I was told to keep the change.

In the 1940s after being discharged from Fitzsimons military hospital in Colorado, I became a reporter for the *Durham Morning Herald*.

Fred Haney, a versatile, workhorse editor, one afternoon asked: "You ever heard of 'Babe' Didrikson?" I knew she was a world-famed woman athlete. "Let's slip out to the golf course for a few minutes while things are quiet. She is giving an exhibition of her golf ability." We went to the course where only a handful of men were eyeballing the "Babe." A larger group was following a male golf trick artist in another area of the greens.

"Babe," whose real name was Mildred, was a rawboned Texas country girl with a mannish voice and friendly chatter. She paused at one point to say, "Fellows, in the flat country of Texas while chopping cotton when a gal's got to go, she sticks her hoe into the dirt and the men don't look. I've got to go."

We men turned away without a word. Our faces were burning. Shortly afterward "Babe" returned with, "Okay, fellows, let's get back with it."

Another shot or two and Fred and I hied back to the news office.

Once I did a Sunday feature about a Durham youth, a gunner on a bomber plane in the South Pacific during World War II. I was told by the feature editor that the story would carry a 72-point (large) headline.

I came up with "Joe Beasley tells of his adventures with the *Vibrating Virgin*."

The newsroom debated the headline. To break the tie we asked R. C. Boutwell, veteran of the Associated Press to decide the issue. A quiet, astute man, "Bout" asked: "Is *Vibrating Virgin* the name of the plane?" Told that it was, he said: "Then I don't see anything wrong with the headline."

It was used. And it did cause comment.

One day "Bout" told me that a tall soldier in uniform had stopped in front of his office to chat briefly as "Bout" was leaving the AP room for a moment. When "Bout" returned he discovered with alarm that his treasured pocketwatch, which he had placed on a table to note time of the news dispatches on the teletype as they came in, was missing. So was the soldier, who "Bout" said was flipping and catching a dollar-size, shiny medallion.

I asked military police at the courthouse to check the bus and train stations for a soldier who might be flipping a medallion. Military police caught the soldier boarding a Greyhound bus and flipping one. "Bout's" watch was recovered.

Oldtimers may recall the old *Durham Sun* building on East Main Street opposite the public library. There, during World Series baseball games before the advent of television, a huge board was affixed next to the back wall of the building. The board was painted to resemble an infield and outfield, and by telegraph a play-by-play of the game was heard and seen.

The board operator called out the balls and strikes and various plays. A white ball attached to a cord would zip toward the batter's box. When the ball was hit the ball would follow the instructions of the announcer. There was also a scoreboard.

It was all great fun and excitement that earned yells and cheers from the large, standing audience. Of course there was betting by the spectators, some of whom passed around a bottle of homebrew or John Barleycorn.

For years, on a shop window of the old Washington Duke Hotel on Market Street in front of the Herald-Sun building, a newspaper employee would print with white paint the scores as they came in during the college football season. This attracted a crowd, too, in the before-TV era.

Norman Reeves, a friend of the late night workers at the *Durham Morning Herald,* operated Reeves Cafe on nearby Chapel Hill Street. After closing his cafe for the night he reopened just for the Herald crew to provide them with coffee and snacks. The cafe was later sold to the Capsalis family and renamed the Palms Restaurant.

There was no engraving at the newspaper in the early days and photographs were marked and rushed to the Durham Engravers on East Parrish Street. There Earl and Mary Wrenn and Jimmy Pulley gave good service and returned the engravings in a hurry.

Deadlines always were strictly adhered to by the editors. The *Herald* and *Sun* both functioned in the same newsroom and the photography darkroom for the development of pictures was adjacent to this room.

Once John Barry, the *Sun's* editor, on noting the time of day, grew impatient and knocked on the darkroom door and yelled "We've got to have the picture." He paused and knocked again, and then forced the door open. Inside, the young photographer was calmly taking pictures of a nude woman.

There was stiff competition between the *Herald* and *The Sun* and verbal strife between the staffs was frequent. The editors, aware of the competition, pretended not to notice.

The company, always keen on Christmas parties and bonuses for the employees, often would give hams to each worker and once distributed beautiful red Bibles.

One year, when the country was dedicated to the World War II effort, there was understandably no Christmas party. Mrs. Ed Rollins Sr., mother of the Rollins children who were joint operators of the company following the death of her husband, entered the newsroom and was surrounded by employees.

A queenly lady with a friendly smile and a warm handshake with each employee, she handed out envelopes containing the bonus to each recipient and said softly with feeling, "Merry Christmas."

One day pretty red rosebuds in slim vases appeared on the desks in the newsroom. The practice continued for some time.

When "Kilroy" of World War II fame arrived, the company printed for distribution small cards with the words "Kilroy was here."

"Kilroy" was a fictitious, ghostly character who appeared everywhere from chalked "Kilroy was here" signs on restroom walls to patches on clothing. It was somehow akin to the way American servicemen showed up almost everywhere.

In the glory days of street sales of *The Durham Sun,* hawkers of the paper would call out: "Read all about it!" And leading the pack, as always, was Dallie Draughon, who with bullhorn voice strode up and down the business sector of Main Street, announcing, with authority, startling news items.

It sounded as if the events occurred in Durham, the state, or nation, but mostly Dallie picked out incidents from other countries. And the imaginative and opportune young man was adept at blowing the news out of proportion such as to stagger the mind with its impact.

Many of his eager patrons soon learned the vendor's style after searching in vain for front-page stories he ballyhooed. They merely shook their heads and laughed. They loved it and kept buying anyhow.

The paper about 30 years ago urged its readers to write in and name their favorite feature. Was it the comics? No. Sports? No. The pattern department? Yes. The good ladies were the most loyal to this feature and wrote in to say so.

Noise has always been a pet peeve of mine. But I do miss the roar of the newspaper press, the metallic clinks of the Linotypes as they knocked out typelines or slugs, the key-pounding of the non-touch typists in the newsroom as they attacked the L.C. Smith typewriters, and the pungent smell of the hot metal from which were cast the forms for the pages.

Progress Would Amaze Paper's Founding Fathers

Ed Rollins and Joe King would be amazed with the changes and progress the *Durham Morning Herald* has made since its debut in 1894. Durham also might not be recognized.

Ninety-four years ago their four-page, 12 by 18-inch, five column tabloid, whose front page was generous with ads, sold for 5 cents a week and was hawked by sales boys along potholed and often muddy Main Street.

In 1906 the five stair-step Zuckerman brothers; Ike, Charles, Jacob, William and Abe, were a familiar and sometimes entertaining sight, peddling papers along streets and in their newsstand. Each lad wore knee britches, ribbed stockings, coats, caps and ties. They carried cotton newspaper bags across their shoulders.

"Extra! Extra! Read all about it!" they'd shout, spicing up some event, oftentimes which had occurred across the continent.

King, a tobacco-chewing printer who also wrote pithy and sometimes biting editorial tidbits, was the first linotype operator in Durham. He even wrote his editorials on the old typesetting machine. King also had a newsbeat and played in an orchestra. Rollins, a sharp businessman, managed the operations of the paper and oftentimes wrote articles. He was well aware of economics.

This writer recalls the time he was told by J. H. Epperson, late director of the Durham County Health Department, that shortly after he came to Durham as a young bacteriologist in the early 1900s, Epperson had occasion to question an article in the paper.

"When I introduced myself to Mr. Rollins, he said, "I know who you are, sir. State your business. I'm busy."

Epperson, a jovial fellow, Kentucky born, whose parents were in the famous Oklahoma Run, said he told Rollins that he wanted an explanation of the article.

"Mr. Rollins glared and said, 'Epperson, let's get things straight. You don't tell me how to operate my paper. I'm just keeping an eye on everything in Durham, including Dr. Cheatham's [Superintendent Arch Cheatham] health department.'"

Grinning, Epperson said, "I thanked him and got out of there. We became friends."

King in the fall of 1894 had bought an interest in the *Herald* from a printer named Gates for a train ticket to Goldsboro and enough money to pay for meals on the trip. Shortly afterwards, Rollins bought a half interest in the paper for $125, and paid the paper's outstanding bills.

The birth of the *Morning Herald* followed a Sunday afternoon meeting of two

The Herald-Sun Newspapers building at Market and Chapel Hill Streets.

unemployed union printers, W. W. Thompson and Zeb Council, in the basement of Temple Baptist Church (then Second Baptist) on Chapel Hill Street. The idea of a morning newspaper came from Gates. The three formed a partnership.

King, foreman of the *Daily Globe*, an afternoon paper in Durham, entered the picture. Thompson quit and his one-half share was bought by Rollins. Zeb Council and W. T. Christian, who earlier had become involved in the paper's operation, also dropped out. Thus King and Rollins became co-owners and operators.

In 1918, shortly before his death, King sold his one-half interest to Rollins and Carl C. Council, a young businessman who had headed the circulation department and advertising, Council long before had served as a paper carrier. The paper expanded and became the *Durham Morning Herald*.

Rollins died in 1931 and Council became president and publisher. With Council's death in 1964, Steed Rollins, eldest son of Ed Rollins, and an experienced newspaperman, became president and publisher.

Steed Rollins retired in 1982 and his brother, E. T. Rollins Jr., also experienced in official capacity with the paper, became president and publisher. When E. T. Rollins Jr. retired, he remained chairman of the board. The council family retains substantial interest in the newspaper, and Steed Rollins Jr., is affiliated with the company.

Back to the 1890s, how was it like in Durham?

Tobacco was king and cotton was queen. Things were humming. New churches sprang up along with homes and businesses of every sort. Schools were added and improved. Entertainment was here and culture was being introduced. Train excursions to mountains and sea shores and to baseball games in rival towns were frequent.

Visitors, after leaving, would often say that Durham was saturated with pungent odors or fumes of tobacco and open-type prives. They said that Main Street, along with its horse troughs, was a giant spittoon.

They said that the lint clinging to the clothing of cotton mill workers looked like snow. Durham was depicted as smelly and a sinful place, with sorry soil and bad water. One of the town's slogans, the "Bull City," fit this citizenry, the criticizers said.

The look-down noses also harked on weird and fearful tales of hoodlums from the Pinhook settlement of West Durham, said this too was an ugly blot on the community, and that East Durham was a place of "toughs."

But censure was certainly tinged with envy of Durham's industry.

Many Durham inhabitants patronized Blackwell's oval-shaped horse race track on a big piece of land later to become the site of Trinity College and Trinity Park School.

Some people seemed to forget that in 1902 Durham had more millionaires than any city in the state, that when the Union Train Station was dedicated here in 1905 Durham could boast of five railroads with 26 trains a day. And, in 1910 Durham had more paved streets and a higher per capita income than Charlotte.

"Truly," it was conceded. "Trinity College and its affiliate Trinity Park School are reputable institutions of higher learning." But, they would add, they are "like an oasis in a desert."

Tobacco sales warehouses, the envious said, were centers of questionable medicine shows, corn liquor vendors, blasphemous drunks and brawlers, and patronized by horse and mule traders, gamblers, painted women, and sellers of everything imaginable except Bibles, testaments, and catechisms.

Admittedly in Durham were raucous sounds of industry paged by factory whistles and horns, cockfights, anvil and horseshoe pounding by blacksmiths, metal wheels on cobblestone streets, gunfire during weekend misunderstandings and on Christmas Eve, singing in religious tent services, outcries of holy-rollers in houses and little churches, river baptisms, calliope-led circus parades, baseball games, singing of spirituals by workers in tobacco company stem-meries, firewagon horns and sirens, band music by the town's orchestras and bands in downtown bandstands.

You name it, Durham had it back then.

And there were the religious-bent who said of evangelists that there was nobody to compare with the great Dwight Moody and Billy Sunday, a Bible-thumping gymnastic-acting ex-baseball player who preached hell, fire, and brimstone.

But tent-fillers who came were evangelists Hamm and Ramsey, "Cyclone" Mack, and "Gypsy" Smith. They were a far cry from the nationally ill-famed Father Coughlan of Detroit and Aimie Semple McPherson of Los Angeles who were active before the Bakkers and Swaggerts and the fictional wicked man on the cloth, Elmer Gantry.

In 1894 there was also a new monthly paper published in Durham, called "The Durham Story Paper." It was short-lived.

Residents through the *Herald* at the turn of the century were being urged while Christmas shopping to buy and send books to Trinity College in care of Professor John C. Kilgo. "He's trying to enlarge the library."

Ellis Stone Company was advertising 20-inch seude evening gloves at $1.75 a pair, ebony gloves, white and black, plain and lace, 69 cents to $1.50. Kron-heimer Store advertised "Ladies fine mohair dress or walking skirts in blue or black, $2.24, black satin petticoats with three ruffies named 'Peco,' 98 cents."

Another advertisement read: "Lost, a large nickel-plated nut off the front wheel of carriage. Finder will be suitably rewarded by returning same to the stables of B.N. Duke." One ad read: "Go to the Little Candy Kitchen opposite the public library for milk shakes, only 5 cents."

The fourth annual banquet of the Trinity college chapter of the Alpha Tau Omega fraternity was held in June, 1903, at the Carrolina Hotel— so named after the owner, Julian S. Carr.

Said the *Herald*: "The occasion was the crowning event of the social side of the order. It was honored by two U.S. senators, Furnifold Simmons and Lee S. Overman, and Judge B. F. Long. The menu cards and the souvenirs and the banquet itself were all in perfect keeping with the occasion. At the hall entrance was a bank of palms and ferns, the Alpha shield of Old Gold, and crimson flowers. The menu cards were in shape of a Maltese Cross. The menu: baked-white fish, Montpelier butter, potato holgraise, broiled young chicken on toast, French fried potatoes, lobster Newberg en case, tips of asparagus. And, crouquettes of sweetbreads aux truffles, early June peas, A.T.O. punch, roast duck, orange marmalade, Russian salad. And Neapolitan ice cream, assorted cake, cheese, crackers and coffee."

In the police court on June 10, 1903: "There were three drunks, one charged with being drunk on Sunday, and this case judgment was held up until the mayor can look into the matter. In the other two cases, plain, old-fashion drunks, were charged a fine of $5 and costs."

From Royall-Borden Company store came this advertisement: "Going to leave Durham? Then you need a trunk, let us show you our stock. Grass carpet and straw matting at cost. Take your afternoon nap on one of our comfortable couches. They are much cooler than a feather bed, and when you do go to bed be sure to have a Royal felt mattress. Mosquitoes and flies do not tickle or bite through our canopies. We have the kind that fastens to the ceiling or the bed."

How astonishing it would be to the oldtimers long departed to know that the textile and hosiery mills (among the world's largest) are no longer in Durham. And the American Tobacco Company, where big tobacco manufacturing really began, along with Bull Durham smoking tobacco, has left us. And Liggett & Myers Tobacco Company, whose Chesterfield brand cigarette once led the world in sales, is operating at reduced capacity. These two companies for years paid more than 45 percent of Durham County's taxes. Those famous tobacco sales warehouses along "Tobacco Row" on Rigsbee Avenue and on Morgan Street are no more.

Gone too is Austin-Heaton Company, a milling plant here which produced the popular Occoneechee, Bon Ton and Peerless flours. Bitter, too, was the departure of the train station and the disappearance of the Durham postmark on mail.

But business in other avenues, nurtured by Research Triangle Park, is flourishing. New construction and promises foretell new progress that Rollins, King, and Council would applaud. And maybe the sad situation of lack of transportation facilities may change.

The trio of old newspapermen would like the new Durham Library, Judicial Building, the magnificent Duke and Durham County General Hospitals. And there is McPherson and Lenox Baker Hospital for Children.

The *Herald,* and its afternoon sister *The Durham Sun,* fill many more pages than the petit clarion of yesteryear. The type now is clearer, there are numerous pictures, some of gorgeous color, there are large presses and working quarters. Equipment circulation is strong, news coverage is good, there is an excellent newspaper library, air-conditioning, elevators, good wages and working conditions, and things are really looking up all over.

Rollins, King and Council would cheer.

4

Buildings and Landmarks

The union train station at the foot of Church Street was a fascinating place, even the cobblestones which flashed sparks when struck by the iron shoes of dray horses meeting the trains.

The excitement engendered by a train pulling in with screaming brakes, hissing steam, smoke, and the odor of coal-burning engines, adding pungent perfume, is unforgettable.

Strangers stepping down from the cars, the bustle of yard workers and freight handlers, redcaps, mail handlers and conductors checking their heavy-chained, biscuit-like pocket watches—how wonderful.

Trunks and suitcases being passed along, candy butchers replenishing their wares, and blind Mr. and Mrs. Raleigh Floyd effortlessly running the concession stand in the station. It was all drama and the gawkers loved it.

Hotels Claiborne (the oldest), the Carrolina, Malbourne, Lochmoor, Washington Duke, the MacArthur, No. 1 and No. 2 Durham, the Grand Central—all history, like the train station, the tobacco sales warehouses, "Four Acres" Duke home, Austin-Heaton Flour Mill, Durham Hosiery Mill, Pearl Mill, Erwin Mills, and American Tobacco Co.

They are some of the important land marks, built with craftsmanship and pride.

Rail Rust and Station Dust

. . . Old-Timers Remember an Entirely Different Union Station

Large and enthusiastic crowds swarmed about Durham's new Union Station—"the prettiest in the South"—when it opened its doors for the first time on May 1, 1905.

The holiday spirit was in sharp contrast to that demonstrated only months prior when the city and several railroads fought bitterly for track and streets rights-of-way.

The first trains to stop at the new station at the foot of Church Street were mixed trains (passenger and freight) of the Southern Railway. These carriers arrived before daylight and but few of the more hardy curious were on hand to see the first tickets sold and the first baggage checked.

Capt. J. R. Renn, the stationmaster, was the busiest person in evidence, organizing his forces, dispatching business, and pausing constantly to acknowledge greetings from the townsfolk.

Renn, the father of Miss Dorothy Renn, was a seasoned trainman, having been a conductor on the Seaboard Railway before moving to the bustling tobacco town of Durham.

Assisting him were R. C. Mullican, ticket agent; Mullican's aide, W. J. Wilson; a Mr. Thacker of Raleigh who was baggagemaster; Thacker's assistant, Tom Ellington; and J. J. Ward, gatekeeper.

J. E. Abernathy, who five years earlier had launched his railroad career with the Southern, was one of the Durham residents who long had awaited the day of the new depot.

It was fitting too, that Durham's fine baseball team was squared off against rival Raleigh that May 1, because hundreds of fans rode the rails to the capital city on that momentous occasion.

The city had completed paving Church Street and a great deal of work had been done on the sidewalk at the time the handsome station, built by Pettijohn of Virginia, launched its career.

Cobblestones, already embedded in the earth in front of the depot all the way to Main Street, gave luster and durability to the area but presented a problem to dray horses unaccustomed to such hard and treacherous pavement.

The building's eye-fetching tower, of mission-type architecture, and the cathedral-like dome inside, were things of beauty all agreed. The artistic masonry, a product of pride which escapes today's bricklayers, was unmatched for adornment in North Carolina, it was boasted. Restroom facilities too, drew much favorable comment, especially from train patrons who long had suffered the lack of such necessities with open protest.

During the scrutiny of station accommodations, attention was brought to the fact that there was no government mailbox for the dispatch of correspondence before the arrival of a train.

A petition was quickly drawn and presented to the U.S. Postmaster General at Washington, asking for a transfer mail clerk at the new station. With that requirement forthcoming, Durham was assured of the most complete and up-to-date depot in the state.

But acquisition of the commodious station was realized only after a long and trying struggle. Credit must be given to Attorney Jones Fuller for obtaining legislation making the station possible.

In 1905, Durham Union Station was frequented by five railroads. On an average day, twenty-six trains passed through.

He introduced the Union Depot Bill (or Fuller Bill) which on Feb. 15, 1903 became law. The measure provided that where two or more railroads served a town the State Corporation Commission (now the Public Utilities Commission) could authorize the erection of a union depot. In appreciation of Fuller's accomplishment, townspeople gave a big banquet in his honor at the Carrolina Hotel.

The union station, property of the Union Station Co. (The Southern, Norfolk & Western, Seaboard, and the Norfolk & Southern Railroads), was completed at a cost of about $50,000. The land on which the station was erected, (the former site of the city market) and other improvements connected therewith, cost an additional $85,000.

The trains of the Norfolk & Western were not entering the new station at the beginning due to litigation over the Pettigrew Street rights-of-way.

Durham's city aldermen, a two-fisted group that asked no odds and certainly gave none in the fight with the railroads, had forbidden the N & W crossing Chapel Hill Street. But the matter finally was compromised and early in May of that year the tracks of the N & W were laid and connections made in a peaceful clime.

Unfortunately, none of the trackage belonged to a main throughline, a fact which as time moved on, became a great disadvantage to Durham. But despite that handicap, in 1905 Durham had more roads and better railroad facilities than any city in North Carolina. In 1906 with a population of 25,000, Durham could boast of 26 passenger trains arriving and leaving here daily.

Tobacco had already brought gold dust to Durham's feet. Records of 1902 showed that with assessed valuation of real and personal property of more than $9 million, here was the wealthiest city in the state.

And now railroads were destined to bring even greater prominence.

It may be well to mention here that figures supplied by Bob Holder of the Durham & Southern, show that the Union Station's building and land as of Oct. 31, 1961, was valued at $103,940.98. The same railroad companies own one-fourth share each of this property.

Ironical it is indeed, referring to Hiram Paul's 1884 History of Durham, to see how Durham's train passenger service today so closely parallels that of yesteryear.

To quote: "Railroad facilities are hardly adequate, only one train a day each way being allowed by the liberal policy of the Richmond & Danville system."

In 1887 charters were secured—that of the Durham & Northern connecting Durham with the Raleigh & Gaston, and the Durham & Southern connecting Durham and Augusta. Five years later a special line connected Durham with Duke Factory. This was known as the Durham Belt Line and tobacco tycoon Brodie Duke was its sponsor.

The same year the Lynchburg & Durham was leased to Norfolk & Western, followed by the purchase in 1889. The Belt Line became a part of that system.

On April 6, 1889, the town council had authorized the Durham & Northern to construct a track up Peabody Street, but unfortunately the street was within the right-of-way of the N.C. Railroad. But the people of Durham were determined that the track should be built.

A group of citizens met at midnight April 9, and working under the supervision of Durham & Northern engineers, by daylight had constructed a track as far as the foot of Corcoran Street. Angered Richmond & Danville authorities immediately secured warrants for forcible trespass. Every one of the workmen were arrested.

The warrants were returnable before Squire M. A. Angier, but as he was a director of the N.C. Railroad he declined to act. The case was heard by Justices of Peace Redmond, Wilkins, and Vickers who after a five-hour session dismissed the warrants.

The tracks to Duke Factory were then completed. The same day, however, a construction crew of the Richmond & Danville arrived in Durham and promptly destroyed the newly-laid rails.

Irate citizens induced police to halt the crew from further damaging the track. Later that day Federal Judge Bond in Greensboro issued a restraining order against the Durham & Northern. The hearing was held May 9 in Baltimore and the Richmond & Danville was restrained from interfering with the Durham & Northern track.

Aroused townspeople, determined that the Richmond & Danville should have competition here, under cover of darkness built a line up Peabody Street. This track became known as the "Moonlight Railroad" and was guarded against assault by the Richmond & Danville.

Further violence followed over the track's right-of-way and several trials were held to settle the controversy. But in 1903 Durham, through court action, lost its right-of-way on Peabody Street, and the Durham & Northern likewise lost.

Thereupon the Seaboard Airline, with which the Durham & Northern had merged in 1901, was forced to negotiate a contract with the Southern. Thus the town and Southern locked horns over the right-of-way on Pettigrew Street, which was just south of the railroad.

In 1904 the Southern disclosed that it planned to build a siding along the street. The City Council at once adopted an ordinance to prevent this.

On the night of Jan. 3, 1905, 50 prominent citizens ignored stormy weather to meet at the courthouse and vote for widening Church Street to the new station. Two days later the same group met and agreed to condemn the Rigsbee property for city and county purposes. This meant that Church Street would be widened to provide a way for heavy wagons and carriages to drive directly to the depot.

On Feb. 1, representatives of the three railroads which owned the depot building—the Southern, Norfolk & Western, and the Seaboard, met here with contractor and architect to discuss work on the northside pavement and the widening of Church Street. The depot passed inspection on Feb. 6.

Late the night of March 22, the Southern Railroad with a large force of men slipped into Durham and layed tracks on both Peabody and Pettigrew Streets. This act opened anew the old railroad war that had waged fiercely for 15 years.

The city secured an injunction and at a hearing in Asheville the suit was withdrawn and the city agreed to appeal its ordinance and the railroad to drop its prosecution of the city.

But the railroad promptly brought suits against the members of the City Council and their bondsman, John Sprunt Hill, for contempt of court. A plea of ignorance by the council resulted in a dismissal of the proceeding.

The extension of Carr Street alongside the Bull Durham Factory and the race between the railroads and the city as to which would reach the property first, had too long plagued the community.

In 1906 the Durham & Southern was organized, bringing trackage between Dunn and Durham, particularly to haul timber as well as tobacco and cotton.

At long last travelers were assured of departure on schedule and on the train they wanted. Fights, torn up tracks, and court action no longer kept patrons in a dither. The busy railroad terminal had become the envy of other towns and cities in North Carolina.

Changing times and lack of a single mainline railroad, however, have combined to make modern Durham one of the poorest rail terminals in the state, passengerwise. Freight business remains, but not like that of the good old days when folks came down to watch operations.

Most of the cobblestones have long departed, falling victim to modern pavement and removal. Glass brick were sealed into the beautiful station tower about 15 years ago, stealing some of its attractiveness in its losing battle with the pigeons. Rail rust and station dust are mute testimony of what has happened.

The Hotel: Focus Of Community Effort Again

The Washington Duke Hotel, then called "the South's finest and prettiest hostelry," opened its doors on Oct. 20, 1925.

It cost $1,800,000 to build, was 16 stories high, and it was the envy of other Southern cities.

Durham was proud of it. It was the product of community effort, created through a citywide campaign to get financial backers.

Now the hotel, called the Durham Hotel, is once again the focus of community effort—this time aimed at saving it. The Homeland Investment Co., which owns it, has announced that the hotel is a money-loser and will be closed unless it can be sold or converted to use for some public purpose.

It is not the first time the hotel has come on hard times since it was opened with such pride and with a glittering celebration that day in 1925.

The open house and festivities made for one of the biggest events in Durham's history. The city at the time boasted a population of 42,258.

According to the Durham Morning Herald there had "never before been such a brilliant gathering of people, women in beautiful dresses of varied hue and men in evening attire, in addition to others who came in regular street attire."

The all-afternoon, all-evening program was arranged by Dr. Robert L. Felts, a hotel project member, and the entire citizenship was given opportunity to see the handsome new giant of the skyline.

More than 500 persons, many from cities as far distant as New York and Illinois, attended a banquet and a ball. A 12-piece orchestra performed that night and remained at the hotel for the rest of the year.

Baskets of cut flowers and potted plants made the lobby and mezzanine a flower garden.

The program was begun with a prayer by the Rev. W. W. Peele, pastor of Trinity Methodist Church. He prayed that the building would be a blessing to the community.

The menu for the opening dinner: half grapefruit, celery hearts, stuffed olives, blanched almonds, cream of tomato-chatley, dinner biscuits, fried filet of sole, Julienne potatoes, braised filet mignon-Washington Duke, new potatoes Rissolee, petit pois, stuffed tomatoes surprise, fancy ice cream, petit fours, after dinner mints and cafe noir.

Judge Robert H. Sykes, one of several who spoke, touched upon the progressive spirit shown by Durham citizens coming together in a work which made possible the erection of "the finest hotel in all of the Southland."

He said the hotel had been "one of the great hopes, dreams and purposes in the hearts, minds and souls of the people for years." It was made possible, he said, through the aid of local civic clubs and all other organizations as well as through individual endeavor.

W. P. Budd, president of the Durham Chamber of Commerce, spoke on "Community Enterprise." He said that "if anybody present doesn't feel like throwing his hat or bonnet into the air from sheer joy over completion of the hotel, something is wrong."

Dr. William P. Few, president of Duke University, spoke on "Washington Duke and His influences."

Few said it was highly appropriate that the people should honor Duke by giving the hotel his name. In his talk he told of the great ideals and the love of peace and humanity which dwelt in the heart of Washington Duke, "the pioneer philanthropist of the South."

The Washington Duke Hotel, later renamed the Jack Tar Hotel and, in this photo, the Durham Hotel, before implosion in 1975.

John A. Buchanan, president of the Durham Citizens Hotel Corp., which erected the hotel, formally turned it over to the William Foor Operating Co. William Foor, president of the operating company, in accepting the hotel, said, "I am proud that we have been selected to operate the Washington Duke. None of the hotels in the South are equal to this hotel, and I speak from knowledge and not for hearsay."

Foor introduced O. W. Donnell, the hotel manager.

Former Gov. Cameron Morrison was called upon for remarks but declined, saying, "Everybody wants to start dancing, so do I."

Dancing continued throughout the night.

On the morning of the opening the Durham Morning Herald had an editorial which in part read: "Certainly in this generation, and probably in the history of Durham, there has been no such achievement on the part of the men and women of this city as will be found in that magnificent 16-story building which will blaze with hundreds of lights this evening in honor of those who brought it into existence . . . near 1,200 persons showed their faith in Durham by subscribing more than $900,000 that was an accomplishment of a great event in Durham.

"It was far greater to the city than if some multimillionaire had come here and erected a million-dollar hotel.

It was a community enterprise . . . it brought the city to a better understanding of each other, and that campaign brought to Durham an improved morale that cannot be estimated in dollars."

But the day after the hotel opened, the paper's editorial page was furious because of the city council's refusal to extend Parish Street to Market Street to serve the hotel. The headline called the action "A Betrayal."

"The action of the council was but a repudiation of the unanimous action of the former council," the editorial said. "The strange thing about it is that of the six members of the former council, including Mayor Manning, who had gone on record favoring the opening of the street, only one had the courage Monday night to stand by that former action . . . For the street opening: Durham Citizens Hotel Corp., representing more than 1,100 stockholders; the Durham Merchants Association, the Durham Chamber of Commerce, large banking interests, and the majority of citizens. Against the street opening: John Sprunt Hill, representing the Durham Loan & Trust Co., owner of 21 feet of land wanted for the extension.

"The citizens and organizations are not 'after' Mr. Hill. They appreciate the many services he has rendered, and the many more services he will probably render. A moral fraud, probably a legal fraud, has been practiced upon every one of the nearly 1,200 stockholders of the hotel."

Sometime later the extension was made and Parrish was opened from Corcoran to Market Streets for a complete loop around the hotel.

When the Great Depression hit, many hotel stockholders felt caught short. Instead of holding on to the stock hundreds sold out for as little as 10 cents on the dollar.

Homeland Investment Co., which had been organized on Feb. 17, 1932, with subscribers W. W. Sledge (president), I. F. Hill and Claude Currie, and with John Sprunt Hill the dominating factor, soon had acquired ownership of or represented 92 percent of the outstanding and unpaid first mortgage bonds.

Federal Judge I. M. Meekins ordered the hotel placed in receivership on July 26, 1932, and named lawyer J. L. Morehead as the receiver. The property was sold at public auction on the courthouse steps on March 1933, and Homeland Investment Co. submitted the highest bid, $149,000. The bid was submitted for John S. Hill, who held approximately $450,000 in first and second mortgages on the hotel.

Stockholders in Atlanta protested confirmation of the sale and Judge Meekins in April of that year refused to confirm it.

A resale was ordered through Southgate Jones, who was named commissioner. On June 3, 1933 Jones held a new auction sale at the courthouse door and Homeland Investment was the highest bidder at $275,000. The only other bid came through Meyers Hotels, Inc. of Atlanta, with $230,000 offered.

Homeland Investment Co. became a member of the Jack Tar Hotel chain in 1960, and the name Washington Duke was changed to Hotel Jack Tar. The affiliation didn't last and in 1969 Homeland Investment changed the name to the Durham Hotel. A motel across from the hotel on Corcoran Street was added and connected by an overhead walk, and the name became Durham Hotel-Motel.

The history of the hotel site is worthy of note.

Back in 1901 Brodie Duke and others deeded the hotel site and adjoining land extending south to Main Street to the city for $36,000.

An impressive Municipal Building, with town offices and a fish and meat market on the first floor and a theater on the second, was erected on the site the next year.

Dr. Blackwell Markham, who is now retired, recalls that his kindergarten graduation exercises were held in the theater part of the building in 1901. He later heard William Jennings Bryan speak there.

The Municipal Building was badly damaged in December 1908, by a fire which swept several blocks of the town, but spirited citizens immediately went to work and restored the building. This time the theater commanded the main portion of the structure and was named The Academy of Music. It was also known as an opera house and a center of culture.

The spacious Academy of Music featured plush red and green chairs in the boxseats, an orchestra pit, and exquisite decorations. Road shows direct from New York, Philadelphia, Chicago and St. Louis came here to entertain. Then came top minstrel shows, musicals, outstanding dancers, ballets, vaudeville, burlesques, magicians, ventriloquists, hypnotists and comedy teams.

As some of these features passed from the scene silent movies came into the opera house.

During its heyday two popular minstrel shows came to Durham at the same time and two blackface characters, one from each show, met. Charles Correll of Illinois and Freeman Gosden of Atlanta, who were to form the two-man team Amos & Andy, were first introduced to each other by the author's father, George Lougee II.

During the early '20s the town decided to erect a new high school on Duke Street. Town offices moved from the Municipal Building into the vacated high school building on Morris Street. The Academy of Music, with new movie houses springing up and its glories of the past lost in a new generation of change, went out of existence. The building was razed. The idea of a hotel on the site began to be talked about.

Durham citizens, anxious that Durham have a first class hotel, launched a move for such a project.

The Durham Citizens Hotel Company received a certificate of incorporation on Nov. 15, 1923. The incorporators were John A. Buchanan, W. D. Carmichael, J. B. Mason, John F. Wiley, K. P. Lewis, L. P. Paschall, E. T. Rollins, O. T. Carver, Nathaniel Rosenstein, and M. S. Llewellyn.

On July 1, 1925, the corporation issued mortgage bonds totaling $950,000, naming John Buchanan as president, R. L. Baldwin as vice president, and Frank Adair as trustee.

When the hotel was completed there had been a total expenditure of about $1,800,000, far beyond the original anticipated cost of just over $1 million.

Fifty years after the Hotel was dedicated, the old hostelry was imploded on December 14, 1975.

Old Gossip Station Was Popular Place

Levy Brothers, a combination delicatessen, newstand, and gathering place for the sporting gentry, was once an integral part of the Durham community.

The genial proprietors, Dave and Roy Levy, were the sons of Jacob Levy, a longtime resident who in the early days operated a basement tailoring shop on the southwest corner of Main and Church streets.

The brothers first had a newstand—"the most popular reading room and gossip station in town," was the way Roy described it—on Main Street only yards away from "Papa Jake."

The business was later moved to N. Mangum Street, just off Main Street, and there it remained until shortly after Dave's death in November 1959.

Before Roy's death in December 1973, he reminisced about the salad days, the days he said so truly were beyond recall. And therein lies this yarn. Roy, a

Brothers Dave and Roy Levy ran a newsstand, confectionary, and delicatessen.

big, jovial jokester who had been a helluva football player for Durham High School, recalled that as a boy he peddled newspapers on the streets, on church steps, and in saloons.

He hawked his wares with such loud outbursts as "Noo Yawk Wurl, Durham Morning Herald, and Richmond Times-Dispatch. Read all about it!"

Roy said Dave, who was 12 years older, would climb into one of "old man Sears' " horse and buggies, click his mouth and flick his whip and be off on another of his three-day trips to Chapel Hill to take orders for men's suits. "On these long trips, Dave, who was a tailor like 'Papa Jake,' had to feed and water the rented horse," Roy said. "This was Durham in the Gay Nineties. Durham was a flagstop hamlet with a well, a watering trough, and stepping stones along Main Street."

Roy, who sold tailor-made shirts and fancy neckties on foot several years before his death, laughed in telling about the happy times on Mangum Street. "Sure, we sold baseball gambling tickets, tip boards, and operated punch boards. You remember, too, even though you weren't one of my steady customers. But we were particular, we didn't flaunt it." And that is nothing but the truth. "But I do know how you liked Mama's cole slaw," he grinned, waiting for an answer. Again, he told it like it was.

Just like a ritual, old man Bob Rigsbee, who owned the building and had a little office upstairs over Roy and Dave's place, came around daily for his $5-a-day rent. "That's the way he wanted it," Roy said. "But it was reasonable for that hole-in-the wall. It was a good location."

In 1902 Roy rode on Durham's first street car. At 12 he thrilled as this magnificent vehicle clammered down the newly-built brick street at the mad pace of 10 miles per hour.

The Spanish-American War veterans were returning from what was then considered a major triumph. Roy said George Lyon, proud and majestic and mounted on a tan-colored horse, led the parade of strutting soldiers down Durham's main thoroughfare.

It was the first time these weary soldier boys had ever seen streets fashioned of materials other than sand or clay.

Roy's father, Jake, held his son's hand and the boy yelled enthusiastically as the parade passed the tailoring shop.

Roy said "old man Sears'" stable was located squarely on Main Street. He said Sears was a man of many trades and callings.

One of his more lucrative enterprises, Roy said, was that of being the sole owner of a hearse in town. Whenever the gentleman was seen washing his "death chariot" (that's what Roy said some folks called it) passersby would always ask: "Who is dead today?" Without fail, the energetic squire would retort with a squirt of stinging tobacco juice, "George Washington."

When Jacob Levy died, Roy, who had outgrown his short pantaloons, went into the newsstand business with Dave, who divorced himself from the tailoring game.

It was 1908 and Carrie Nation, with her hatchet and bluenoses, outlawed alcoholic drink. Durham's 21 saloons operated a while longer on a small-time bootleg basis, but the flourishing days were gone.

"I can remember being chased out of 'Happy Patty's, place on S. Mangum Street when I'd go in to sell newspapers." Roy chuckled. "Patty didn't like for anybody but men to come into his saloon. I guess he was afraid someone would tell who they had seen and he might lose their trade."

He said that with Durham becoming "arid as a desert," there were weekend excursions to Virginia for alcoholic excitement. "I'd say a great percentage of the town's males would take a train at the Union Station and visit Virginia where they could get stinking drunk legally," Roy laughed.

He said these episodes were rip-roaring, and many a passenger returned to Durham with a demijohn of his favorite toddy. And many a gay blade was given a smarting going-over by his wife or mother when he stepped or staggered from the train after the safari.

Roy recalled that the Elks Club minstrel players used "Papa Jake's place as a dressing room because Stoke's Hall, the site of their performances often proved inadequate for a change of clothes to costumes."

Enjoying a chat about the days of yesteryear, Roy remembered when eggs sold for five cents a dozen and good suits were available for $7.

Charlie Clark and Jack Summerfield were the town's pride and joy along fisticuffs lane. Prize fights were an art and science at the time.

Roy recalled visits to Durham by President Teddy Roosevelt, William Jennings Bryan, President Woodrow Wilson, Will Rogers, and muscular Jim Jeffries, one of the all-time great pugilists.

As to the old blue laws here, Roy grunted. "I used to sell cold drinks illegally on Sunday to discreet customers," he said. "But I won't tell you the price I asked for taking a chance on the Sabbath, unless it's off the record."

He said that the delicatessen business was great at one time, and that the nonpareil, Jack Dempsey, and the great Rubinoff, he of the "magic violin," had come in to enjoy the cold cuts, slaw, pumpernickel and rye, and the draft beer.

Roy said that the brightest spot of any day was when a returning serviceman would enter and yell, "How's about getting off your fat so-and-so and drawing me a beer, you old so-and-so!"

Dave was an orthodox Jew, but Roy wasn't. Dave made like he didn't notice when Roy ate a ham sandwich and told jokes about the Hebrews. But that was Roy and people loved him. You couldn't dislike him because he was honest, even to telling about the time he gave his wife Margaret a diamond ring. She took it to a jeweler to be sure it wasn't glass. "I don't blame her," Roy said, "I'd have done the same thing."

The way Roy told it, the past was mellow and rich with memories. Those were the good days, sir.

Requiem for an Old Courthouse

She Had Her Weddings, Deaths, Birds

The sedate old lady on the south side of the street, with her dirty gray face and faded red wig, unchallenged for 62 years, faces painful but sure desertion.

The Durham County Courthouse, built in 1916 through civic pride by craftsmen with foresight and enterprise, stood defiant and unscathed when assailed in 1954 by Hurricane Hazel, the most devastating force since Billy Sunday.

Now the grande dame, this formidable, four-story bulwark, this august tribunal, is destined soon to join the infamous modern day junk heap of discarded has-beens.

There is a new, untarnished girl on the block, on the north side of the street, eyeballing the old in disdainful confrontation. This is the handsome new building, the new Judicial Building, a name that somehow seems to say that her $9.8-million cost makes her more than a courthouse.

But what of those family jewels, the Confederate monument, the plaques commemorating the Durham dead of World War I and World War II, the tableaus of Squire Angier and Dr. Bartlett Durham? Will they yet stand on the lawn and piazza of the divorced building? And what about the flag pole?

County Manager Ed Swindell, who has lived most of his days in Durham, says there are no plans for the old courthouse, and that statues and adornments will remain as they are.

There is a flag pole on the lawn of the new Judicial Building and landscaping is coming. The big transition will come in late summer, when much of the equipment and the files will be moved across the street to the new headquarters.

Magistrate offices will be in the basement, the sheriff's department will have about one-half of the first floor, getting out of the basement it has occupied since 1965 when the police department moved into its new building about a quarter of a mile north.

The sheriff's offices were on the first floor of the old courthouse for many years, through the regimes of Sheriffs John Harward and E. G. "Cat" Belvin. When Sheriff Jennis Mangum took over, his offices were moved to the then fairly spacious basement.

The new courthouse's jail will occupy the seventh floor, while the courts will take over the third, fourth, and fifth floors. The county manager's offices will be on the sixth floor. Other county offices will occupy the remaining space in the Judicial Building.

The old courthouse, together with the land, cost $363,466.76, an impressive sum of money in 1916. Constructed of Indiana limestone, the building was designed by Milburn-Heister and built by George A. Fuller Construction Co., nationally known firms.

The structure consists of a full basement; the first floor, which was occupied by the sheriff and county offices; the second floor, which was used by other county offices and Superior Court and Recorder's Court; and the third floor, which was used by health, welfare and county school offices. The county and city jails and jailer quarters were on the fourth floor.

In 1925 Mrs. B. N. Duke donated to the county a bronze bust of M. A. "Squire" Angier, a prominent member of the board of commissioners and later mayor of Durham.

The Junior Order of United American Mechanics next erected on the courthouse lawn a water fountain dedicated to World War I veterans. The people of

The old Durham County Courthouse.

Durham County on May 10, 1924, he erected on the lawn a statue of a Confederate soldier.

Next came a bronze tablet of Dr. Bartlett Durham, founder of the city of Durham whose remains were later to be removed from a county grave to the city cemetery. The tablet is on the front of the courthouse.

Later, a bronze tableau inscribed with the names of Durham servicemen who died in World War II was erected on the lawn next to "Johnny Reb."

Just a few years ago several county offices, which were begging for space, moved into the County Building which occupies the site of the old YMCA and Lochmoor Hotel.

The new Judicial Building is expected to take care of the county's needs for many years to come, but that's what they said when the two other courthouse buildings were erected.

Especially so back in 1887, when the county commissioners shackled the taxpayers with a $20,000 bond issue that was to earn the commissioners the dubious title of spendthrifts.

The clay bricks for that courthouse were burned by a brick mason employed by John W. Evans, then superintendent of the county poorhouse and workhouse.

The contract for that courthouse and jail was $19,900. The land cost $2,485 and was part of the site for its successor. The structure was not ready for use until 1889 because there were political pitfalls then as well as today.

As courthouses go, the 1889 building was short-lived. Then the 1916 courthouse opened, and it has survived a full six-plus decades.

These are just some of the memories:

Mrs. Elizabeth O'Kelly, a public health nurse, gave more "shots" with the needle than anybody could ever count on the third floor. A lot of the kids lined up each summer for what they called "swimming shots," in reality, typhoid protection.

Winos and loafers used to sprawl along the front steps of the courthouse, spitting tobacco juice and getting sick on such stuff as aftershave and bay rum and vanilla extract.

But they finally were discouraged by courthouse personnel who with pin-point bombing from two floors above, dropped paper bags of water atop the unwanted loungers. A J. "Buck" Gresham and policeman G. F. Partin could have accepted some of the credit for the evacuations.

Prisoners on the fourth floor would dangle long strings from their cellblocks to the sidewalk below so that friends could tie on cigarettes, drugs, and liquor to be quickly hoisted to the cells.

One prisoner set his mattress afire and firemen, who discovered all 11 of the courthouse fire extinguishers to be dry, had to run a hose up through the elevator shaft to quench the blaze. Fellow prisoners, understandably frightened, yelled loud and long for help, attracting pedestrians and motorists alike.

Lay preachers visited the jails and led prayer and singing, but protests of other prisoners caused the visits to cease.

There was a horse trough in front of the courthouse alongside the street. Once, when a polite lawyer swept his hard straw hat from his head in bowing to a pretty woman, a horse who was watering from the trough seized the straw and chewed it up. The lawyer had purple words for the horse when the woman was out of hearing distance.

A prominent garden club planted flowers on the lawn amid fanfare, and members were later miffed when the wrong seed came to bloom.

A New Yorker with one leg in a cast and his fiancee from Connecticut, also with one leg in a cast, were married in the basement by a magistrate. The man, a writer, said that both were riding on his motorcycle when he ran into the rear of a truck in Manhattan. (There was no waiting period for marriage in North Carolina if you had the proper papers.)

Roosting birds from the upper ledge of the courthouse were messing up the sidewalk below, so the county installed flashing orange lights aimed at making them leave. It caused insomnia, but the dirty birds finally left. Fred Copley, then courthouse custodian, years ago fired a shotgun blast into the maple tree on the west side of the building. A few birds fell, the rest never returned.

When the second-floor Superior Courtroom was remodeled to permit space for additional courtrooms on the third floor years ago, plans had to be altered. It turned out that iron beams extended across the entire space and couldn't be removed.

The old oil portraits of famous Durham attorneys that once graced the walls of the old paneled courtroom were removed forever.

Moot courts, plays, political meetings, and election returns, once were frequent in the old courthouse.

A once gifted prizefighter, while a jail trusty, swallowed roach powder and died. A Durham woman who felt stigma on being jailed for the first time on her first drunk, hanged herself with an old khaki army blanket in her cell.

Plaster fell often in Superior Court office, prompting employee and visitor alike to look upward when entering.

District Judge Oscar Barker died on the bench, and a Mrs. Nowell of Raleigh who was pleading her own civil case in Superior Court died while arguing before the bench.

The courthouse basement used to become extremely warm when old court records were burned. But the occasion was much sadder when confiscated contraband whisky was poured down the drain, and when illegal slot machines seized in a raid at Hope Valley Club were smashed alongside the courthouse furnace.

Prisoners on many occasions have dashed from courtrooms and fled down the steps to freedom or capture. Deputy Sheriff C. P. Fogleman, on duty in a courtroom, once fired his pistol at an escapist, careful to knock plaster into the fellow's face rather than hit him.

Civil rights demonstrators, laughing on the way to jail and then yelling from their cells, chanted when they were released.

County officials once put out the word that they wanted the flagpole painted. One fellow agreed to accept the job and responsibility until he learned it was necessary to climb the pole to paint it; there were no plans to place it flat on the ground as he thought.

There was a young uniformed soldier who bolted from the courthouse after breaking out in sweat just before he was to repeat marriage vows before a magistrate.

The eagles etched into the sides of the courthouse and the sword of justice engraved over the door leading to the basement on the west side of the building once prompted a drunk man under arrest to shake his head and say: "The eagle is getting ready to drop on me and when I get upstairs the judge will put that knife into me."

A black man named Thompson once ambled into Superior Court office, throwing a pair of long dirt-laden cowbones on the floor. He ran out the front door of the courthouse and met the Durham High School band which was marching westward on Main Street. He led it for several blocks amid cheers until apprehended.

S. O. Riley, then court clerk and magistrate, was called "Marrying Sam," and often was addressed by letter as "Esso Riley."

Willis Holmes Jr. whistled "The Wabash Cannonball" as requested by Judge of Recorder's Court A. H. "Bus" Borland during a court session.

Police Detective Capt. W. E. Burgess, the heaviest man on the force, nimbly kicked his foot above his head.

Military police from Camp Butner were arrested for selling whisky in the courthouse basement where they had quarters.

W. T. Nash supplied meals for jail inmates before the county installed a kitchen.

World War II soldiers were naturalized in Superior Court.

Heavy brass cuspidors were kept shined in the courthouse and sometimes "accidently" kicked over.

The first person on probation in North Carolina was placed on probation by then-Solicitor W. H. Murdock; Bruce White was probation officer.

Elevators were manually operated, and Channie Lloyd and Obie Lloyd were the favorite skippers.

Police and deputy sheriffs once received huge bags of fruits, candies and nuts, and cigarettes at Christmas. Merchants were appreciative.

Many auctions were held on the steps at the courthouse door, and Bill Farthing has probably held most of the sales.

The U.S. Postmaster was Amazed

In the Days a 3¢ Stamp Ensured Prompt Delivery

Fifty years ago this month on a cold afternoon, a big, balding Irishman with a booming voice mounted a platform in front of Durham's spanking new post office.

A rousing band concert came to an abrupt end and dignitaries of various stature pressed forward to pump the hand of beaming James Aloysius Farley, U.S. postmaster general and a gumchewing, political mastermind. Then they ceremoniously claimed folding chairs on the odorous Carolina pine-slab rostrum.

Big Jim acknowledged the efforts of the band with a nod. He gave a half salute to the freshly scrubbed Boy Scouts forming a cordon about the new flag pole to make room for the flag raising ceremony.

The postmaster general sat down, first cautiously testing his weight with the strength of his chair.

When the cheers subsided and the photographers were satisfied, Dr. David W. Scanlon, pastor of First Presbyterian Church, gave the dedicatory prayer.

Handsome and bouncy, Mayor Will F. Carr welcomed the visitors to Durham, saying this was an event long-awaited by its citizens.

Congressman William B. Umstead of Durham stepped forward to say in a nasal tone that he was pleased to be present even though it meant his first absence from duty in Washington since his election to office.

J. Elmer Long, former lieutenant governor and chairman of the Durham Chamber of Commerce post office committee, next presented Farley; colorfully and lavishly listing the veteran politician's many accomplishments.

The whistles and hurrahs that rent the chill air brought a wide grin to Farley's round face.

With typical Irish gusto his resonant voice thanked his "friends and constituents." Then he launched into high praise of Durham and "the great State of North Carolina."

Farley congratulated "the Old North State" for its able representatives in Washington, a state which he said was "standing stalwartly behind the administration of Franklin D. Roosevelt."

Farley mentioned the names of Senators Josiah Bailey and Robert Reynolds, as well as Representatives Umstead, Robert Doughton, and others.

He paid tribute to the progress of North Carolina, saying the state had led the nation the past two decades, "this being particularly true with regards to industries, good roads, and schools."

Farley turned to the operation of the Post Office Department and told of its aims and achievements, pointing with pride to its employees' dedication to service.

He summed up this devotion with the old post office motto: "Neither snow, nor rain, nor heat, nor gloom of night stays these couriers from the swift completion of their appointed rounds."

Recognition was given to T. C. Atwood and Howard Weeks, architects for the new post office, and to Henry C. Ashmead, government engineer for the project.

Then came the real surprise, an act which brought amazement from Farley. A representative from the American Tobacco Co. presented him with a certified check slightly in excess of $300,000, purchasing for Durham the post office, which actually cost less than the value of the check.

It was a check for internal revenue stamps to be affixed to Durham tobacco products. Moreover, the check was not an extraordinary expenditure, but rather a representative daily tobacco tax payment.

It was pointed out to Farley that Durham tobacco plants the previous year paid nearly $10 million a month (drawn, of course, from all over the world), enough to build the government a post office every day of the year.

Farley and his aides had arrived in Raleigh shortly before 8 a.m. on the day of the dedication. After breakfast in that city, the postmaster general attended mass in a Catholic church.

Farley arrived in Durham about 10 a.m. and retired to his room in the Washington Duke Hotel for a rest. An hour later he was touring plants of Liggett & Myers Tobacco Co. and the American Tobacco Co., where he appeared fascinated with the transformation of weed into cigarettes.

Farley topped off the morning with a visit to Duke University, where he was a luncheon guest of Duke President William Preston Few.

At 4 p.m. the postmaster general visited Durham Postmaster James K. Mason where he accepted the invitation to serve as a postmaster here for one hour.

Postmaster Mason, it was noted, enjoyed the distinction of being the only Durham postmaster to serve under four presidents: Harding, Coolidge, Hoover, and Roosevelt. Mason also was to serve under President Truman before the postmaster died in 1946.

Farley was honored guest that night at the annual dinner of the Durham Chamber of Commerce. Carl C. Council was chamber president, and attorney R. M. Gantt of the Durham County Democratic executive committee presided.

Mayor Carr presented Farley with a silver-headed cane as a gift of the chamber. Governor J.C.B. Eringhaus, in a brief speech, pointed out that the State of North Carolina ranked second only to New York in contributing money to the federal government. The postmaster general, introduced by Umstead, used the occasion to praise President Roosevelt's courage, integrity and humanitarianism.

In explaining the drastic measures necessary to get this country on an even keel, Farley said that everyone knew that one of the main causes of the situation in which we found ourselves was that the agencies and individuals were "living beyond their means."

Farley left Durham at 9:30 p.m. to return to Washington where the government's emergency airmail service was under fire.

Malbourne Drew GIs, Elite

Durham's handsome Malbourne Hotel, which fell to the iron ball 53 years after it opened, catered to families and traveling salesmen but enjoyed the patronage of the GI and the elite.

Guests included the inimitable Billy Sunday, Roy Rogers, Tom Mix, Guy Lombardo, Diane Barrymore, and ex-President William Howard Taft.

The Malbourne, on the northwest corner of Main and Roxboro streets, opened for business at 6 p.m. on June 16, 1913, with a dinner. It advertised that it was in the business center of Durham, on the street car line to and from all principal parts of the city.

"We have spared no time or costs in making The Malborne one of the handsomest and best equipped in the South. Every room is an outside room, steam heat, telephone, hot and cold running water in each room. Rooms single or en suite—with or without bath. E. I. Bugg, proprietor."

When the doors opened fully 700 persons visited the hotel for a personal inspection. Supper was served American style at the opening but then became European or a la carte.

The Durham Orchestra furnished music for the occasion. The lobby was nicely set with palms and potted plants. The floors were tiled while the walls were beautiful white marble wainscoting height.

The lobby and writing room were built together. The office was in the rear of the lobby on the right, while just opposite was the elevator. Stairways wound around the elevator shafts.

The late Neil Graham quit school at age 17 to take a job at the cigar stand the day the hotel opened. He wanted to bring in revenue for his family.

Two weeks later Graham was made night clerk. He worked from 7 p.m. to 7 a.m., seven days a week, and was paid $50 a month. Then came World War I and Graham enlisted in the Navy. Immediately after he was discharged from

The Malbourne Hotel.

the Brooklyn Navy yard, he took a train home. Within hours he was back at his old job at the Malbourne.

Early in World War II, Bugg appointed Graham manager of the hotel, a position he held until the hotel closed in 1966. Graham was the last person to leave when the doors were locked, for the first and last time.

Graham wasn't the only long-time employee at the hotel. There was a cook with 48 years of service, bellboys with 42 years, a housekeeper with 35 years, two maids with 38 years each, a clerk with 30 years, and one with 24 years.

During the Great Depression years, about 80 percent of the hotels in the nation changed hands or went broke, but not the Malbourne.

During World War II, nearby Camp Butner poured out soldiers by the thousands, and the Malbourne on occasion would fill up early.

Rather than turn away the soldiers, Bugg permitted them to sleep on the lobby chairs, sofas, and the floor. As many as 50 men at a time would be sleeping on the lobby floor during the weekend and Graham once said he had to step over and around them to get to the desk.

Bugg never charged the soldiers without a bed a cent, but would give them every accommodation he could, including free baths in the public rooms.

The hotel was popular, and two men, T. O. Wilson of Roanoke Rapids and J. W. Dillard of Lynchburg, once said they had been patrons of the Malbourne for a combined total of more than 80 years.

The Durham Bar Association, in March 1915, gave a dinner at the Malbourne in honor of Taft, who at the time was a distinguished professor of law at Yale. He had served as president of the United States, and following his time at Yale was to become chief justice of the United States.

Taft had given a lecture at the University of North Carolina, beginning at 7:30 p.m., and it was nearly 10 p.m. when he arrived at the Malbourne, escorted by members of the Durham bar, including W. G. Bramham, J. L. Morehead, and R. H. Sykes.

The lobby of the hotel was crowded with enthusiastic onlookers who applauded and cheered as Taft made an appearance. Taft was the biggest man ever to be president at 6 feet, 2 inches tall and weighing more than 300 pounds.

Smiling and waving, Taft moved through an aisle in the lobby to get to the banquet room where guests sat patiently waiting to begin the dinner that had been scheduled for 9 p.m.

There were Durham, state, and national dignitaries, court officials, and deans of the law schools of this state. The bar dinner committee was composed of Victor S. Bryant, Jones Fuller, R. O. Everett, Sykes. and Morehead. S. C. Brawley was bar president.

The bill of fare read: "Martini, Lynhaven Bay oysters on the half-shell, mock turtle soup, celery hearts, salted almonds, queen olives, sauterne, North Carolina shad, maitre de hotel; shoestring potatoes, Tennessee milk-fed broiler on toast with Smithfield ham splints, champagne, creamed white potatoes, asparagus on toast, sifted green peas, fruit salad, a la Malbourne; tutti frutti ice cream, assorted cakes, Roquefort cheese, saltines, demitasse, cigars."

Talks were made by Bryant and Judge Clark. Bryant took the occasion to inform His Honor that there was no violation of laws of North Carolina in the refreshing beverage. The martini, Bryant said, was North Carolina product.

Bryant presented Taft as "a profound lawyer, a just judge, and a patriotic citizen."

Taft, who demonstrated humor and wit as well as sagacity, talked about his controversial appointments and stands, and said, in part: "I think I have seen Durham all over the world . . . and while I do not smoke I'm glad to take away the present from the company—the subject of the picture." He was referring to a gift of Bull Durham smoking tobacco, and a handsome pipe in a plush case of the Yale colors, which were presented as a gift from the American Tobacco Co.

"I had a talk with General Julian S. Carr and found in him what I doubt not will be found in all Durham people—a willingness to admit Durham is really a great town, a town of quiet, modest strength which yields the expression after the treatment."

Taft left the banquet at 11:45 p.m., although the dinner was but half served. He went to Raleigh through the country and there caught a northbound train for his home.

The Malbourne was famous for its good food, and in its later years Graham's wife, Mary, was in charge of the hotel's Coffee Shoppe.

During World War II a substitute worker inadvertently ran up the American flag upside down on the Roxboro Street side of the hotel. A soldier home on furlough, his chest decorated with ribbons and medals, and his face flushed from a sojourn at a beer oasis, spotted the grave mistake from the YMCA across the street.

"They've got the union [the group of white stars on the field of blue] upside down. That's a sign of distress. Hell, this country ain't in distress, the enemy is!" he shouted. Then, "I'm going over to that hotel and tell them off!"

Unmindful of the street traffic, the irate soldier bounded over to the Malbourne, taking two of the stone steps at a time. He was followed by three or four young men who wanted to watch.

The GI stopped at the desk. "Where's the boss?" he thundered.

"Hello boys, what can I do for you?" amiable Mr. Bugg asked, smiling. The soldier stated his case, challengingly.

"You are absolutely right, it is a bad mistake," Bugg said. "I had no idea the flag was upside down. It will be made right and now. I apologize."

Then he placed his hand on the glowering soldier's shoulder. "Now I want you boys to be my guests for lunch in the dining room. It's time to eat." Tactful and gracious, he ushered the hesitating and sheepish group into the dining room. It was just an example of Bugg's quiet and friendly diplomacy.

Bugg died at 71 years of age on Jan. 22, 1957. His heirs turned the hotel over to a group of New York and Connecticut residents who gave mortgages and deeds of trust in the acquisition of the property. Graham continued as manager.

In 1960, the Bugg heirs foreclosed against the group. The heirs then sold the property to the Durham Redevelopment Commission. The County Judicial Building now stands on the hotel site.

When the stately old lady was being destroyed by way of the iron ball to make way for the county building, the wrecking or razing crew had a real job on its hands. In those days they built with craftsmanship, pride, and good materials.

Said the crochety old straw boss of the Cleveland firm doing the wrecking: "We've knocked down buildings up to 20 stories all over the country, but this is the toughest SOB I've ever seen."

Now the once-gracious hotel with the classy name is but a memory of great parties, banquets, teas, and headquarters for the greats and near-greats. It was the traveling man's good friend. And who can forget these peerless pictures: greetings by Bugg, Graham, and L. C. Curtis; the cosmopolitan allure of over-stuffed leather chairs on the sidewalk where patrons read their newspapers, enjoyed a cigar, and savored the penetrating giggles of vaudeville dancing girls at the adjacent Orpheum; and the cozy, summertime sun basking of Clerk of Recorder's Court Sam O. Riley on the rooftop of the hostelry.

Patrons Ate Under Canvas

Durham Cafe Served 'What Anybody Wanted'

William Frederick Adcock, a farmer turned restaurant operator, once cooked food and served customers in a tent on Parrish Street.

"That was my first cafe," Adcock once recalled. "We served about everything anybody wanted: stew beef, Brunswick stew, quail, rabbit, oysters, country ham, biscuits, corn bread, squirrel, fish, and real thick soup."

Asked about chitterlings, he drew up proudly and answered: "I said anything a customer wanted."

Adcock died at 97 in December 1958.

He was once told that Channie Lloyd, considered a legend by oldtimers at the courthouse, had a fine recipe for preparing and roasting possum. W. F. (that's what Adcock like to be called) nodded seriously. "Channie was a good cook, all right," Adcock said. "I don't believe I ever had any calls for possum. Too many other things available."

Adcock said that when he was five minutes old, his uncle Ben Ellis put Adcock's father, Robert Adcock, into a wagon bound for a Confederate Army camp "and we didn't see him again until I was 17 years old."

Adcock said he was born on a farm near Knapp of Reeds in Granville County, but his family moved three days later to Durham County.

"I went to a one-room school house at Mount Tabor," Adcock said. "When I was just 7 years old, my mother gave me a little piece of ground on which I raised a patch of tobacco. Uncle Ben brought it to town and sold it for $38.50."

He kept the 50-cent piece as long as he lived. He said that the coin was minted in 1821, and that Durham banker Gene Umstead had offered him $3.50 for it.

Adcock said his Uncle Ben once gave him a quarter for three quail and a rabbit, and that he also kept the quarter.

Robert Adcock returned to his family in 1878, having fought for the Confederacy, participated in the Indian wars and done a lot of log-camping out west before he got homesick.

W. F. Adcock and his wife Janie Wilkerson Adcock had 12 children. Eight were born on the farm, twin girls were born at their home on Ramseur Street, and two were born in his last home at 1207 E. Main St.

On coming to the city with his family, Adcock took a job at the old Commonwealth Cotton Mills but quit after one week. He couldn't support a family on 50 cents a day, or $3 a week.

He secured a job at a hosiery mill but soon departed to clerk in Gladstein's uptown clothing store. Later, he worked three days a week in a Main Street tobacco warehouse and drummed ("got it ready to bring in for sale") tobacco in the country three days a week.

But Adcock grew restless working for someone else. He opened a grocery business, which quickly went under. Then he got into food catering, an enterprise that he was to follow for many years.

Adcock said a good bowl of soup with crackers could be bought for a nickel, 15 cents bought a bowl of Brunswick stew, and a quarter bought an entire meal.

He moved his business, which was still in a tent, to Mangum Street, but a law was soon passed prohibiting the use of tents for food establishments. Adcock moved to Orange Street, but soon afterward, he lost his restaurant to the big fire that destroyed nearly every building in downtown Durham. Then, he moved back to Parrish Street, where he stayed until he retired around 1940.

His son Frank, who had assisted in the business, took over the operation of the cafe. But the elder Adcock found time to sit around and keep an eye on things—"ride shotgun on the stagecoach," somebody said admiringly.

Mostly, he wanted to keep in contact with old friends and cronies and solve world and town problems.

Adcock acknowledged he was recognized far and wide as a champion Brunswick stew and stew beef cook. In fact, he said that anyone who had doubts had only to ask around to be enlightened.

I was a believer, having sampled his succulent makings often.

Adcock bristled when asked about his politics. "I'm neither muskrat, polecat, Democrat, or Republican," was the stock answer he would shoot back. "I have always voted for the man I wanted, but my father was a Republican. I am a lifelong Baptist, that's exactly what I am!"

W. F. had eyeglasses but didn't use them to read, partly because he was always misplacing them. He once said he read the *Herald* and *The Sun* everyday without spectacles.

The only advice he said he had was for people to mind their own business. "That's what I always tried to do," he said impishly, a twinkle in his sharp eyes.

Frank Adcock, a quiet, friendly, and determined man, closed his restaurant on Church Street during the 1960s and later opened Adcock's Kitchen on Holloway Street. His career has exceeded his father's by many years.

But old W. F. was the pioneer who enjoyed the swashbuckling days when Durham was a boom town and when you could bring in a fresh-caught catfish and have it transformed into a beautiful stew.

Smelly Emptiness, Sorry Memories

Ugly and forgotten—virtually swept under the rug—Durham County's antiquated brick jail still stands, defiant, in the heart of the city.

Dwarfed by Main Street buildings and camouflaged by a cavernous, fenced-in lot, which runs southward along Church Street, the squalid bastille serves as a hitching post for parked cars.

After dark, it becomes a rendezvous for wine fanciers and other tipplers who prefer to socialize with their own gentry, in friendly shadows of night.

Built in 1916 with materials salvaged from its hard-featured predecessor which was razed to make way for the present courthouse, the lockup was discarded after but a year of use. The jail accommodations were provided on the fourth floor of the courthouse.

As isolated as a pit privy, the two-story former penal place broods in its burial ground a stone's throw from the Union Train Station.

Inside the barred and locked old jail there is nothing but debris, smelly emptiness, and sorry memories.

According to ex-Sheriff E. G. "Cat" Belvin who during its regime served as jailor as well as one of the county's three deputies, the box-shaped structure long ago was deprived of its guts.

The tough metal cells, he pointed out, were sold to Granville County and yet remain in use. The tomb-like jailhouse became a storage place and was used for this purpose until recent years.

Belvin disclosed that the old jail had four cells, two for white inmates upstairs, and two for black inmates on the first floor.

Women of both races were placed in the more splenderous confines of the County Home prison unit.

Chuckling, the ageless Belvin recounted that the jail boasted a zinc bathtub. "We had to force most of the inmates to take a bath in it," he said.

A battered coal stove gave off enough heat to cut the chill.

"But the old jail," Belvin championed, "was made out of good stuff, not much to look at, but rugged. It had strong cells, heavy doors, and thick iron bars which made the thought of escape seem silly."

Belvin said there were no professional bondsmen in those days and little vis-

Sheriff E. G. "Cat" Belvin at the old Durham County Jail.

iting with the prisoners was permitted Fingerprints and photographs of the captives were unheard of.

"They hated to go to jail or to the roads and I didn't blame them for that," the retired sheriff remarked.

"Prisoners used to have to work from sunup to sundown. Now a lot of them are bored for lack of something to do."

Recorder's Court was held on Church Street in the building unit now housing a beauty shop and a real estate firm. Superior Court cases were handled on Parrish Street in the building now used by the Durham Notion Company.

When a man was sentenced to the roads he had to walk all the way to the prison camp on Watts Street extension, wearing handcuffs and 18-inch leg band chains.

The meals for the jail inmates were cooked by Sankey Bynum, who also cooked for the late Sheriff John Harward.

Ironically, Sankey was killed accidentally by a car driven by a relative of Sheriff Harward.

"People those days respected as well as hated the old jail," Belvin said. "They didn't fare as well then as they do now. Lawbreakers seldom fear arrest and imprisonment any more."

Old Mart

Usual Fly Catch: 2 Bushels a Day

"With its flies and its dirt, the old municipal market was a monstrosity at best."

That's the way the late Jesse H. Epperson, longtime director of the Durham County Health Department, described the market on Foster Street.

The market, which was of white brick with a red tile roof, was on the site of the current Central Civic Center, originally built in 1935-37 as a national guard armory through funds supplied by the Work Progress Administration, a federal agency established by President Franklin D. Roosevelt to help create jobs. The market was closed in the late 20s.

There was a small weigh-scale building at the rear of the old market on the southeast corner of Morgan Street. Besides serving as a weighing place, the small brick house was used as an office for the clerk and had a public toilet on the other side. It later became just a toilet.

Most of the market's rear space served as a vending place for vegetables and fruits, most of which were brought in by farmers.

At the southern end of the market, fish odors vied with the stench from a large livery stable and flies had the choice of many dishes in the section.

Inside the market the concrete floor sloped in every direction and the few drains were not too effective. There were about 13 stalls in the market.

Meat was thrown upon marble-slabbed tables and a customer could look through various piles of carcasses and pick over the flesh at will.

"There was no mechanical refrigeration, just ice boxes, and no display counters. Butchers brushed flies away and hacked away at a beef carcass," Epperson said.

He said cuts of meat were placed on a piece of pink wrapping paper and weighed on scales that hung over the chopping block. You picked out your fish and it too was weighed on the same scales and then wrapped in a newspaper.

Meat falling off the block dropped on the sawdust-covered floor. It was picked up by the butcher and dipped in discolored water to wash off the debris, and then wrapped.

Epperson said the butchers would always smile and say, "I'm sorry it fell off the block, but it's all right now."

Dr. Arch Cheatham, under whom Epperson served as bacteriologist and food inspector, had fly traps placed inside and outside the market. The catch totaled from one to two bushels a day.

"You just couldn't miss," Epperson said.

Stall privileges were sold at auction at the city's four wards. There were two wards in East Durham and two in West Durham. At the time, both East and West Durham were outside the city.

Epperson said the sausage mills in the market were "nasty things," and the grease on the wooden floors "was so thick you could skate upon it."

Epperson said the slaughtering of animals was carried on in the woods—there was only local meat at the time. The animals were knocked in the head and then strung up with wire or ropes in trees. Much of the meat became fly-blown and was declared unfit for consumption.

During World War II, a carload of western beef supplied by one of the country's great meat-packing companies arrived in Durham "hot." The ice had melted in the meat cars. Health department sanitarians immediately burned the meat in an incinerator so it would never reach a Durham table.

At the time, the federal government was operating the nation's railroads.

Before his death, Epperson once reminisced about the early days of the health department. He said that a lot of people were indifferent or just plain scared where a vaccine was concerned.

"Meats were not inspected thoroughly because of lax health regulations," he said. "We looked for smallpox like we looked for winters. We looked for typhoid fever like we looked for summer. And we were never disappointed. Just how anybody lived is more than I can understand."

As health laws grew teeth and inspections became rigid and constant, people became more aware of sanitation. The butchers at the old city market either went into business at another location and abided by the new, tough ground rules or they just called it quits.

That brought an end to the city market era. Soon the vegetables, fruits, and other products from the farm were not available outside the market. There was no longer homemade molasses, sweet milk, buttermilk, cream, chitterlings, sidemeat, souse meat, crackling bread, cider, honey, walnuts, scaly barks, and hickory nuts. There was no longer any homemade lye soap, goose grease, creasy greens, collards, turnip salad, turnips, gourds, and preserves.

Produce markets began to spring up on the outskirts of town, and finally, the curb market arrived. And then the Agriculture Building was erected on N. Foster Street as a clearing house for farm folks who started coming back into Durham to bring the produce back to the sales counter.

Remember the Reo?

Carpenter Once Sold Them and Chevrolets

You look at Marcus Guy Carpenter's many citations, plaques, silver trays, and scrapbooks, and you wonder how he managed to crowd in so many achievements in just 80 years. Modest, and preferring to point out the accomplishments of others, the soft-spoken Durham native was in the automobile business more than 60 years.

Now retired, Carpenter was born June 3, 1893, to James E. and Lena Lloyd Carpenter. He attended Edgemont graded school and was a member of the patriotic Durham High School class of 1918.

His father operated a general store, first in the Albright section of town, a part of the Holloway Street-Hyde Park Avenue community. He also had an automobile agency and was a universalist minister. The elder Carpenter filled the pulpit when the regular preacher was absent, and he also preached most weekends in schools and churches in the rural areas.

"Together our family attended Sunday school and church and Wednesday night prayer meetings," Marcus Carpenter said. "I served as Sunday school superintendent, president of the BYPU (Baptist Young People's Union), and held most every office in church. I am so glad I was raised in a Christian home."

This church disbanded in 1918 and most members transferred to Universalist churches in the eastern part of the state.

As a young boy, he lived on Alston Avenue, selling the paper Grit and The Durham Sun on downtown streets, and he carried a Durham Morning Herald route. These jobs brought him money for clothes and entertainment. "My regular customers downtown included A. A. Murdock, R. L. Lindsey, and Nello Teer. Carl Council was circulation department manager of the papers, and Mr. Ed Rollins, the publisher in later years, would put one arm around my shoulder and say to those around, 'Marc trained on my paper route. That's where he got his good business sense.' And he was pretty much right," Carpenter said.

At age 12, Carpenter had a harrowing experience that has happened to few people. While he was delivering the Herald near an old coal chute in East Durham, he was bitten by a rabid dog. "A Mangum boy was also bitten by this mad dog. Many people in the neighborhood thought placing a madstone on the wound was a sure cure for the bite. But this treatment failed and he died a horrible death."

"My parents took me by train to Raleigh where the state could give the Pasteur treatment to prevent rabies. The treatment was in its infancy and was awful to undergo, but it saved my life," Carpenter said.

He said arrangements were made for him to live with a friend of the family in Raleigh while undergoing the treatment. "Each day I was carried to the second floor of a building on Fayetteville Street, and my father was usually on hand to assist and comfort me."

"I was placed on a wooden table in the middle of a hall. Nearby were cages of hundreds of rabbits. I can hear the noise now of those rabbits popping their hind feet on the floors of the cages. The doctor, or chemist-bacteriologist, would use a syringe to eject serum from a rabbit's spine and immediately shoot the fluid into my stomach with a blunt needle."

"The pain was intense. The treatment started with one shot the first day and increased each day, until I was receiving seven shots each day. After that, the seven were reduced by one shot a day until I had had 49 shots in the 14-day period. I became so sore I could not walk, talk, or take a deep breath without severe pain. I begged to be left alone and I preferred death to the treatment," Carpenter said. "Everyone should be thankful that the treatment today has become refined and much less painful."

"At that time my father and his brother, J. W. Carpenter, together with their father, Duane Carpenter, were running a partnership business at the corner of Church and Parrish streets. They sold groceries, feedstuffs, wagons and buggies, and Metz automobiles and Kohler trucks. The truck was one-cylinder and had a buggy dash, solid tires, and a hand crank on the side. The vehicles were serviced from a hand-operated sidewalk gas pump."

"After school I helped out at the store and assisted my father in making car and truck repairs. There were no such things as mechanics and father read repair instructions from factory manuals," Carpenter said.

Crackers, soda, salt, sugar, and pepper were weighed out, packaged, and tied up in brown paper sacks.

"We'd put the sacks on the counter because we knew that on Saturdays we'd be busy. At that time, Main, Mangum, Church, and Parrish streets were all full of individually owned stores," Carpenter said.

"O. K. Ferrell ran a feed store on Parrish Street, and the place was known as a 'blind tiger,' and popular with those who liked a drink. Ferrell became a big landowner. There was also a Bill Ferrell, known as 'Watermelon Bill,' who grew watermelons so large that four filled his wagon bed."

Carpenter said folks would gather around the pot-bellied stove in the Carpenter store and just visit and talk.

"I remember the time the county commissioners came in and sat down and started bragging about buying crushed rock to cover the road between town and the country home. My grandfather, who had a long white beard, tugged it fiercely and shouted, 'Squire (Squire Wilkins was board chairman) you have put a debt on the county that our children and grandchildren will be paying for a long time to come.' "

Carpenter said his father, a Republican, and John T. Salmon were two of the city councilmen who held out for building the dam at Lake Michie when there was opposition.

Carpenter said his father was cited for heroism in 1937 when he leaped from a boat, fully clothed, and saved a 5-year-old boy from drowning at Beaufort.

Carpenter was too young for the draft in World War I, but was large, and people on the street began to look "hard" at him. "It was a patriotic time and those not in military service would catch it," he said. "I finally ran away and got a job in the shipyards at Norfolk. When my time for the draft neared, I quit and went to Chapel Hill and volunteered for officers' training school. Several of us were selected and we were waiting for a truck to take us to Fort Gordon when the Armistice was signed."

Returning to Durham, he went back to work for his father, who earlier had obtained the agency for Fords but then had the Reo and Chevrolet dealerships.

"I sold the Durham Traction Co. (later to change to Durham Public Service Co. and Duke Power) its first fleet of trucks. They were the Reos. You'd buy the truck and then buy the body, which would have to be mounted like a bus," Carpenter said. "I also sold the first fleet of school buses in the state. They were also Reos and were bought by Orange County."

Laughing, he said, "I induced Houston Walker of Hillsborough to buy a hearse and start a funeral home business. He and his brothers were operating a flour mill at the time."

Believed to be the only man living who was in the automobile business in 1910, Carpenter said his rules for business success were similar to those of his father. "Each night I would write notes of what I would try to accomplish the next day. I listed 100 people. This included fleet users, public officials, preachers, and key people in factories and other places where groups of people worked together. For over 50 years while in business, I contacted each one every month. Then I would make contacts at meetings, in homes and businesses, and by mail. One day every week I would leave Durham at 7 a.m. and make trips to Bahama, Roxboro, Shakerag, Hillsborough, and then Durham, stopping at every filling station, grocery store, and other businesses, seeing farm leaders and customers. I offered help if needed, hearing complaints and giving and accepting advice."

Carpenter was manager of Carpenters for more than 50 years, was potentate of the Sudan Temple which had more than 10,000 members, was president of the Widows Fund, president of the Durham Chamber of Commerce, president of Durham Gas & Oil Co. for many years, director of the state Dealers Association, president of the Durham Shrine Club several times, chairman of the East-West Expressway commission, a director of Durham & Southern Railway, a member of the Durham County General Hospital planning board, a member of the Kiwanis Club for more than 40 years, active in the Durham Centennial program in 1953, a member of Durham Masonic Lodge for more than 50 years, plus many other affiliations.

In 1951 when Carpenter became Shrine potentate, the city honored him by closing off Main Street from Five Points to Roxboro Street, and staging the biggest square dance in Durham's history.

The Sudan band and orchestra entertained 6,000 Shriners and thousands of townspeople who turned out for the colorful tribute. "The firm discipline and love I received from my parents created habits that brought satisfaction and happiness to me," he said. "I have worked to improve my Christian life, my health, and my desire to support myself and family and to help others where possible and practical," he said.

"If there is one thing I can say about myself, it is that I am honest."

5

Capitalists, Businessmen, and Artisans

Durham has had its share of capitalists and business leaders, but few today share their wealth for the betterment of the citizenry.

In the days of Durham's glory, you would have to think of the Dukes, General Julian S. Carr, George Watts, W. T. Blackwell, John Sprunt Hill, Eugene Morehead, C. B. Green, E. J. Parrish, W. P. Few, H. O. Reams, Robert F. Morris, the Mangums, James Southgate, and perhaps several others.

In recent decades you would think of George Watts Hill, Dr. George Carrington, Howard Easley, Nello L. Teer, and possibly a few others.

Artisans of the past here should include the brickmasons, imaginative architects, and metalworkers, who all practiced craftsmanship and pride.

Fleeting examples include the eagles and the scales and sword of justice on the face of the old courthouse, the brickwork on the old tobacco warehouse which is now Brightleaf Square, the Snow Building, the Carolina Theater, and the old S. H. Kress building.

Long gone structures of beauty were: "Four Acres," the Duke home with its iron picket fence, bamboo reeds and superb grounds, Union Train Station, with its Italian and Spanish design and cobblestone pavement on S. Church Street, the Flatiron building at Downtown Five Points, the copper and tile roofs of several Durham homes, and the heavy, decorated bricks of so many sidewalks of yesteryear.

A Doughty Multimillionaire with a Twinkle in His Eye

John Sprunt Hill was Durham County's wealthiest man during the past half century. But he was more than that.

He was Durham's grand old man.

Hill, who shared birthday honors with Saint Patrick of Ireland on March 17, died in July 1961, at the venerable age of 92. He had planned to live to be 100.

His illustrious career rivaled that of an Horatio Alger hero.

When he died the inventory of his estate showed a valuation of $17.3 million. But this wasn't a true picture since most of his vast holdings had been parceled out earlier to his three children and grandchildren, not to mention his philanthropic gifts, here and elsewhere.

Be that as it may, the friendly but formidable No. 1 citizen was a man's man, an individualist who made it on his own.

I had the privilege of lunching with the white-haired, handsome patriarch on many of his birthdays at his mansion at 900 S. Duke St., and then writing a yarn which was never off the record. Hill said that perseverance, good health, and "getting in on the ground floor" brought him success "and a life filled with adventure."

He completed high school in Faison at the age of 12, and graduated from the University of North Carolina in 1889, with a senior-year average of 99, which brought him the honor of being valedictorian.

Hill taught school for two years and then returned to UNC for a year of law. He won a scholarship and studied advanced law at Columbia University.

Jobs were short and breadlines long in New York. Things appeared hopeless. "I remember walking into three-story library at Columbia and a woman shouting at me, "What are you doing here! Don't you know we are having a cholera epidemic and 187 have died? Now you are quarantined and can't leave." Hill said he told the woman that hogs in his hometown had cholera.

"She asked me what I could do. I told her I could lecture on Blackstone's commentaries on law, and on Miner's Institutes on Law, had librarian experience, and had given lessons in boxing. She exclaimed, 'You are the man we need!' "

Hill remembered a contact he made in Chapel Hill. Soon he was working as a law clerk in the law offices of Peckham-Warren-Perkins.

A prominent New Yorker had taken $758,000 from the estate of his wife and her sisters. Nobody would take the case for prosecution.

But Hill, a gambler at heart, offered to represent the estate provided the pay was good and if he was furnished a bodyguard.

"They accepted my offer, but said I was a damned fool Southerner who didn't care whether he was killed or not," Hill chuckled.

He employed a lawyer, a country barrister named Brewster, to assist him. Hill said brewster dropped dead the second day of the court hearing.

"I then hired Abram Miller, another able attorney. After addressing the jury for two hours, Miller went to dinner. He was never heard of since," Hill said.

"There I was with an eight-day-old law license. The judge asked: 'Mr. Hill, what will you do now?' I told him I'd fight it alone."

He said the jury convicted the defendant and the man committed suicide that

John Sprunt Hill, capitalist and philanthropist.

night at his home. "But I had won my spurs in the legal world," Hill said modestly.

Hill met Annie Louise Watts, daughter of George Watts of Durham, at a girl's finishing school in New York, and they later married.

While playing golf with his father-in-law at Poland Springs in New York, Hill met the son of a man named Croker, the boss of Tammany Hall. Hill soon became attorney for this powerful Democratic organization, mostly because of his first successful venture in the courtroom.

In 1900 he joined the military and became a horseman courier for Gen. Nelson Miles in the Spanish-American War. "I escaped the bullets as well as the typhoid fever epidemic," Hill said.

When George Watts became ill in 1903 and went to a German spa for his health, Hill was induced to come to Durham.

"He offered me $8,000 a year and a fine home. So my wife and son (George Watts Hill) and I moved to Durham, and we never regretted it." Besides his family, Hill also brought to Durham $125,000 he had earned, "and a fine and remarkable young man named Sidney C. Chambers to work in my office."

Hill said that at the time, "Durham had 6,000 people, 19 saloons, and a shoestring form of government." He said that "worst of all, money was being loaned at the fantastic rate of 26 per cent interest, 6 percent for the bank and 20 per cent for the lawyers who handled the loans."

Hill and his wife soon established Home Savings Bank and the Durham Bank & Trust Co., and offered loans at 6 per cent, with no other costs. Later, as chairman of the North Carolina Banking Commission, he was induced by Gov. Locke Craig and President Woodrow Wilson to go to Europe "and find ways of lending money so that an ordinary person could borrow without being cheated."

Upon his return, Hill established credit unions for the first time in the nation's history. The first was at Lowes Grove. He next inaugurated the farmers' mutual exchange program.

About 1915, people in Durham concluded that the old courthouse was a sorry spectacle. There was talk of hiring an Atlanta firm to remodel the building.

"General Julian S. Carr was attorney for the building committee, and he made a passionate speech for the project and a fiery denunciation of me for daring to speak up for a new and modern fireproof courthouse," Hill said.

"Branding me a young upstart, the general roared that he would ride with blood up to his bridle for Durham County. His talk set the crowd to nodding their heads."

"I quietly produced a picture of the general in his full uniform holding a Confederate flag and standing in front of the old courthouse. 'General,' I said, 'we need a fine courthouse.' "

"The general, tears in his eyes, said, 'Young man, I withdraw what I said about you. I'm for a new fireproof courthouse too.' I was made chairman of the building committee," Hill smiled.

When the courthouse was dedicated in 1916 it was hailed as one of the finest in the state.

Asked where he had obtained the name "Sprunt," Hill grinned widely. "Old Dr. Sprunt, a preacher at Kenansville, would come to Faison and stop by our home for a bit of brandy as well as conversation. I was a new baby and the old Scotchman, warmed by the brandy, insisted I be named after him and become a preacher, too. That's how it happened."

Hill nodded and held up a finger. "I want to say now I've always been a Prohibitionist and have led fights against the abuse of whisky. However, I have always championed the ABC system. It has been highly successful in dealing with a worldlong problem."

Conceding that his business attainments had bordered on the fantastic, Hill said, "It's astonishing about how everything I've touched has turned to gold. Get in on the ground floor when you can, then the plums will fall your way."

"I've never borrowed a dollar in my life, they've borrowed from me. As long as you can do that you will be all right."

Although he cornered the market in many transactions, Hill shared his good fortune with his fellow citizens. And he championed the poor. He gave sites for schools and parks and donated property for city advancement. The University of North Carolina benefited magnificently. Many of his gifts were made anonymously.

Emphasizing his good health, Hill said he had ignored strong drink, tobacco, and bad habits. "I've been in excellent shape ever since I boxed at Carolina and helped instruct students in the manly art of self-defense. Golf helped, but not boxing."

In one interview, Hill sported a green tie and had a green hat set in jaunty fashion upon his head. The redoubtable gentleman made the motions of an Irish jog. "I've kissed the Blarney stone twice at Killarney Castle at old Lake Killarney. They held me down by my legs. The luck of the Irish has always been with me. But I will admit, the Wall Street Journal is my patron saint," Hill laughed.

The doughty capitalist always contended that he was "a country boy at heart." He became a builder of roads as State Highway Commission head and was known as "Father of Rural Credit in North Carolina." He served in the state legislature as a representative and was also a senator.

When the "bust," or the Great Depression, came in the '20s, Hill bought up real estate, giving much of it away "to prove I wasn't trying to skin anybody."

The congenial multimillionaire always gave a bottle of Old Granddad whisky to this reporter after the interviews. Hill said a friend who didn't know better always gave it to him at Christmas. The reporter in turn gave the fifth to his drinking colleagues at the newspaper office.

Hill fought strongly against adding fluoride to the city's water supply, inserting large ads in the newspapers suggesting that the chemical was a poison.

He acknowledged, with a twinkle in his eye, that possibly he was against fluoride because members of his family were for it. And he once told this reporter—and it was printed—that if the chemical were added to city water he would dig a well in his front yard.

Then the health director, J. H. Epperson, an admirer of Hill, but equally adamant, said, "He's got that privilege, all right, but if the well water is not up to our standards, by God, I'll put a cement cap on the well."

Fluoride was never added to city water here until after Hill's death.

Just for kicks and comment, Hill used to wear unmatched socks. He wrote pretty good poetry, gave hearty handshakes, and said he never tired of admiring a good-looking woman.

He expressed disappointment that the George Watts mansion adjacent to his home was torn down and the land sold, later to become the site for Blue Cross-Blue Shield.

Hill said he would see to it that this would not happen to his home. That he did, leaving the lovely old mansion to be used by women's organizations in Durham.

Hill, at 84, Still 'Interested' in a Kaleidoscope of Area Ventures

George Watts Hill, who at 84 is in "damn good health," says "you never lose interest in what you have put so much into. I work in Durham and sleep in Chapel Hill. God has been good to me and I have tried to help Him."

A tall, handsome man given to modesty, wit, and memories of his father (the late John Sprunt Hill, Durham capitalist and philanthropist), he commutes five days a week in his 1966 Cadillac to his 15th floor office on Corcoran Street.

Hill's keen mind is a kaleidoscope of architecture, finance, health care, Durham ventures, and yes, prize guernsey cattle. When verbal ping-pong about a proposed civic center, hotel, and office building seemed to reach a stalemate, he had architect Frank DePasquale design a model complex for such a project. Hill gave it to the city which in turn asked and received his approval to exhibit the attractive glass-enclosed model in the lobby of the downtown Central Carolina Bank. "I give the project my blessings."

As to construction of buildings—he has been involved in many, Hill said— "I love to have an affair with a bulldozer, its safer than a redhead."

In a reminiscent mood recently, Hill recalled his days at Durham High School (class of 1917), and at the University of North Carolina.

"The old high school building became city hall, and is now the Durham Arts Council headquarters on Morris Street. We called Donnie Sorrell 'Radiator' Sorrell because he always sat beside the radiator in Miss Lila Markham's classroom."

"Billy Carmichael was a fine basketball player, and he and May Waller, a classmate, were later married."

Smiling, he said, "I was upset because James Leyburn and Martin Holton beat me out in class scholastics. They got scholarships to Trinity College and Davidson College. I got my scholarship to UNC and gave it to Billy."

Hill said that his father once told him that he made a grade average of 99 plus during his days at UNC, but was beaten out by a student who had a one-sixteenth better average.

George Watts Hill (at left) with photos taken from the Washington Duke Hotel corner-stone before its implosion in 1975.

"Dad lived on the southwest corner of the South Building one year and Mott Morehead (John Motley Morehead) lived next door. They had kerosene lanterns in those days, no electricity. Neither one had 50 cents to his name."

"When I graduated in 1922 we had 2,300 students. Jonathan Daniels and I were classmates. He was smarter and graduated in three years and went on to become editor of the *News & Observer* and an aide to President Franklin D. Roosevelt in the White House," Hill said.

Hill said he was football manager when Carolina's football games were played on old Emerson Field. The donor, Emerson, founded Bromo-Seltzer. Brothers Bob and Bill Fetzer were the coaches.

"I remember sitting on the ground at the UNC-Virginia football game and counting out $16,000, the total gate receipts. I had the money in two tin boxes, like lunch boxes. I watched the game with the money at my feet."

Hill said he studied geology under Collier Cobb and attended but two classes and passed the course.

"Cobb was a little, short man who liked to say: 'We're where we are because of what we are.' "

Hill went two years to UNC Law School which was headed by Lucius Pope McGhee. "I passed the bar in August, and was number 2 leading the state bar exams in Raleigh. There were 66 questions with four sub-questions for each one. Funny how you remember such things."

Grinning, he said: "I thought I had busted the hell out of it. I got on the 'rattler' sleeping car that night for Asheville, the home of my bride-to-be, Ann McCulloch, from Baltimore."

He said the list of those who passed the bar was not in the Asheville newspaper the next morning. "All hell broke loose because we were to get married September 24."

"Ann said: 'The invitations have all been engraved. What are we going to do?' I said we can't get married until I pass the bar and am able to support you," Hill related.

Smiling again, he said, "Finally I called the *News & Observer* in Raleigh and they said, 'Yeah, you passed the bar.' But Asheville didn't print any names of those who were from east of Greensboro. That cleared the way. I was in good graces once more."

Then, "Ann's father was an Episcopal minister and headmaster of the Oldfield School for Girls, the oldest preparatory school for girls, at Glenmore, about 15 miles north of Baltimore."

"He married us in Christ Church. I remember flags hanging on both sides of the church."

Hill said the honeymoon was for 10 months. "My father sent me to southwest Korea to visit a Presbyterian mission station which my grandfather George Watts had supported. Now he was dead and the mission wanted money, money, money."

"We spent Christmas with missionaries, then went on to Shanghai to see about my family's stock in British-American Tobacco Company."

"It turned out that B.A.T. would build a factory and operate it three years in China and then the Chinese would take over. They repeated this plan several years."

"B.A.T. made Lord Nelson and Lady Hamilton cigarettes. These two had quite a party with public liaison, but never married. The cigarette sold for one cent gold, American money. That's the way they expressed it," he said.

"We planned to spend the summer in Europe and I had cabled my father from Cairo to send $3,000 to me at a hotel in Rome. The money was there when we arrived."

"Then on July 25 mother sent me a cablegram instructing us to meet her in London. We did, and the vacation ended. We returned to Durham."

"When we arrived here I found that my father had taken $3,000 out of my savings account, leaving me just $3.61. That was just like him," Hill chuckled.

"Ann and I lived first in Watts Carr Sr.'s rental house on the southeast corner of Morehead Avenue and Willard Street. I went to work for $250 a month, big money then, in the old Durham Loan & Trust Company, now Central Carolina Bank. His father was bank president."

Hill said he was working in the bank when the bank holiday came suddenly. "President Herbert Hoover called my father and asked if he could stop the bank failures which started in Florida and moved into Georgia, etc. My father said he would try."

"That was the time when the First National Bank here busted. We needed some cash in the bank. My father sent me to the Federal Reserve in Richmond to get $500,000 and bring it back to Durham."

"I had an old Buick and I went alone to get the money and bring it back in a bag. A few days later he sent me to Charlotte and I came back with $750,000 cash," Hill said.

Shaking his head and grunting, he said: "I had a puncture about 11 o'clock that night, several miles before I reached Pittsboro. I was alone and nobody around knew I had the money. It was dark as hell. I jacked up the car and changed the tire, putting in a new tube. I'll never forget it. Father was glad to get the money, all right, shrugging off my mishap."

Hill said the money stopped the run on the bank, and Durham Loan & Trust took over banks in Mebane and Hillsborough.

"In 1933 when President Roosevelt came into office, he declared a bank holiday. Our bank closed and we bank people all 'went fishing,' as the saying goes."

Hill's wife died in 1974 and a year later he was married to Anne Gibson Hutchison of Huntington, W. Va.

"We've been married 11 years. There are 12 Anns or Annes in our family, so you see we like the name." His secretary is Mrs. Ann Hall.

The present Mrs. Hill has two daughters and one son by her previous marriage. Hill has two sons, G. W. Hill Jr., and J. S. Hill II, and a daughter, Mrs. Dudley Hill Campbell.

Hill built a new home in Chapel Hill and gave the large house he built in 1937 along with its 90 acres at Quail Roost to UNC at Chapel Hill as a conference center.

"My son John and his wife live down the hill from the big house at Quail Roost, near the dairy farm. The guernsey herd I owned has been replaced by the 25 horses they own," he said.

Hill, an Army officer during World War II, is a brain and spearhead in the creation of Research Triangle Park. He is a member and chairman of Research Triangle Institute.

He served for 23 years as secretary of the foundation, remains chairman of the board of Central Carolina Bank. He and his first wife started Durham Academy in 1933. He is also a board member of the N.C. School of Science and Math, Durham Community Foundation.

Hill recalls with satisfaction and pleasure his leading role with the late Dr.

Wilbert C. Davison, in the establishment of a plan in 1933 to enable people to pay for medical care.

He was a trustee of Blue Cross-Blue Shield of North Carolina until his retirement as trustee in 1974, and was the oldest trustee of the plan in America, having served for 41 years.

From the very beginning up to today, the success story of Blue Cross-Blue Shield reads as a tribute to its humane founders.

"I've had a lot of fun and always spoken my mind, good, bad, or indifferent," Hill said. "Say, that old Cadillac of mine has 165,000 miles and runs like a top. It doesn't have all of these fancy do-dabs which cause so much trouble."

George Watts Hill Retires From Blue Cross-Blue Shield

George Watts Hill, who with the late Dr. Wilbert C. Davison established a plan in 1933 to enable people to pay for medical care, retired Wednesday as a trustee of Blue Cross-Blue Shield of North Carolina.

"My term has expired under the new rules and because I am 72, I'm not eligible for re-election. It is a good rule," Hill said.

At the annual meeting of the board Wednesday, Hill was named an honorary trustee for life. Board Chairman W. C. Harris Jr. of Raleigh and President Thomas A. Rose of Chapel Hill paid tribute to Hill for his service and contributions to the organization.

Hill goes back further than any other trustee of the Blue Cross-Blue Shield plan in America, having served for 41 years. There are 74 of the organizations covering all 50 states, Canada, and Puerto Rico.

It was back in 1927 that Hill and Dr. Davison, who had just arrived in Durham from Johns Hopkins Hospital in Baltimore to become dean of the newly created Duke University Medical School, decided to work on a cooperative arrangement for prepayment health care.

"We were using the insurance principle to pay in advance for a program which Dr. Davison told me was in operation in England," Hill said. North Carolina at the time had a serious shortage of both hospitals and doctors, ranking fifth or sixth from the bottom of the nation.

There was also the problem of money. Hospitals had a constant flow of patients who, although not indigent, did not have the cash to pay their medical bills.

As chairman of the board of trustees of Watts Hospital, Hill knew the need for a prepayment plan. He had also developed an early interest in the subject from his father, John Sprunt Hill, who had studied cooperative medical care plans in Europe for the U.S. government as early as 1913, and from his maternal grandfather, George Watts, who was founder of Durham's first hospital, which was named for him. "I had been helping Dean Davison with his plans for Duke Hospital and at the same time I was handling the business affairs of Watts Hospital at the request of my father, who was president of the board of trustees of Watts," Hill said.

It was 1929, he recalled, "and the stock market blew all to hell. People had no money to pay doctor bills." Hill said he was returning to the states from Europe when "Black Thursday came with the fatal crash." The ensuing depression delayed plans for a prepayment medical program, but in 1933 the two men brought it to life again.

"A man from Raleigh by the name of Snyder had started a little hospital pay association or something like that, and we brought him into the picture and incorporated the Hospital Care Association," Hill said. A board of directors was organized with 50 per cent being appointed by Watts Hospital and 50 per cent by Duke Hospital.

"I gave them an office in the Trust Building, rent-free for a year, and put up $250 capital. Charles L. Medlin of Cary was the first enrolled member and we later employed Elisha Herndon as president of the firm," Hill said.

The first four organizations or corporations to enroll in the association were: the Durham Herald-Sun, the University of North Carolina at Chapel Hill, Duke University, and the old Durham Loan & Trust Co., now Central Carolina Bank & Trust Co. The four are still subscribers. Eventually the association occupied the mezzanine of the Trust Building, then moved to the second floor of the Temple Building (now Guaranty Bank), and next occupied more spacious quarters on Geer Street. Later the association built a structure on Duke Street. In 1968 Hospital Care merged with Hospital Savings Association of Chapel Hill to become Blue Cross and Blue Shield of North Carolina.

Two years later Hill was chairman of the building committee for the $10-million Blue Cross-Blue Shield Service Center on the Durham-Chapel Hill Boulevard, which was dedicated in 1973. "We have 225,000 square feet in this building and employ 835 people there," Hill said. "We continue to use the Durham office building on Duke Street for all government business."

Hill said his lifelong interest in hospitals and medicine "probably dates back to 1917 when I had a 'football knee' and was a patient in a New York City Hospital for three months.

"The first job I had after I married Ann McCulloch of Baltimore and returned to Durham was to study out and build the Laura Valinda Beall Pavilion in memory of my Grandmother Watts with funds left by my grandfather, George Watts, in his will when he died in 1921," Hill said. "This increased the hospital by about 40 beds, giving it a total of about 135 beds."

He pointed out that George Watts first built Watts Hospital on the corner of

W. Main Street and Buchanan Boulevard, near where McPherson Hospital is now, in 1895. The new Watts Hospital was built in 1909. "I was president of the Watts board of trustees when its first bond issue for building funds was held. This resulted in a new wing being built in about 1954," he said.

"One of the greatest satisfactions in my life was to see us have over 1.5 million people in North Carolina covered by Blue Cross-Blue Shield, out of the state's five million population. It has meant the difference to them in escaping financial catastrophe. It has paid so many bills for so many people."

The Hospital Care Association was the first statewide Blue Cross-Blue Shield plan and the fourth in the country. Had there been no stock market crash and depression in 1929, the Durham Hospital Association (as it was then called) would have been the first prepaid voluntary health service plan in the United States.

Hill retired from the Watts Hospital board of trustees 10 years ago, "except for 'Friends of Watts Hospital.' "

Executive Worked Her Way Up

Lost Scholarship Started Her on Way

The disastrous flu epidemic of 1918 cheated Maggie Allene Morris out of the scholarship to Trinity College she had won as she graduated from Durham High School. "The Trinity campus was quarantined and they wouldn't let the town girls and boys enter," she recalled. "Every family was hit by the dreaded disease—it was a major calamity which ravaged Durham. My mama, 18 of her boarders, and the cook got sick. Mass burials were common."

Miss Morris, who now observes her 49th year with J. Southgate & Son general insurance, has been affiliated with an insurance agency longer than any other woman in Durham and possibly in the state. She is called "Miss Insurance."

The youngest of 10 children she was born "in a house at the point of Wilkerson Avenue and Pettigrew Street." Her parents, James Leonard Morris and Mary Eleanor Morris, had moved here from the Reedy Creek section of Wake County.

"I first attended Edgemont School and then Durham High where I was a member of the patriotic senior class. Our colors were red, white, and blue, and the boys all wanted to join the military. We girls in the class volunteered for various war-effort endeavors and sold war savings stamps and bonds," she said.

With her long-sought scholarship to Trinity knocked out, a disappointed Maggie Morris found a job "looping government socks" at Durham Hosiery Mills in Edgemont. She was paid about $2 a day.

She attended night classes at Atlantic Business College in the old Lochmoor Hotel. "A Mrs. Summers, who was Superior Court stenographer, ran the school. She would take the class into court, have us take down the evidence, return to school and transcribe the evidence," Miss Morris said.

On Saturdays she worked at Mrs J. L. Council's general store, earning 10 cents an hour the 10 hours she was there. "In February 1919, I decided I wanted to attend school during the day, so I quit my job at the mill," she said.

Two months later, Miss Morris went to work for the Durham Motor Car Co. which was where the W. C. Lyon Hardware Co. is now.

"We sold the Reo, the Paige, the Liberty, and the Hudson automobiles," she said. "I was office secretary, bookkeeper, stockroom clerk, and also priced every item and made out sales papers." The salary was $10 a week.

On Sept. 22, 1924, Miss Morris went to work for J. Southgate & Son, a leading Durham insurance agency and the oldest in North Carolina under the same firm name. The business was established in 1802. "I was office secretary, working from 8 a.m. to 6 p.m., six days a week. I was paid $150 a month, which was good money then," she said.

Miss Morris turned all of her wages over to her mother, who paid their rent, bought groceries and clothes, and paid all other expenses.

"Papa was dead and all of the other children were out on their own," she said. "Mother and I lived in the G. C. Farthing home at 403 McMannen St."

When Miss Morris received her first raise, she didn't tell her mother, but put money in a savings account at First National Bank. "I had $1,000 on deposit when the depression came in 1929 and bankruptcy followed," she recalled. "I was able to recover only $550 of my money and that over a period of six years. Our firm, like so many others, was hard hit and lost heavily. Our large accounts and many small individual accounts carried us through."

In 1940 Miss Morris, who had risen from stenographer to bookkeeper, was made secretary-treasurer and became Tom Fuller Southgate's secretary.

Southgate died in July 1956 and left Miss Morris one-fourth of his company stock. His will provided that she would have a job with the firm for as long as she lived.

Long active in various aspects of insurance, Miss Morris organized the Durham Association of Insurance Women in April 1948 and was its first president. She later became regional director of the North Carolina Association of Insurance Women. The association of insurance women has named her "Insurance Woman of the Year" on three occasions.

Asked about changes in the insurance business, Miss Morris said there had been more changes during the past 20 years than in her first 29 years in insurance. "Everything is so specialized now," she said. "There are so many ways coverage can be written and extensions made by endorsements. You have to be on your toes to keep up with these changes. You have to know where to find the answers."

Asked about the really sharp people she has found in the insurance business, Miss Morris was quick to answer. "Mr. Southgate was the most knowledgeable man of his time, and was so recognized. I have no reason to think this wouldn't be true today if he were living."

Hobbies? Miss Morris smiled when asked. "Just living and being involved with trying to do for others. That's it," she said.

He Has Memories of Lakewood Park

Marvin "Firecracker" Mangum may have stretched it a little when he championed sale of his fireworks by referring to the Biblical injunction, "Make a joyful noise unto the Lord."

"Of course there were complaints and reports of injuries, but he sold a lot of fireworks during the Christmas season," says Robert Edward Lee Jr., better known as "Cotton" Lee.

Lee, who has lived in the Lakewood Park area since he was a boy, retired from his City of Durham job in 1965, after working as a draftsman for 43½ years.

Now 78, and living at 1609 Lakewood Ave., with his wife Cecelia, Lee yet haunts the woods, fields, swamps, and rivers, hunting, fishing, cooking for friends, and "enjoying my lifelong marriage to the out-of-doors and my love of God's wildlife creatures."

"Firecracker" Mangum first ran a little grocery store on Lakewood Avenue, where he also sold fireworks, and he later operated a fireworks stand on Chapel Hill Road near Pickett Road. That was long ago.

Mrs. Lee said that people were mostly poor when she was a girl, but that they usually ate well, and put up a Christmas tree even if it had to be decorated with real wax candles (which they had to watch if lighted).

"Sometimes there were bits of cotton, loops of crayon-colored paper, strings of popcorn, and maybe a star," she said. "And stockings were hung but no one expected much. I first remember Mama waking me on Christmas morning and telling me that an old man had brought me a doll. But who can forget that delightful cedar tree fragrance."

Her husband grinned. "I first knew of a real Christmas gift when my father, who worked at a furniture store, gave me a single-barrel shotgun when I was 15. I later acknowledged to him that I had long known the identity of Santa Claus but didn't want it known for fear of being cut off."

As to his name, Lee said he had always been proud of being named after the illustrious Gen. Robert E. Lee. "I had a signature of the general and I passed it on to our son, R. E. Lee III, in Alabama."

Laughing, Lee recalled the time an employee of Miller-Hurst Co. (They were on Morris Street opposite the old City Hall) said he had been told that Ulysses S. Grant was looking for Lee.

"I told him in seriousness that if he saw Mr. Grant to send him to my office."

Asked about the nickname "Cotton," Lee said it was tied on by Bill Murray, who with his father W. R. Murray operated Murray Music Store. "My hair was sandy, all right, so the name has stuck all these years."

Lee said that his old community was once noted for its Lakewood Park, which was advertised as "the Coney Island of the South."

"I saw the roller coaster being built by a man who also ran a popcorn stand," he said. "He made little pressed popcorn biscuits and put syrup or molasses on his popcorn. I sold the stuff at five cents a bag, making a penny on each bag I sold. It was called 'Razzle-Dazzle' popcorn. I'd yell, 'Razzle-Dazzle popcorn, five cents a bag. Good for the ladies and good for the babies.' "

Street cars came to Lakewood Park regularly, open summer cars with people hanging on the sides, going to and from the amusement park.

"At first the park had a long earthland dam lake for swimming. They'd rent you a bathing suit and let you swim for a quarter. Sometimes the boys would steal the lake water cutoff and drain the lake. Then the boys would capture turtles, bullfrogs, muskrats, and snakes from the mud. Later the park built a new concrete pool a couple of hundred yards away," Lee said. "The first dollar I made was selling a dozen pair of frog legs to Mr. T. E. Cheek, a banker. I got the frogs out of the old lake."

Lee said that carnivals often came to the park, along with huge one-man balloons that offered rides. "They also had high horse dives into the pool, a dance pavillion, merry-go-round, shooting gallery, skating rink, bowling alley, lots of confectionary stands, swings and slides, and tables and benches.

"There was also a casino which offered plays and opera, and stock companies. I remember how frightening was the play, Dr. Jekyll and Mr. Hyde. I can't forget the grim-faced, wooden, Chinaman who turned a crank for the organ to play lively music for the merry-go-round. He wore a queue (plait of hair)."

Lee had an older brother, Wallace Lee, an electrician who was also a musician, a magician, and ventriloquist. He entertained throughout North Carolina, usually in schools and at Duke University.

"He published books on double-talk and trick mathematics, but he never helped me on math, despite the fact he was an awfully good brother," Lee said. "Wallace, who has been dead a long time, had a lot of fun in stores, on the street, and in buses, 'throwing his voice' and making double-talk."

Lee may be the only living person who attended school in the building on Morris Street which at first was Durham High School, and then worked in the same building when it became City Hall.

"I worked first for the city when it carried on its business in the old Academy of Music building, which was to become the site of the Washington Duke Hotel. Durham had its first city manager at the time, R. W. Rigsby. While I was in Durham High School I was a member of the co-op class taught by Miss

Maude Rogers, I was in the class half the day and worked also in the machine shops of Liggett & Myers and the American Tobacco Co. I took double doses of drafting in school. I guess I became a self-educated man."

Retirement Doesn't Dim His Interest in Durham

Marcellus Arnold Briggs, a native son of Durham who cast his lot with his hometown, has excelled as a business executive, an educator, and churchman. At 88, he is in retirement, but he maintains his interest in civic affairs.

Briggs is a tall, wiry man with a ready smile, wit, and hearty handshake. He was one of the ramrods for Durham's centennial celebration in 1953 and he plans to participate in the local observance of the nation's bicentennial.

Briggs was born April 17, 1887, the son of Peter M. Briggs, a lawyer who became bookkeeper for the Blackwell Durham Tobacco Co. "There were four of us children and we lived on Dillard Street, right behind where the bus terminal is now located. Adjacent to our yard was a neighborhood tennis court," he said.

At the time, Main Street didn't go directly east across Dillard, it swerved to the left because the old Bryan home was situated in the intersection, Briggs said.

He attended Morehead School, which had 10 grades, and he graduated in 1905 at the time W. J. Carmichael was principal. "Morehead was the first school in North Carolina to have classes in shop and mechanical drawing. The school magazine, the Messenger, started when I was in the senior class and I was the editor-in-chief," Briggs said. "We published about six times a year and it later became the yearbook of Durham High School."

Briggs said that on graduating from high school he received a scholarship to the University of North Carolina, and John Hall Manning received one to Trinity College. "We swapped scholarships because I wanted to go to Trinity and live at home," Briggs laughed. He became southern intercollegiate tennis champion at Trinity and was senior class president. He was also editor-in-chief of the Archive, the college publication.

"Just before graduation in 1909, the president, Dr. John Kilgo, told me there were 39 in the graduating class and that he would make it 40 because he was resigning to become a bishop in the Methodist Church," Briggs said. "He also told me, 'Arnold, your class is in deficit of over $300 (for the Archive) and the class can't graduate until we get the money.' "

Briggs said he was wondering how to collect the money so quick when C. W. Toms, a tobacco company executive and a member of the college board of trustees, gave him a check for the entire indebtedness. "He said, 'You can repay me when the money comes in.' So the money was turned over to Dr. Kilgo and the class graduated. I didn't tell him where the money came from. Several months later we repaid it all."

After graduation Briggs taught English in high school at Chester, S.C. A year later he returned to Durham and for three years taught English at Durham High School—in the building that is now City Hall.

"After three years I was made principal while E. J. Green was superintendent of city schools. The first time I walked into the principal's office I noticed a large picture of a hunting dog pointing, nose and tail straight out. The picture carried one word, 'steady.' "

When Briggs became principal there were two teachers in the high school who had taught him. They were Miss Lila Markham and a Mrs. Shaw. "There was discipline in the schools then. I wouldn't have lasted two weeks the way schools are run now," he said.

While he was principal, Briggs said, he was instrumental in the school presenting "The Merchant of Venice," at the Academy of Music (site of the Durham Hotel), with rented costumes from New York, and the presentation of a musical comedy entitled "The Captain of Plymouth."

"We had basketball, football, and baseball at high school then, but there were no coaches. Our basketball team one year won the state championship, the players walking all the way back from Chapel Hill where they won the title," he said.

The playground and ball field of Durham High School then was at the rear of the school, the site now of Carolina Theater. "The playground was divided, one-half for the boys and one-half for the girls," Briggs chuckled. "We had no cafeteria and most of the students brought their own lunches or bought apples from Henry Faucette, our janitor."

In 1916 Briggs went to work as a salesman with Carolina Rolling Mills, a Durham flour mill owned by Gen. Julian S. Carr which manufactured Occoneechee and Peerless flour. The mill later became Austin-Heaton Co., named after Carr's sons, Austin and Heaton.

In 1920 Briggs became a charter member of the Durham Kiwanis Club. Today he is the only living charter member. "I was first introduced as 'Mr. Occoneechee,' and I presented my wife as 'Peerless,' " Briggs laughed.

Briggs moved up in his business and in 1932 was made president of the firm, which in 1961 was sold to Harris Milling Co., a Michigan enterprise. "I remained on until 1963, at which time I retired, having had 47 years with the company," he said. The mill was torn down in 1970.

Briggs served as president of the National Soft Wheat Millers Association. He also was a member of the board of directors of the Millers National Federation for 27 years.

For many years wheat came into Durham from a radius of 40 miles, and as many as 100 trucks would be unloaded at the mill.

Briggs recalled that he joined Trinity Methodist Church in 1900 at the age of 13. He has been chairman of the board of stewards twice, superintendent of the Sunday school in 1927, and taught the men's Bible class for many years. "I've been practically everything but janitor at Trinity," he said.

Briggs was instrumental in establishment of the Depositors National Bank (now N.C. National Bank) after the old First National Bank failed during the depression. He became a member of the board of directors of the Durham & Southern Ralroad during that time.

"I was interested in Durham's Centennial in 1953 and we came out with a net profit of $4,000 which I presented to Mrs. Mary Duke Biddle for the Durham United Fund," Briggs said. "We had borrowed $7,000 from the city of Durham, and the city council was greatly surprised when we paid this back. The council never thought we would."

Briggs also served for 24 years as a member of the Durham City Board of Education. "One of the things I've really enjoyed and really got a lot out of through the years, was having been associated with milling officials all over the United States," Briggs said. "They thought as I did, and were conservatives. I've never changed."

Briggs' wife, Frances Watts Markham, died many years ago. They had three children, Miss Frances Briggs who is a professor at Commonwealth University, in Virginia; a son, M. A. Briggs, Jr., who is minister of music at First Baptist Church in Wilmington; and daughter Miss Marcella Briggs of the home.

Briggs still enjoys his church, walking, and reminiscing. He has many of his school periodicals, keeps up with what's going on in the world, and hopes that before he dies a little gentility of yesteryear will return.

Chapel Bells Rang Out 'Annie Laurie' for Metal Master

At 4:30 p.m. on June 2, 1935, Anton Brees, noted carilloneur of the Mountain Singing Tower, Florida, in a prelude to the service dedication of the magnificent Duke University Chapel, gave an impressive carillon recital. *America* was his first rendition. At 5 p.m. Edward Hall Broadhead, chapel organist, opened the service with *My Inmost Heart Doth Yearn,* by Brahms.

But the first tune played on the great bells at the chapel came earlier, impromptu, without much ado, and was dedicated to a Durham sheet-metal master, William M. Mutter. It was the old Scotch favorite, *Annie Laurie.*

The late Frank Mutter of Glendale Avenue, son of William M. Mutter, and himself a skilled craftsman, once said it came about in the following way. The Mutters were placing lead-coated copper inside the tower of Duke Chapel when they met a Scotsman who had come to Durham from Europe to install the costly bells in the chapel.

The three became friends when the Scotsman learned that the elder Mutter came from his old home, Dundee, in the same country. The Scotsman insisted that the first song be in honor of Mutter.

When Temple Baptist Church was remodeled years ago and a 14-foot concrete cross added, Frank Mutter was hired to install copper in the cross. Mutter recalled that the architectural inspector called his boss, W. P. Budd of Budd-Piper Roofing Company, to say that the cross was setting crooked.

"I knew this was not true because I had been careful with the level, but the inspector was reluctant to take my word," Mutter said. Laughing, Mutter said he got the inspector to crawl up the shaky wooden scaffold with him. When the level showed that the cross was setting true, Mutter said, the inspector patted him on the back and said he was sorry.

"I jokingly told him that I ought to push him off the scaffold. The man turned pale. He looked down to the ground far below and without a word climbed down with quite a speed for a man of his age and size. He thought I was serious."

Asked about lightning rods, Mutter said. "We put a lightning rod through the cross. It's the thing to do because it would be rather expensive to erect a scaffold to the top of a steeple for a repair after lightning struck."

The biggest copper job Mutter ever had a hand in was at St. Mary's Catholic Church in Wilmington. He said what made the work so difficult was that the top of the church was built in the shape of a cross and the wings of the buildings were round.

The entire roof was of tile construction and workmen had to drill through the roof and install wooden battens to anchor copper to the roof. He said there is not a nail or any wood in the more than 100-year-old church except the pews and the heavy doors which have brass hinges and screws. Everything is arched and keyed-in.

The biggest copper job in Durham, Mutter said, would be that at Duke Chapel, rivaled only by the 20 tons of copper placed atop Duke's Perkins Library to support and protect the roof.

Mutter recalled working with the first sheet metal firm in Durham, which had a shop at the site of Happy Patty's saloon at 113 S. Mangum St. "I helped them on occasion to make copper pipe for customers' whisky stills, then so popular, but that was a long time ago."

A native of Portsmouth, Va., Mutter began working at 17 by making gun powder for sale to the Russian government, while employed by E. I. DuPont & Company at Hopewell, Va.

When the United States entered the war against Germany in 1917, DuPont ended its contract with Russia and began making gun powder for this country.

Two years later Mutter was transferred to Wilmington, Del., to take a fore-man's job, but soon resigned to join his father, who had opened a sheet metal shop in Portsmouth. Seven years after that, Frank's brother William was drowned in a fishing accident. Upset, the elder Mutter moved with his family to Durham.

In 1939 Frank went to work at the Norfolk Navy yard where the government was making metal furniture for ships. Mutter was supervisor of 3,000 men in the metal shop. England was at war and America was beefing up its fleet.

One day his boss came in with a set of blueprints, pointed at a drawing and asked, "Can you make this?" Mutter looked at it and answered, "Yes." It was a halfround, stainless steel gutter, 32 feet in diameter—a gas seal for the turrets of the big battleship guns. Mutter thus became supervisor.

In 1946 he returned to Durham where his foreman's job awaited him. For several years he also taught his trade in a Durham school.

Mutter lamented that Durham had been gutted by changes. Cornices had disappeared and classical design and intricate work had become a thing of the past. A lack of pride in work and an increasing grasp for more money was to blame, he said.

Mutter said the Duke Chapel architecture and the craftsmanship of Ameri-cans, Scotsmen, and Italians that went into the chapel's creation, along with the dream of the Duke family and the awe-inspiring atmosphere, make it a shrine of sanctified beauty.

His widow, Essie Mutter, still lives at the home at 1908 Glendale Ave. Their son Robert is a Durham bank executive, and son Frank Jr. is retired from a United Airlines office in Washington, D.C., and is living at Murrell's Inlet, S.C.

So when the mighty bells and organ send forth their triumphant sounds today as the 50th-reunion services of Duke Chapel get under way, somewhere there will be echoes of old *Annie Laurie* for kindred souls of the past.

6

Politics and Law

Wiley P. Mangum of Bahama, educator, was once, for a short while, vice-president of the United States.

Attorney Dan K. Edwards of Durham was mayor, state legislator, and district attorney assistant secretary of Defense under General George C. Marshall, U.S. spokesman for NATO, administering this office from London and Paris. Edwards was also a major general in the Army during World War II.

Durham has had many outstanding attorneys and several excellent judges. Attorney William B. Umstead was a U.S. Senator and Durham's only state governor. Attorney William Bramham was once the commissioner, or czar, of all organized minor league baseball.

Off The Record with "Marryin' Sam" Riley

He has been called "Esso" Riley, "Marryin' Sam," and "Here Come da Judge." He takes the handles in stride. He is Samuel Oscar Riley, a courtly, white-haired man with spring in his heart and his step, who held public office longer than anyone else in Durham County's history.

Riley was clerk of Recorder's Court for 47 years, and at the same time was a justice of the peace for 39 years. Then he served on the city council and became one of the first three District Court judges when the district system was set up in Durham.

A Democrat, Riley was never defeated in a political race and often led the ticket. He said he never spent a cent campaigning.

His age? Riley, now enjoying his retirement, shakes his head and winks. "I might want to marry again," he says.

Riley, a widower who has been married twice, was born in Durham County, about four miles west of the courthouse. Although he never was a lawyer, he became interested in the law when he was a boy. Sometimes he skipped school to sit in on court.

But his first job wasn't in the court system; it was in a tobacco warehouse owned by his father, John Jefferson Riley, and R. T. and W. L. Umstead. After his father's death, Riley bought tobacco for Liggett & Myers and R. J. Reynolds.

In 1916, the year the courthouse was built, he ran for clerk of Recorder's Court against R. A. Harris, and was elected by 86 votes. "The job paid $1,000 a year, court was held every day except Sunday, and Paul C. Graham was judge," Riley recalled.

Prohibition was the law but genuine corn whisky and East Lake rye were readily available. Public drunkenness, fighting, and gambling cases took much of the court's time. There were few traffic cases because there was little motor vehicle traffic.

The penalty for drunkenness was a fine of $5 and the costs ($3.85), plus jail fees and meals. This was true six days a week, but intoxication on Sunday brought a fine of $10 and costs.

"In the old days there was always a large crowd of spectators when court was held. Outside of courtroom activity, baseball, church, and watching the trains come in, there was little recreation or entertainment except a silent movie or a vaudeville," Riley said.

As clerk of the lower court, he handled all of the official business with the help of a parttime clerical worker, Miss Nina Horner (later Matthews), who recently retired as long-time manager of the Durham Social Security office. Later his staff grew larger.

"In 1917 I was appointed a magistrate. There were only two magistrates in Durham at the time, R. C. Cox and R. A. Harris," Riley said.

A couple of weeks later he performed his first marriage. The wedding was held in his office in the courthouse after the soon-to-be groom showed his $3 marriage license. There was no set fee for the magistrate's service but on most occasions the groom handed the knot-tier a small sum of money.

Riley was clerk of court during World Wars I and II, and recalls that in the days of nearby Camp Butner in the early '40s, "a lot of girls came here from distant places to marry their boyfriends before they were shipped out."

Chuckling, he related how he was awakened late one cold December night at his home on Cole Mill Road by a telephone call from police headquarters. The call was urgent. "I was told to come down to my office in the courthouse and marry a couple. I dressed, and still sleepy, drove to the courthouse."

"A young soldier and his fiancee were pacing the floor outside my office. He had his license gripped tight in a sweaty hand. I told the couple there would have to be at least two witnesses to the ceremony. The soldier left, promising to return with witnesses."

"I gave the girl a magazine to read and I got busy with some office work. Way past midnight, hours later, we heard footsteps clanging against the tile floor of the corridor and the hallway. I opened the door and to my astonishment I found that the soldier had brought a good portion of his regiment with him. The witnesses, laughing and wise-cracking, filled the main office, the private office, the consultation room, and part of the hallway."

Following the brief ceremony, all of the soldiers wanted to kiss the bride, he said. "It took a long time. I got home before daybreak."

As to marriages he performed, Riley said some brides-to-be came to his office with babies in their arms, some pregnant. One couple was blind, another crippled, and many singles were rolled up in wheelchairs.

"I had a lot of couples to come in while intoxicated. I told them to sober up and return. A few of them did. I married couples from every state in the union and my largest fee was $50 and the smallest just 50 cents," he said.

On one occasion the soon-to-be groom remarked that he had only $5 to his name, and Riley told the man to use the money to buy his wife a wedding present.

"They came in wearing fancy clothes, overalls, or scanty attire. Sometimes the bride held flowers in her hand, once in a vase. And occasionally a couple I had married returned to get 'unmarried.' I referred them to a lawyer," Riley said. He once estimated that he had married 12,000 couples. They didn't call him "Marryin' Sam" for nothing.

Riley said that as a judge he never divorced a couple he had married while serving as a magistrate or "jaypee."

Riley said the most difficult cases he ever tried as a judge were those concerning custody of children. "There is often heartbreak and bitterness in the proceedings," he said.

Riley believed in a decorous courtroom. In fact, he ended his career as clerk of Recorder's Court because he felt the court wasn't being run properly.

Riley stalked out of the courtroom one day in March 1963 and announced he was quitting because the prosecutor and judge had ignored his pleas to quit ramming cases through so fast he couldn't record judgments fully as the law required.

He said the court was skipping the requirement for having witnesses take oaths and was rushing cases so that some witnesses didn't even get to testify. He turned in his resignation a few days later. The next month he was elected to the city council. He served for three and a half years, then stepped down to go on the District Court bench. He retired in 1970.

Although he bore himself with dignity, and insisted on it in court, Riley knew how to have fun. He says he's had a lot of fun, from taking sun baths atop the old Malborune Hotel to organizing a washboard band and dancing the fox trot at Lakewood Park pavilion.

Recalling his sun baths on the hotel roof with attorney James R. Patton, Riley said, "My good friend, E. I. Bugg, owner of the hotel, told us that the legs of our cots were sticking in the roof, causing leaks. That broke it up."

Riley, who has been a widower since 1959, lives alone at 819 Buchanan Blvd. He has a daughter, Elizabeth Riley Morrison, by his first marriage, who lives in Greensboro.

"I feel as young as I did 30 years ago. I've always had good health and I attribute this in great measures to walking. But I don't walk downtown, it's too depressing to see so many buildings gone," Riley said.

Roosevelt In Durham: 'Articulate... With Fire, Fervor'

Visit In 1905 Described As 'Bully' By Local Attorney

The rugged fellow with the walrus moustache and pince-nez surveyed the wildly cheering audience with a wide, toothy grin. Then with the jaunty ease of a Canadian logroller, he brushed aside his guard and secretary who sought to hold him to the safety of his flatcar.

"Get away!" he commanded. "We will walk to the platform."

He was the 26th president of the United States, Theodore Roosevelt. The time was Oct. 19, 1905, and the place was a railroad siding opposite old Trinity College in Durham.

The Republican chieftain, fondly called "the Rough Rider," the "Trust Buster," and "Teddy the Great," was the third president to visit the tobacco town of Durham. He followed James Buchanan (1859), and Andrew Johnson, (1866), the North Carolinian who was nearly the victim of impeachment.

Two Durham attorneys, Victor S. Bryant and Reuben O. Everett, remember well Roosevelt's momentous visit here. The occasion followed the announcement of September 1905, by Secretary Pogue of the North Carolina State Fair, that Roosevelt would attend a luncheon sponsored by the N.C. Agricultural Society. This was hailed as a highlight of the 45th annual State Fair.

A Durham committee composed of Mayor P. C. Graham, Victor S. Bryant Sr., W. A. Erwin, General Julian S. Carr, W. T. O'Brien, John F. Wiley and T. B. Fuller, was named to consult with Governor Robert B. Glenn in behalf of having the President visit Durham. Members of the committee next made a trip to Washington and telegraphed back that Roosevelt would make a stop in Durham of fifteen minutes, the same length of time scheduled for Charlotte.

There was a stipulation that the president would not leave his train in Durham, because when he did so, someone in his party was always absent when the train was ready to resume travel.

The State Fair opened on Oct. 17, and the report that Roosevelt would be coming attracted huge crowds, as was anticipated. Governor Glenn, in opening the fair, said it was the greatest in state history, and would feature the appearance of the president and the showing of a new invention, the cotton picker.

The Governor took the occasion to say he hoped to see the day when temperance would by the vote of the people, by legislation, or through the uplifting influence of the churches, pervade the state and the Bible take the place of the bottle and the pistol in the pockets of erring young men.

President Roosevelt's train was scheduled to reach Raleigh at 1 p.m. on Oct. 19, arrive in Durham 1:55 p.m., and leave on the trip west at 2:10 p.m.

The Southern Railway flatcar to be used as a speaker's platform was scrubbed and handsomely decorated with silk and bunting. A plush carpet was placed over the car.

Police Chief J. A. Woodall had men on all sides of the car for protection to the nation's leader. A general holiday was declared in Durham and schools, banks, and many factories and businesses were closed.

The Southern Railway issued a handsome souvenir for the president's southern trip in the form of a small book giving his schedule, miles to be traveled, names of those in his party, and a map of his 4,000-mile trip.

With the president was his wife, high officials, reporters and photographers. A crowd estimated at more than 15,000 persons was on hand when the train arrived 12 minutes late.

Roosevelt, who had become president on Sept. 14, 1901, following the assassination of President William McKinley, strode toward the freshly erected rostrum some 100 feet away from the rear of his train. Whistles and bells from town factories and mills roared a welcome, but it was the football yells by the Trinity College student body gathered south of the speaker's stand that brought the famous grin from the President.

"As I came in, gentleman, I felt as if I was at a football contest," he bowed and said in appreciation of his greeting.

On all sides of town had been placed miniature flags, bits of bunting, banners and the president's picture. The yard engine which brought his train was also appropriately decorated.

Over the gate at Trinity College swung a large banner which read: "Trinity college Welcomes the President of the United States."

The president while speaking stood on a Persian rug. One of his conductors said arrangements in Durham were the best he had seen on the tour. The throttle of the presidential train was handled by Engineer Miles Glenn, a Durham man, who was enjoying his place in the sun.

Mrs. Roosevelt was presented with a bouquet of American roses by Mrs. George W. Watts. A few minutes earlier the president spoke to a gathering at the Corcoran Street crossing when his train stopped for water.

He tried to talk but the whistles at the Bull Factory were going so strong he could not be heard. The president laughed and said, "Well, I'm glad to be in North Carolina today and glad to meet North Carolina people."

At his official stop opposite Trinity College on W. Main Street, he was introduced by Mayor Graham. The major portion of the president's well-received speech was directed to students and graduates of Trinity. Roosevelt paid a warm tribute to the Confederate soldier. He said he had traveled across the union "and found the average American to be a pretty decent fellow, and the only way to get along with the other average American is to know him. I don't care whether he lives in the North, South, East or West, or whether he be a wage earner or a capitalist, or whether he lives in town or country, the important thing is that he shall know his fellows who live somewhere else and work somewhere else. And he shall understand that fundamentally both of them have the same feelings, the same convictions, are striving for the same ideals, and that they achieve those fields best if they stand shoulder to shoulder in righteousness together."

Lawyer Victor S. Bryant says he was a boy when his father took him by buggy to hear the president's speech. "President Roosevelt was articulate, and spoke with fire and fervor," he recalled.

Bryant says he remembers that while the president was speaking a member of his party tapped Roosevelt on the sleeve and said, "Time to go. The engineer says it is time to go." The president turned to say: "You tell that engineer to wait. This is the finest audience I've had in a long time."

Everett commented: "He always made a good talk. It was bully. You know that was the president's favorite expression, 'Bully.'"

Roosevelt was assistant Secretary of the Navy under President McKinley, and with the outbreak of the Spanish War in 1898, he helped organize the 1st U.S. Volunteer Cavalry and led the "Rough Riders," an inexperienced but dramatically tough fighting unit.

He later became Governor of New York by a scant margin, and enemies in effort to resist his desire to succeed himself as governor, helped lift him to "the honorable seclusion of the vice presidency.

His popularity as president brought him the presidency in the election of 1904 in the race against the Democratic nominee, Alton B. Parker.

Retired from the presidency in March 1909, after declining to seek another term of office in 1908, Roosevelt gave his support to the candidacy of William Howard Taft, his Secretary of War.

Taft became the next president. At the urging of Roosevelt, who never forgot his warm reception in Durham, President Taft later came to Durham and attended a banquet of the Durham Bar Association.

He Remembers Washout at First Lady's Party

Trailor D. Young, director of food services at the Durham Hotel, once catered a luncheon for Mrs. Eleanor Roosevelt. It was a washout.

"Six weeks before Franklin D. Roosevelt became President of the United States, I was hired as director of food and beverage services at the Congressional Country Club in Washington," he said.

"Mrs. Eleanor Roosevelt was giving her first luncheon as the wife of a president and it was being held as a coming out party on the terrace off the main lobby of the club."

"There were at least 1,500 guests and we really rolled out the red carpet in her honor. Shortly after the food was served, a thunder storm developed and you have never seen so many well-dressed people completely drenched. Talk about being mad as a wet hen, those ladies were really upset. They were soaked and so was the food. Mrs. Roosevelt, a gracious host, tried hard but failed to hide her disappointment. She was all wet, too."

Young is a native of Robinsonville in Martin County.

His father, Nathaniel Young, was a tobacco warehouseman and after the family (there were two girls and three boys) moved to Walkertown in 1908, the father became involved in tobacco markets in North Carolina, Georgia, and Tennessee.

When Trailor Young graduated from high school in Walkertown, he accompanied his father on trips to these markets.

"When the depression came in 1930, I had $1,800 in the Merchants Bank in Winston-Salem but I couldn't buy a pack of cigarettes," he recalled.

Young struck out on his own, first taking a job as a checker in the food stockroom at the Robert E. Lee Hotel in Winston-Salem.

Eighteen months later the head waiter, a German named Pete Schmidt, told Young he would get him a job in the Congressional Country Club in Washington if Young would agree to take Schmidt along.

"Pete had worked there so I readily consented to a move," Young said. "I got a job as the food and beverage director of this swanky place located eight miles north of the District of Columbia in the Glen Echo community."

During his 10 years at the club, Young said, he had the privilege of knowing six presidents of the United States, U.S. Postmaster James Farley, "who put F.D.R. in office," and "King Fish" Huey Long, "who started playing golf on the club course at the crack of dawn, usually playing alone and always accompanied by his caddy and two bodyguards armed with submachineguns. Long was a very controversial fellow at the time. You may recall that he built the Huey Long Bridge in Louisiana in honor of his daughter."

Young knew the late FBI Director J. Edgar Hoover. "He was one of the quietest people I've ever seen," he said. "He walked like a tiger tracking down his prey. A brilliant man with the most piercing eyes I've ever seen. He was a true patriot, a dynamic, kind figure. Nobody, not even a president ever dared cross him, and I don't think there will ever be a person capable of taking his place."

Chuckling, Young recalled his first meeting with the late John L. Lewis, the labor leader.

"I remember well his bushy eyebrows and menacing scowl. He came up to me at the buffet line on a Sunday night, slammed a heavy hand against the table and with a glare and a command, snapped, 'I want a cut out of the center of the beef. Rare!' Those bushy eyebrows, beady eyes, I can see them now." Young grinned. "The man never changed expression. He was hard as a rock, a rugged piece of merchandise. Of course, I gave him the cut he wanted, what else."

Young was a friend of General "Billy" Mitchell, famed U.S. Army pilot who because of his persistence, this country built planes instead of warships, and because of his defiance of his superiors, was court martialed in 1925.

"About 10 years after his death, Congress authorized the Medal of Honor for Mitchell because early in World War II, events confirmed many of his predictions," Young said.

Young knew Herbert Hoover, Franklin D. Roosevelt, Harry Truman, Dwight Eisenhower, John Kennedy, and President Richard Nixon. "Kennedy and Nixon were junior senators when I met them at the club, but, of course, they were to become presidents," he said.

Entertainers and movie stars, sports celebrities and Miss Americas, all have been familiar figures at the club, Young said.

"I knew Bing Crosby when he was singing with Paul Whiteman. He was a popular fellow," Young chuckled again.

The late Prince of Wales drew a lot of attention and admiration when he was a guest at the club and was "a style-setter," Young said.

Shaking his head and smiling, he added, "What a club. Everything was wide open, we had five bars. On the inside we had bowling, tennis, swimming, and billiards, and outside there was a lake which, when frozen during the winter, was used for ice skating.

In 1939 Young returned to North Carolina to work for the Sedgefield Country Club in Greensboro. "I had worn out three automobiles between Washington and Norwood, courting Bess Thompson, whom I married upon my return. I felt like I might be better off in North Carolina than spending so much time on the highways," he said.

In 1940, Young returned to the Robert E. Lee Hotel as director of food and beverage services. "I opened up a roof garden there and we had name bands playing for dances on Saturday."

Blake Nicholson, father of Blake Nicholson Jr. who is manager of the Durham Hotel, was assistant manager of the Robert E. Lee. In 1941, he and Young went together to the New Ricks Hotel in Rocky Mount.

"I left in 1958 to go to the Sheraton Hotel in High Point, but five years later I went with the Holiday Inn in Salisbury. I remained there four years and then went to the Commodore Yacht Club in Charlotte, a private club on Lake Wylie," Young said.

He said this club had 300 slips for anchoring boats. "We had anything from a $200,000 Chinese sloop to a little runabout. We had 'em all."

At this club Young had his first experience in helping layout and plan an 18-hole golf course. He remained at the club until 1970 when he came to Durham.

Asked if he had ever become restless or temporarily fed up with the food and beverage livelihood, Young laughed. "Yes, I did, once. It was in the 1960s and I felt a need to get away from it all. Bess and I returned to Norwood where we have a home and property. I just took it easy, planted a little garden and hoed and tended it six days a week for something to do. Then I got to itching to return to work."

Young said Blake Nicholson Jr., who had been working with his father at the New Ricks Hotel in Rocky Mount, took over the assistant manager's post in the Durham Hotel, then became manager in 1970. "So old friendship prevailed. I came to Durham to work with him," he said.

Young said his profession has been interesting and rewarding and that he has enjoyed his contacts with the public. "You meet people at all levels, what with conventions and group meetings. You're at the pulse of everything. You ask if work is my hobby. No, it's my life."

Durham's Dan K. Edwards, Hero and Statesman

When Gen. Douglas MacArthur said old soldiers never die, he could have been thinking of men like Maj. Gen. Dan K. Edwards of Durham. Edwards retired this year as commanding officer of the 30th Infantry Division of the National Guard after a lifetime of soldiering.

Now 60 years old, the general still has the bearing of a soldier and he remains as tough as spring steel.

A hard-jawed man of medium build, Edwards always wears the World War II white sidewall hair style. He goes bare of head, walks rapidly, and speaks softly but with authority. His unwavering blue eyes are a part of his authoritative directness.

He keeps in shape by regularly walking from his home at 406 Buchanan Blvd. to his downtown office two miles away and by using barbells.

A cigar-chomping man who eats rapidly but caresses his scotch on the rocks, the general's main concerns have always been his family, his country, a G.I. wherever he may be, his church (Duke Memorial Methodist) and the practice of law.

He was a champion wrestler and a boxer during his school days, and he loves to ride a horse, snow ski, swim, and play golf. His quiet diversion is classical music, which he enjoys with closed eyes, a half smile, and a cigar puff.

Daniel Kramer Edwards was born in Durham Feb. 17, 1914, son of the late Eva Marie Kramer Edwards, whose family built ships, and the late Duke Prof. Charles W. Edwards. He attended Durham High School and graduated from Duke University in 1936. He finished the school of law at Harvard College in 1938 where he made Phi Beta Kappa.

Edwards returned to Durham to practice law and in 1939 he joined the National Guard and enlisted in the Army as a private. Two weeks after Pearl Harbor he married Mary B. Partin of South Carolina. They had five children before her death: Katherine LeRoy, who is the wife of Dr. Walter Pepper of San Francisco; Dan Edwards Jr., a Duke graduate who will receive his degree from the University of North Carolina Law School in June; Claire Eagan, who is married to Fred Daughtery of Durham; Jane Harrison, who is undergoing medical technician training at Fort Sam Houston in Houston, Tex., and Marie Fulmer, who is attending art school in Camden, S.C., where she is also an instructor in horsemanship.

Several years ago, Edwards married Mrs. Virginia Dooley Duncan, wife of the late Harmon Duncan of Durham. The Duncans also had five children: Richard Duncan Edwards and Lucille Duncan Edwards, who live in the Edwards home; Joe Duncan, a student in California; Clayton Duncan of Atlanta, who is getting a doctorate in English at Berkeley, Calif., and Mike Duncan, who operates a ranch in New Mexico.

Mrs. Edwards, an experienced equestrienne, participates in fox hunts and has jumped and ridden horses in many states as well as in Ireland. She has skied on snow slopes throughout the country and in Italy. She has been affiliated with many organizations and civic endeavors.

As an infantry officer, captain, major, and then lieutenant colonel, Edwards fought through several campaigns in New Guinea and the Philippines on the bloody island road to Tokyo. Edwards emerged with a Distinguished Service Cross, Silver Star, Bronze Star with four oak leaf clusters, the Air Medal, Purple Heart, and last but not least in his mind, the Combat Infantryman's Badge.

Major General Dan K. Edwards

Through Buna, Hollandia, and Biak in New Guinea and Leyte and Palawan Island in the Philippines, Edwards served as operations officer, task force executive officer, and more notably, as aide to Gen. Robert L. Eichelberger.

How Edwards won the Purple Heart has become a renowned episode of the Pacific war. On Jan. 10, 1946, Eichelberger told of the exploit in Asheville as he was being honored at a dinner upon his return from Japan, where he was in charge of occupational forces. "While wading through swamps and being fired upon from every side by Japanese snipers, Col. Edwards led his men forward under almost impenetrable conditions into the fight," Eichelberger said.

"Then from dense vegetation from the roots of a tree, a sniper opened fire, Edwards fell into the line of fire to protect me and just four feet from me Edwards was hit. The bullet ripped through his side, tearing through his back and taking with it a part of his pelvis, making a hole almost as large as my fist. But Col. Edwards kept directing his men, at the same time yelling aloud to make the Japanese think they had wounded me."

Glancing at the stoic Edwards, Eichelberger continued: "Finally we inched forward through a hail of fire, carrying Edwards to one of our field doctors. After one quick look the medic explained to me that Edwards was as good as dead. 'Hell,' I said, 'He can't die here.' So we placed him in a jeep and I drove the jeep myself through the swampy jungle. We got him back to a field hospital and an operation was performed to remove chunks of metal and loose bone. The next morning Japanese planes bombarded this hospital, shredding tents and killing most of the patients and personnel."

"Edwards, blown from his cot, took refuge in a native hut. The next day he was put on a plane named 'The Chattanooga Choo Choo' and evacuated to Port Moresby. From there he was taken to a general hospital at Brisbane, Australia. Within three months after he was hit, Edwards was back in action. I can only say that 'Eddy is my No. 1 man for the Army,' " Eichelberger said.

After the war Edwards returned to his law practice and to the National Guard. Following stints as regimental commander of the 30th Division he was named commanding officer of the 1st Battalion Group, the 120th Infantry. Then came promotions to deputy commander and commander of the 30th Division.

But as he was moving up in the National Guard, he also entered other arenas of public service. He was elected to the state House of Representatives and began serving in 1947. He was credited with leading the work to enact the Powell Bill, which provides annual aid to North Carolina's towns and cities for street work. Edwards and Rep. Oscar Barker of Durham also sponsored a bill that increased the salaries of county officeholders.

Edwards resigned from the legislature before his term ended because he had been elected to another job—that of mayor of Durham. In the same year, 1949, he received the North Carolina Jaycees' Distinguished Service Award, and in 1950 he received the Durham Jaycees' Young Man Of the Year Award.

Two weeks before Edwards' second term as mayor expired in 1951, President Harry S. Truman appointed him assistant secretary of defense under Gen. George Marshall.

In Washington, Edwards maintained a daily schedule that would stagger many an executive. For example, on an August day in 1951, Edwards conferred with two assistant general counsels concerning a senatorial trip to Europe; attended a consultation on the Armed Forces Reserves Act; attended a conference with Deputy Secretary Lovett; met with the dean of the Duke University Law School; visited Capitol Hill and conferred with Congressman James Richards, chairman of the House Foreign Relations Committee, met with representatives of the State Department and his own staff in his own office, and planned transportation and itinerary for personnel to visit foreign countries.

His secretaries called it a typical day.

Edwards' staff in the Defense Department consisted of approximately 80 members, including attorneys and their secretaries. His job primarily concerned legal and legislative matters, such as the Mutual Security Aid Bill and the International Criminal and Geneva Convention. He also attended special engagements including receptions at embassies for foreign dignitaries and gave numerous speeches, sometimes filling in for General George Marshall. At the same time, he conducted Red Cross business as a member of the organization's board of governors.

Edwards was with the Defense Department during the Korean war and dealt with the problems of that conflict as well as continuing the establishment of the Department of Defense as a unified operation with a coordinated legislative program.

"There was also the excitement created by President Truman relieving General Douglas MacArthur from his command in the Pacific, and the subsequent hearings in the Congress participated in by Gen. Marshall," Edwards said.

In 1952 Edwards was made United States representative to the North Atlantic Council, with offices in London and Paris. The Defense Department was involved in the North Atlantic Treaty Ordinance (NATO) effort, although Edwards' part in that was somewhat indirect until he moved to Europe. "In Europe we were engaged in coordinated effort among the NATO member nations developing logistic systems in support of the military forces on the continent, negotiating status of force, agreements, coordinating in connection with what was called Off Shore Procurement—that is to say, the purchase of military goods from European sources," Edwards said.

His files on most of these matters are incomplete since he was constantly dealing in classified things "and could not maintain memoranda or files on most of the things we were doing." After his work in Europe in 1952, Edwards returned to Durham, but there was more public service ahead.

In September 1961, Gov. Terry Sanford, who had served under Edwards in the military, appointed him to succeed William H. Murdock as solicitor of Durham County Superior Court. Murdock had resigned to become U.S. attorney.

In 1963, while serving as solicitor, Edwards ordered the body of a slain 17-year-old exhumed from a Person County cemetery to recover a bullet from his body. The bullet compared with one fired from a pawned pistol. This action, rare in court annals, resulted in the conviction of the slayer.

Edwards resigned from the solicitor's office on Dec. 31, 1970, to devote more time to his work as attorney for the Durham Redevelopment Commission and the Durham Housing Authority, and to his first love, the National Guard.

In 1965 President Lyndon B. Johnson promoted Edwards to the rank of brigadier general, and in 1969 President Nixon promoted him to major general.

In January, the 30th Infantry Division was deactivated. Gen. Edwards presided over the retirement ceremony, and days later he, too, stepped aside. On March 9 at Fort Bragg, as the highlight of a military ball, the old soldier was recognized for his career. He was presented with the Army Distinguished Service Medal, the National Guard Bureau's Meritorious Service Award, and a large oak plaque mounted with bronze cutouts of three states. They were North Carolina, South Carolina, and Georgia, the three states whose men made up the 30th Infantry Division.

Participating in the service for Edwards were Lt. Gen. Richard J. Switz, commander of the 18th Airborne Corps at Fort Bragg; Lt. Gen. John J. Tolson III (Ret.), secretary of the state Department of Military and Veterans Affairs; and Major Gen. William M. Buck, state adjutant general.

Actually the general doesn't feel retired now, just deactivated, like the 30th Division. And he hasn't faded away because "old soldiers never die."

Edwards has mixed emotions about retirement from the guard. He says it this way: "About my participation in the Army National Guard—it's a good thing that the law and regulations fix a time limit on service in the Army and its reserve component, otherwise, I would be tempted to stay on indefinitely. I am glad that I now can pursue the practice of law without having to explain to people from time to time that I am not a full-time general. I have found that this is a problem that besets mayors and legislators and other part-time people."

"I am grateful that during the last quarter of a century the nation found it important to have an Army reserve component. Many years ago, a funny thing happened to me on the way from law school to the practice of law. I found myself in the Army for a period of some six years for World War II purposes."

"The associations, interests, and activities I experienced during that period continued to be sufficiently fascinating to keep me at least partially in the system. The Army National Guard provided a good means to be in both civilian and military worlds during these years. And I enjoyed the association with other soldiers and the activities, even though part time, incident to military service during all these years."

"I hope that, in addition to my own satisfaction derived from all of this, the nation has benefited from the National Guard in general. I believe it has. And the service of guardsmen as reserve component people of the Army and the importance of their contribution may have been the best kept secret of recent times. They deserve more credit than they have received."

After 37 Years, He Quit Politics

Alexander Hawkins "Sandy" Graham, retired lawyer and former lieutenant governor, says he has had to "pull in my horns."

At 86 he remains as tough as a lightwood knot but as gentle as the Salvation Army woman with an armful of The War Cry.

Basking in the glow of his memories and fretfully independent, Graham prefers to talk about beaten biscuits, and about putting up tomato juice, jellies, and pickles from his own garden instead of his political achievements.

"I retired from politics after 37 years. I figured I had performed my duty for the state, so I quit," he said, "but I do keep up with politics and a few other things, too."

Graham lives on St. Mary's Street in his homeplace, a beautiful, huge two-story house on a 59-acre tract that abounds with flowers, shrubs, and trees. It is steeped in history.

His nickname "Sandy" originated from an uncle named Sandy, and Graham explains that "it's easier than saying Alexander."

He said his grandfather, Gov. William Alexander Graham, who was born in Mecklenburg County, bought the homeplace in 1842 from a Mississippi bishop.

"My grandfather also was a United States senator, served as secretary of the navy from 1850 to 1852, and ran for vice president on the Whig ticket," Graham said. "He was in Washington a lot and while away the home burned down and he didn't rebuild it. He had seven sons and all served with the Confederate army."

His great grandfather, Gen. Joseph Graham, "was a colonel at the time of the American Revolution and was in charge of the defense at Charlotte. He became a general before he was 20 during the Indian War."

Graham said that while his grandfather was a captain, he headed a regiment at Guilford Battleground. "Cornwallis had an outpost three miles west of Hillsborough along Eno River. Capt. Graham, on horseback, brought a detachment here and killed 16 British Redcoats. They were buried on one side of the Eno and I never heard of anybody digging them up after the raid. The Americans then rode back to Guilford. The calvary in those days covered a lot of territory."

Graham said Cornwallis' outfit placed a road of cobblestone downtown at the time his army occupied Hillsborough.

Returning to the history of his homeplace, he said his father, John Washington Graham, who graduated from UNC in 1857 and taught law there for a year until he was old enough to get his law license, rebuilt the place about 1867.

Ill-fated, the home burned again in 1893. Five years later he rebuilt. More than a half-century later in 1947-48, Sandy Graham remodeled the home.

Graham graduated from UNC in 1912, and sometimes walked the 14 miles from Hillsborough to Chapel Hill. "I was young and didn't mind it, but you could go by horse and buggy, which I sometimes did, and you could charter a car."

From UNC Graham went to Harvard Law School, rooming with Col. William Joyner of Raleigh.

He began law practice with his father in Hillsborough in 1914, working out of their office in a little wooden building with a front porch. "There were country magistrates. We did a lot of work involving wills, lands, and debts," Graham said.

Then came World War I in 1917. Graham volunteered and was accepted, being sent first to officers' training school in Fort Oglethorp, Ga., where he was commissioned a second lieutenant. About two weeks after that, on Aug. 28, 1917, he was married to Kathleen L. Long of Graham, the sister of J. Elmer Long. "The next day I reported to duty at Camp Jackson. There were other camps to follow before we sailed to England," he said. "I was in a little fighting and was fortunate." He was regimental adjutant for the 81st "Wildcat" Division.

In a scrapbook kept by Graham's daughter-in-law, Mrs. A. H. Graham Jr. of Durham, there is a note mailed by Graham to a relative, in which he said: "Just a few days before the end of the war we were in severe fighting just east of Verdun. I went 'over the top' with a Jay Ward, and was near him when he was killed by machine gun fire. Not far away a Lt. Smith was killed by German artillery."

When he returned from the war, Graham resumed his law practice and soon afterward went into politics. His first office was that of chairman of the Orange County Democratic party, a post he held from 1919 to 1947. "The Republicans were in power when I took over. They had every office except that of register of deeds. Somebody said I was the oldest chairman in point of service in North Carolina," Graham said.

He went to the state legislature in 1921 and served continuously through 1929, the session in which he was speaker of the house. "In 1933, I was elected lieutenant governor and served four years with Gov. J. C. B. Ehringhaus." Graham was appointed a state highway commissioner in 1945, and served under Gov. R. Gregg Cherry.

"Then I returned home and started back to practicing law. My friend Bill Umstead (Gov. William B. Umstead of Durham who died about 22 months after going into office) persuaded me to go back into politics as chairman of the State Highway Commission once again. I served out my term under Gov. Luther Hodges," he said.

Graham does not see a bright future for the Democratic party. "I think the Democratic party and the Republican party have about seen their day. There will be two new parties, the conservative and the labor party."

"It's been bad when the president of one party sees the great control of Congress by the other party. There has been a stalemate."

Reminiscing, Graham said that staves for whisky barrels once were manufactured in Hillsborough, and at one time the country's largest yard selling railroad crossties were in his town. 'They were all plain, white oak, a lot hewn by hand. It was a great business for the farmer in the winter."

"Years ago there were copper mines here and three little hills. One had a big hole which the young folks called 'Panther's Den.' Piedmont Minerals has bought one of the hills to get fire clay which it sells largely to General Electric and Westinghouse. Before that one of the hills was sold to Southern Railway Co. for ballast. They'd crush it up and chuck it around the railroad crossties. Prison camp labor was used for this at one time."

"The other hill has a fire tower on it as a lookout for fires At one time, and it was done quietly, U.S. Army personnel were stationed in huts there. I never knew exactly what it was all about."

"There used to be water troughs on the streets here for horses and mules. There was a water pump in the middle of town and a lot of the tin dippers were stolen."

"There were no window screens and flies were bad. A lot of folks while eating had servants keeping the flies away by fanning the air with a branch of a tree."

Graham was asked if he could recall anything unusual about the old type of lawyer. "The old lawyers used to carry a flask in their little grips along with brushes and combs and extra-stiff collars. Lawyers would make the circuits just like the judges and would make them by horse and buggy. It was rough in winter and that's when the flask came in," he said.

Recalling incidents while he was in the legislature, Graham said during his first session in 1921, "Old man Buck Duke came down to Raleigh from his home in Charlotte by his private train car. There was a great fight about the utilities commission. Duke had gone around to several industrial plants and obtained signed contracts. Later on he found that the contracts were too low and he wanted to do away with the contracts. But the industrial concerns wanted the contracts held."

"A Sen. Outlaw from Wayne County was opposed to Duke's position. Mr. Duke referred to him as "Sen. Outrage. The contracts were held for the session but later the Public Utilities Commission was organized and given powers to control rates."

About 1936, while Graham was lieutenant governor, John Sprunt Hill, a senator from Durham, was strongly advocating the establishment of alcoholic beverage control stores although personally he was a teetotaler, except for liking beer. "The session opened with prayer and a little minister took it upon himself to deliver a prayer very much opposed to Mr. Hill's position. This made Hill furious. As soon as the prayer was over he rushed up to the presiding officer's desk and asked that the prayer be expunged from the records. I told him I couldn't do that, that the prayer was already half way to heaven. He took it in good faith after that, and of course the ABC system went into effect in 1937."

An athletic man despite his age, Graham was aptly described years ago by a Raleigh newspaper: "His conservatism is as much a part of the lieutenant governor as his deep-voiced dignity."

Walking erectly over his vast, well-kept lawn recently, Graham proudly pointed out the 130-yard long, 48-year-old English boxwood which is in a serpentine line. "They were rooted and nurtured by my wife, and she had over 3,000 flowers planted in front of the boxwood." There are firs, oaks, pecans, and cedars. Graham's grandfather planted a Japanese fir that was a gift from Commodore Perry. An old, separate, outside kitchen has been turned into a workshop which Graham frequents.

Another structure is on the site of a house which once served as quarters for seven slaves, and there is a smaller house behind the home. Several years ago the state prisons system did away with most of its security dogs, offering some of them for sale to the public, Graham said. "I went to Sanford and got Lobo, a big German police dog. He was quite a fellow. But Lobo died and I've got another big dog for security, Jason. And then I've got Queen, a German shepherd, who is something of a receptionist. She greets everybody who comes on the premises."

Mrs. Graham, who died about a year ago, called the Graham home "Montrose," and Graham has worked to keep it in the tiptop condition she always favored.

Hobbies? "Well, I hunted and fished up to two years ago. I last hunted quail. Now I visit around some, read, and keep up with things." In the home are beautiful oil portraits of Mrs. Graham and Graham and of ancestors. There is a handsome chandelier and vintage furniture no longer available today. A steel roller machine of yesteryear makes beaten biscuits.

There is a massive, solid mahogany bed that once belonged to Gen. William Bailey, the grandfather of Mrs. Graham. He was a Georgian who served in the War of 1812. "The general used up nearly all of his money organizing and equipping troops for the Civil War. He later moved to Florida," Graham said.

The bed, nearly 200 years old, had to be taken apart before it could be brought into the home. It was moved to Hillsborough by truck from Danville.

Graham was a member of the original Tryon Palace Commission and he recalls that the palace was rebuilt by William Muirhead of Durham.

Graham has two sons, A. H. "Sandy" Graham Jr., a Durham lawyer, and John W. Graham of Raleigh, a graduate of West Point who is an engineer and a colonel in the army reserves. There are seven grandchildren and one great-grandchild. As to religion, Graham said he is an Episcopalian. His father at one time was a Baptist, and there have been Presbyterians in the family. Many of the ancestors are buried in Hillsborough cemeteries. "I'm not too pessimistic for the future," Graham said. "I think we'll weather the storm. This I believe. People are not as patriotic today, and many want more and more, and, want it now."

Most Folks Call Him Judge Patton

His name is James Ralph Patton, but most folks call him "Judge." He has been a judge and a lawyer of the "old school" and for 24 years was a member of the board of the Raleigh-Durham Airport Authority. Now 78, Patton is retired, but he still maintains his interest in both the law and the airport.

Patton was born on a Friday the 13th. "Like Macbeth I think I had a caul on me when I was born," he says. (A caul, a membrane that sometimes covers a newborn child, was once believed to an omen of luck.)

In an interview, Patton reminisced about his career and about growing up in Durham seven decades ago.

As a boy living on Morris Street next door to the Imperial Tobacco Co. of Great Britain, he said, he could hear the black people singing spirituals in the stemmery. "It was sweeter than a symphony orchestra, I'll never forget it," he said.

Patton's father was the tax collector for the city for 45 years, and living in the business area was both convenient and interesting.

"I attended Fuller School on Cleveland Street and I had to pass a blacksmith shop en route," he said. "It was a curiosity I never tired of. A horse and buggy or mule and wagon was the sole means of transportation about town."

He recalled that when he was a boy there were saloons in Durham, but he remembers best the tantalizing odors from the bakery shops and the home-made candy shops, and the many joys to be found at the drug store soda fountains.

"Doctors made house calls but most people depended on other remedies until they got so sick they had to call him to cheat the undertaker."

"The cure-alls were such products as castor oil, Cardui, Lydia Pinkham's compound, asafetida, turpentine, calomel, Epsom salts, mustard, plasters, flaxseed poltices, flaxseed for objects in your eye, and quinine, argerol, and bicarbonate of soda," Patton said.

Patton said he carried his school books in a strap and many a time wished he had carried more books in his head than on the strap.

Durham High School was on Morris Street—now the building is City Hall—and Patton recalled that W. D. Carmichael was superintendent and Ernest Green, principal.

"Mac Campbell taught history, coached football, and also played on the high school team. A coach could play along with his players in those days," Patton said.

Patton was president of his senior class in high school.

"I had always had a penchant to go to the University of North Carolina. My grandfather, George Washington Jones, had gone there. I was an only child and it seemed the thing to do."

Shaking his head and grinning, Patton recalled that he and the late Gov. William B. Umstead of Durham were roommates in their freshman year.

"Bill and I said our prayers every night before going to bed. This seemed to needle our other roommate and he let us know it. Before moving out he said, 'You fellows are always saying prayers. I don't. You make me feel like an s.o.b.' "

While at UNC he was editor-in-chief of the Yackety-Yack, the school annual, was commencement marshal, chief manager of the commencement ball, and a member of the Order of Gimghoul.

Upon graduation Patton entered Harvard Law School in the fall of 1917, and there enlisted in the navy and also attended the Ensign School.

His roommate one year at Harvard was the late Superior Court Judge Henry L. Stevens of Warsaw, North Carolina's only national commander of the American Legion.

Upon graduating from Harvard Law School, Patton returned to Durham. "I felt obligated to return here, I had a definite obligation to my parents," he said.

After hanging out his shingle in a one-room office in the old Geer Building on the northeast corner of Main and Corcoran streets, Patton decided to go into partnership with old classmate Umstead.

"Bill and I took quarters over the Court Square Drug Store on the corner of Main and Church streets, and we grabbed every kind of case that came along," Patton chuckled.

The building was torn down several months later and Patton and Umstead dissolved the partnership, preferring to go it on their own.

"That was the first and last time I ever had a partner or associate," Patton said. "I moved back to the Geer Building (later the Wachovia Bank Building) and there I remained until they tore the building down. I next moved to the North Carolina National Bank Building."

Chuckling softly, he added, "The old times are coming back, the memories are many. I remember years ago that some fireworks, they were legal then, were some way ignited in the Durham Book & Stationery Co. on Main Street, and pretty soon it seemed like downtown was going to be destroyed. A steam engine drawn by brawny horses arrived at the scene in a hurry, with Fire Capt. Claude Turner in charge. It was a spectacular thing."

Patton said the first important legal case he was involved in was the private prosecution of Buck Carden, who shot and killed his wife. He was convicted and died in the electric chair.

"I've tried thousands of cases all over the state, and usually as a defense attorney," Patton said. "Criminal law has stuck with me a long time."

A man given to flowery and pungent phrases, Patton in his speeches to the jury has quoted from the Bible, Shakespeare, Byron, Lord Tennyson, Dante, and Aesop's Fables. On some occasions he has sugar-coated his barbs with jokes tailored to the austerity of the judge presiding.

Always fascinated by words, Patton has been a devotee of both poetry and prose. "My mother used to say that the three finest books in the world were the Bible, Shakespeare, and the dictionary," he said.

Patton once spent a term in the state legislature, coming out to run for the judge of Recorder's Court. He served eight years as the recorder and "saw nature in the raw."

As judge, Patton once tried a genuine prince of the Congo. "He was a fine specimen. I don't recall the charge but he came clear," Patton said.

On another occasion a Dr. Buzzard, who was charged with false pretense, came before Patton in court. "He was a mystic character and conjured visions of fortunes for a fee. He used a surveyor's instrument which he said brought him information of buried treasures.

"One fellow once dug a deep trench but found nothing of value. That's when the good 'doctor' met his Warterloo."

Patton said he once tried a preacher on a charge of drunkenness and while the trial was under way the preacher gave him a little book the preacher had written.

"The title of the book was 'Be Kind to a Man When He's Down.' That got next to me. I asked the preacher what he thought I should do to him. He told me a couple of days of rest at the County Home would prove beneficial. I followed his request," Patton laughed.

"We tried a lot of gambling cases involving slot machines and prostitution, but no drug cases," he said. "The kingpin of the slot machine business in North Carolina came before me once. He was a man of wealth and influence. During the hearing I received a telephone call which threatened me with death. Dr. Runyon Tyler, a good friend, stayed all night on my front porch to protect me."

Patton said law and order is not closely pursued like it has been in the past, and it is a sad commentary on the times.

"There has been a transition in the attitude of the people. I always thought that the three great deterrents of crime were the family, religion, and public opinion. But this is a new day. We're all so lackadaisical about crime. I just don't know what has happened to the high ideals people once had. The affection and neighborliness has all but evaporated in the air," he said.

Durham's First And Only Executions Drew Crowd

White Man, Black Man Hanged In 1907

It was a morbid but laughing and jostling crowd that gathered about the old wooden jail to witness Durham County's first and only legal executions.

It was Friday, Feb. 8, 1907, a bone-chilling day, with snow and sleet and an indifferent sun.

The scaffold and trap had been erected in the outer court of the jail and the fresh pine slabs exuded the fragrance of the forest. The iron lever that was to spring the trap had been borrowed from another county, from which an expert in such things had come to help Sheriff John Harward make arrangements for the double hanging.

The noose was also borrowed. It was fashioned of unstained white linen strands which had been used in four other hangings in North Carolina.

John H. Hodges, a Virginian, a middle-aged white man who had boasted of killing his estranged second wife, Mattie High Hodges, in front of their children, elected to die first.

The second condemned man was Freeman Jones, a 25-year-old black man who confessed that he had dragged a 60-year-old white woman out of her home and intended to rape her.

Long before 10 a.m. the crowd outside the jail was stamping impatiently, attempting to fight off the cold while speculating on how the men would die.

Several who had witnessed other executions out of Durham expressed fear there would be some hitch, saying that hanging was new here and the sheriff and his deputies were inexperienced at it.

The scaffold was set up in the corridor of the old part of the jail, giving the hangings a privacy that could not have been obtained had the instrument of death been erected outside the jail.

Only a limited number of tickets were issued and except for newspapermen, physicians, and lawyers, no one saw both executions.

Promptly at 10 a.m. Sheriff Harward appeared. Those who had tickets lined up. The gate swung open to admit them, and then the heavy iron door of the jail swung shut with a resounding thump.

Standing directly before the door was the new scaffold. It was smaller than those usually used, but the trapdoor was much larger.

Quarters were cramped and spectators huddled together.

Suddenly the door opened and a hush fell on the group. John Hodges was being led in by Harward.

A man seemingly in the prime of life and of perfect physique, he wore a mustache, had clear and sparkling eyes and thin hair sprinkled with gray, and his jaws showed the tenacity of a bulldog.

Hodges was cool and self-possessed, and some of the crowd at first thought him to be a deputy sheriff. A photographer took his picture.

At the direction of the sheriff, he stepped to the flooring of the scaffold, the noose that dangled before him not daunting his courage.

In his hand he carried a Bible bound in black cloth. After looking over the crowd he turned to the sheriff and said, "I want you to give this Bible to Mr. Pleasants (deputy sheriff James F. Pleasants). He loaned it to me, and it has been a great comfort."

Hodges asked for and was given a chair. He removed his shoes and sat down, still composed. On the chair which was moved to him sat Tom, a cat given to him as a kitten by Sheriff Harward.

The photographer asked Hodges to pose standing up with the cat on the chair. Hodges obliged.

Asked if he wanted to say anything, the condemned man nodded. "Boys," he said, "I want to tell you all that I am ready to go. God rest my soul and help all whisky drinkers. I have prayed hard and believe God has forgiven me for my sin. I have been well treated. My hopes were downed by whisky. It not only downed me, but my wife and children. When you drink it will send your soul down."

Asked by his lawyer, W. B. Guthrie, if he had any hard feelings toward anyone, he said, "No, I'm ready to meet my God."

One spectator who was becoming ill asked to leave. He was let out of the room.

The sheriff had forgotten the black hood which is placed over the head of those condemned to hang. He left hurriedly and returned shortly with it. He tied Hodges' hands and feet.

The noose was adjusted and pulled tight. Hodges asked that it be removed for a moment, and it was. He raised the black hood, peered again at the crowd and said nothing. Then he shook hands with the sheriff and thanked him for his kind treatment.

"Are you ready?" Harward asked.

"Yes," Hodges answered clearly.

"Goodby, John."

"Goodby, Sheriff."

The sheriff went to the front of the scaffold and pulled the lever. The body plummeted and came up suddenly at the end of the rope. Then it hung limp and lifeless. No struggle, no twitch.

Drs. Julian Smith, N. M. Johnson, and J. M. O'Kelly examined the body and found no pulse.

The lever was pulled at 10:30 a.m. and at 10:50 the body was cut down and turned over to the J. S. Hall & Co. undertaking firm.

The crowd dispersed, and a new group was allowed to come into the death chamber.

A few minutes after 11 a.m. Freeman Jones was brought in. He, too, displayed no nervousness and was just as cool as Hodges as he marched to the steps leading to the scaffold.

Jones' eyes roved about the crowd and then to the sheriff, who was seemingly casual about his task.

Jones was in his stocking feet. Although there was no sign of fear he appeared somewhat dazed after noting the dangling noose.

Jones' lawyer, R. O. Everett, asked him if he was guilty of his crime.

"I deserve what I am getting, for it is only justice," Jones answered. Then he related that he had gone to the Jack Barker home on June 18, 1906, and finding the door unlocked, dragged the screaming woman outside and threw her down.

Jones said the screams of the woman and her elderly mother, who lived with her, attracted the attention of a black man who lived nearby.

The neighbor came to the woman's rescue, and Jones said he ran.

Jones said that when he entered the Barker home, Mrs. Barker asked what he wanted, and he told that her husband, a fugitive from justice for selling liquor, had asked him to come there and wait for him.

Mrs. Barker ordered him to go elsewhere and wait, Jones said, but instead he grabbed her.

The sheriff pinioned Jone's arms and legs, adjusted the same black hood and pulled the lever.

The trap slipped from under Jones at 11:33 a.m. and 19 minutes later he was pronounced dead.

His body was placed in a pine coffin and taken to his home in East Durham.

Hodges' body, strange to say, was taken to the home of a brother of his murdered wife.

Hodges sat up until 2 a.m. on the day of his death, listening to bible verses read to him by fellow prisoners who still shrank from him.

Then Hodges went to bed, accompanied by his cat Tom.

He had bragged about killing his wife in cold blood and said he did not regret it. The slaying occurred in February 1906 at her home in West Durham.

Mrs. Hodges had charged him twice with assaulting her, and on one occasion he would have been sent to the roads for it but a friend paid his fine.

After she instituted divorce proceedings Hodges went to her home and started beating her. A son tried to intercede and was knocked down, and when a daughter tried to shield her mother with her body, Hodges pulled out his pistol. He shot his wife through the heart and threw her to the hearth.

Jones, 25, was also married but had no children. Considerable sentiment was shown in his behalf, and letters were written to Gov. Robert B. Glenn, pointing out that Jones had been drinking at the time and had not actually raped the woman.

Glenn refused clemency, and then for the first time Jones confessed to the crime.

In later years men sentenced to die were executed at Central Prison in Raleigh, and the counties in which capital crimes occurred were spared the obligation of putting people to death.

An 'Old-School' Lawyer Takes His Shingle Down

William H. "Bill" Murdock, one of the most versatile and active attorneys in Durham history, a lawyer of "the old school," has closed his law offices. "I've enjoyed the head-butting, the conflicts, and the opportunities to help make justice prevail. After nearly 55 years in the profession I hated to quit, to sell my law books and to take down my shingle. But there always comes a time. My health helped make the decision," he said.

Murdock, a Durham native, enjoyed great success in the courtrooms, and more than one attorney has said that the stalwart could win more when he lost than most lawyers could when they won. The retirement of the tall, erect, and handsome man whose insight, vigor, and alertness belies his 78 years, deprives the courtroom of a legal giant.

Murdock graduated from Durham High School in 1921 and went on to Trinity College and the University of North Carolina, where he earned his law degree in 1927.

He joined the law offices of J. L. Morehead in the old First National Bank Building. At the time, Paul C. Graham was judge of Recorder's Court and Hugh Scarlett was prosecuting attorney.

"Courts were altogether different then," Murdock said, "serious, dignified, and there were longer sentences given, few appeals and rarely a continuance. Courts were held every Saturday morning and lasted until every case on the docket was heard."

He said Tom Pendergrass was superintendent of the Durham County roads and the rock quarry on Newton Road, now known as the Broad Street extension. The county had to handle the construction and maintenance of its own roads and convicts did most of the work, including breaking up rocks with sledge hammers in "the rock hole."

Murdock said the misdemeanor prisoners wore vertical stripes on their uniforms and felons wore horizontal stripes. "While out of the workhouse most of the prisoners wore ball and chain on their legs, even when leaving a courtroom. There was no radio or television in the jails."

W. H. "Bill" Murdock greets President Lyndon B. Johnson, who appointed him U.S. Attorney of North Carolina

In 1928 he was elected prosecuting attorney of Durham County Recorder's Court, serving for two years. In 1936 he was elected judge of this court, succeeding Judge Walter Bass. Two years later he was elected solicitor of the 10th Judicial District, succeeding Leo Carr, who was to become a Superior Court judge. Marshall T. Spears was resident judge at the time.

"North Carolina's first State Prohibitition Office was established in Durham about 1937, and R. Bruce White was its first probation officer," Murdock recalled.

As solicitor, Murdock was responsible for the processing and prosecution of criminal cases in five counties: Durham, Orange, Alamance, Person, and Granville. "The job paid $4,500 and I received $1,500 for travel expenses." Murdock said. "I had no secretary and I had to pay my own office rent and for supplies. It was pretty rough in the old days."

Murdock's first big case in Durham County was the prosecution of a man named Clarence Rogers for the brutal murder of young Howard Moore, a Durham Sun carrier.

Rogers was convicted and sentenced to be executed. While on Death Row at Central Prison he killed a guard, and he was later electrocuted. Murdock said that in the old days people flocked to the courtrooms to hear the trials. "There isn't as much interest in trials now, perhaps because there are so many legal technicalities, defendants' extensive rights, continuances, and leniency.

"There hasn't been an execution in North Carolina since 1961, and the last person to die in the gas chamber from Durham County was executed in 1944," he said.

Murdock said there was a strict code of ethics if the old days as to courtroom dress and decorum. All attorneys wore dark blue, black, or dark gray suits. There were no mismatched suits or sport coats, no arguments with the judge.

Murdock was solicitor when women first served as jurors. "Mrs. J. P. McGuire was one of the women on the first mixed jury. The case I prosecuted was that of a man who was candidate for mayor, and charged with assault. He was convicted by the jury."

During World War II, in 1944-45, Murdock turned down a commission "and a desk job," to get into the action as a gunner's mate in the navy. He served aboard a munitions carrier in both the European and South Pacific theaters of operations.

In the early 1950s Durham county provided Murdock with his first assistant, Bruce White, who worked only in Durham.

In 1961 President John F. Kennedy appointed Murdock, then the dean of North Carolina solicitors after 23 years, to the office of United States Attorney for the Middle District. After President Kennedy was assassinated in 1963, his successor, Lyndon B. Johnson, commissioned Murdock to a second term.

When Republican Richard M. Nixon was elected president, Murdock gave up the office after completing nearly eight years.

As solicitor, Murdock, a modest man, was known as fearless and fair. A keen judge of human nature, he spent less time in selecting jurors than did defense attorneys. Often he favored as jurors persons who had been indicted or tried on the very charge held against the defendant. Unlike many of Durham's astute criminal lawyers, Murdock did not resort to flowery expressions, Aesop's fables, or the Bible, to convince a jury. Neither did he wheedle or needle a witness or berate or belittle the opposition. Skilled at the game of cat and mouse, Murdock would set a trap and at the right moment lower the boom. His wit and personality, plus his sense of timing in the use of bare knuckles and kid gloves, proved formidable weapons.

"Never," he once warned, "never antagonize a woman on the witness stand." And when a trial was ended and a jury's verdict or the judge's sentence was contrary to Murdock's feelings, he did not show it. Any criticism came from others. "To fight crime effectively you need preparation as well as ammunition. Nobody likes to go hunting with a switch," he emphasized.

Murdock married Christine James of Durham in 1926. There were three children: Mrs. Phillip Hutchings Jr., Mrs. Frank Creel, and W. H. Murdock Jr. Mrs. Murdock died in 1947, and Murdock in 1965 married Mrs. Marie Dane Grantham, a widow with one son, Kenneth Grantham.

The Murdocks live at 1006 Gloria Ave. Murdock, who used to follow the dog and horse races and circuses (he is an honorary ringmaster of Ringling Brothers, Barnum & Bailey Circus), and was fond of playing poker and golf, now keeps up with sporting events through newspaper and television.

Sanford Remembers Depression

His parents gave him zeal for education and politics, and the Great Depression fired his dedication to eliminate poverty, ignorance, and injustice.

James Terry Sanford, named after two grandfathers, James K. Sanford of Sanford and David Terry Martin of Salem, Va., has always preferred the name Terry Sanford.

Sanford, the president of Duke University and governor of North Carolina from 1961 to 1964, was born in Laurinburg: "In the middle of town, a block and a half from the Conferederate monument."

His parents were Cecil L. Sanford, merchant, Methodist leader, and political official, and Elizabeth "Betsy" Martin Sanford, an inspirational schoolteacher.

"My first job came when I was in the second grade, selling magazines and newspapers for my brother Cecil, who was a year older," Sanford said recently. "He established his commercial credit early."

U.S. Sen. Terry Sanford with wife Margaret Rose at a Durham voting machine.

He said that at a young age he became acquainted with every part of town, especially so around the Chatwyn Hotel where he sold out-of-town papers. "The *Saturday Evening Post* brought 5 cents, and I earned enough to make it interesting."

Sanford said he worked part-time cutting meat for A & P and Pender stores. Meat wasn't pre-cut in those days. He also played ball and was active in the Boy Scouts, becoming an Eagle Scout and assistant scoutmaster.

"I finished in the Laurinburg High School class of 1934, and 30 years later while I was governor, we held our reunion in the Governor's Mansion," he said. "Just about everybody came except the glamor boy of the class, who was in Arizona. I always figured he was no longer the glamor boy."

Nodding, he said that he learned more in scouting than in any other institution. "My father was deeply interested in politics," he said. "He registered the first black in Scotland County, in the late '20s. We were big for Al Smith when I was 11. The next time we had an election was in 1932. Everybody was for Franklin D. Roosevelt."

Sanford said he remembered the depression well and the "Hoover Carts" (horse-drawn wagons made with car chassis, wheels, and tires) way back then.

"My father's and grandfather's hardware store went bankrupt during President Herbert Hoover's reign," he said. "Their store was named 'Sanford & Son.'"

Sanford said that his father got a job unloading brick for $15 a day. "We made do, and we had a good garden."

Laurinburg had few extracurricular activities and Sanford said he never saw a basketball game until he went to Chapel Hill.

"After Cecil graduated from high school in 1933 he worked at a drugstore and bought himself a cow," Sanford said. "He built a stall in the garage. At the end of the year he and three other town boys entered the University of North Carolina as freshmen."

"I believe our father, a devout Methodist, wanted Cecil and I to go to Duke University, but Duke, a private school, cost a lot of money. So I went to Presbyterian College in Maxton. It cost about $50 and I earned that during the summer by cutting grass and painting windows."

He said that he hitchhiked the seven miles to the college every morning. "I worked to pay the tuition and when Christmas came I figured I had been there at Presbyterian College long enough," he said, smiling, "I had two or three piddling jobs and saved enough money to go to college."

He said that a friend, Jesse Lewis, had told him that if he went to Chapel Hill he would arrange for him to enter UNC.

"I delivered the student newspaper for $5 a week, which covered my food, and I also worked at a Franklin Street cafe," he said. "My father helped pay my tuition and in 1935 my mother entered a pick-the-winner football contest and won a Plymouth car. But she chose $500 instead of the car and helped Cecil and me. It was her first and last time in such a contest."

Sanford said he was taking a general education course. "I started to major in math, and ought to have, but I began taking courses in political science, economics, and psychology," he said. "I also took advanced courses in writing."

By then his father had become a UNC fan, although Duke still meant a lot to him, he said.

Sanford had a part-time job officiating intramural games and became one of the first lifeguards and swimming instructors at UNC. During the summer he ran a boys camp and helped teach some of them that had polio how to swim.

"Bill McCachren (now head of Selective Service of N. C.) and I leased a high class boys camp on Lake James in Marion," he said. "We hired 'Red' Laird of Davidson College as director and we were his assistants. After two summers—I had law back of my mind for two years—I went back to UNC and entered law school, graduating in 1946."

After two years in law school he went into the FBI, but World War II intervened. "I was active there one year and was on leave to go into the Army," Sanford said.

He went in as a private, wanting to see action. "Cecil was on an aircraft carrier at Pearl Harbor," he said. "I volunteered for the Parachute Infantry which gave me $50 a month bonus. The recruiting officer also said I would have no KP and would have a steak every night. That certainly was not true."

On July 4, 1942, while in the FBI, he married Margaret Rose Knight of Hopkinsville, Ky., whom he had met at UNC. By November of that year he was overseas and in plenty of time for the Normandy invasion, The Battle of the Bulge, and the end of the war in Europe.

Sanford then volunteered to go to Japan and was enroute back to the United States to prepare for action there when the war ended. "We volunteers on ship were lucky, and were discharged," he said. "I went back immediately to Chapel Hill and re-entered law school. My wife was working with the UNC Dean of Women and I was assistant to Albert Coates at the Institute of Government."

Two years later the Sanfords moved to Fayetteville and he opened a law office. "I went there with the intention of running for governor—there was no doubt in my mind about that," he said.

In 1960 on a platform of more taxes for education, he was elected governor.

Going back to his teen-age days, Sanford said the devastation of the depression and particularly how it affected a small town could not be forgotten. "I saw hard times and suffering and this made people have compassion and concern," he said. "It offended you to see people abused and discriminated against. Yes, the depression made a deep impression."

Sanford said that from the time he saw Gov. Max Gardner in Laurinburg he made up his mind to be governor. "We were privileged with seeing Roosevelt's 'New Deal,'" he said. "I was and still am, of the opinion the government can be better run, people could do a lot better, I still believe that is possible."

Sanford said that as governor he proposed a sales tax, "and I take part of the blame. If we had not had a sales tax we wouldn't have all the school improvements we've enjoyed. We couldn't possibly have developed the community colleges. I'm very proud of the fact that the Legislature had the courage to think of the children instead of their political careers. The people that complained were those who said I did what I said I would do."

Smiling, he said, "I ran a little for President of the United States in 1972 and 1976. I ran a little, but not much." Sanford had been a member of the State Senate and president of the Young Democratic Clubs.

He had cut all of his ties with his law office in Fayetteville to run for governor, and after his term he opened a law firm in Raleigh.

"I got two grants and did a study of the American States here at Duke," he said. "My book, *Storm Over the States,* (dedicated to the memory of W. Kerr Scott, Governor of North Carolina) was a product of the study. In December 1969 I became president of Duke. I had no problem making the transition to Duke because of the warm feeling of my father for Duke. I say when I came here they talked about staying five years. I've been here 15 years and I hate to leave. It's been a very rewarding, great experience for me. I've enjoyed every day of it."

The Sanfords have two children, Terry Sanford Jr., and Betsy Sanford, both of Durham. His brother Cecil lives in Hillsborough, and there are two sisters, one in Philadelphia and the other in Berne, Switzerland.

Sanford was in the N. C. National Guard from 1948-60. In 1960 he was the first southern leader to break with the Solid South and announce his support for John F. Kennedy for president. And he seconded Kennedy's nomination at the Democratic National Convention in Los Angeles.

Sanford also wrote the books: "But What About the People?" which was dedicated to his parents, and "A Danger of Democracy—the Presidential Nominating Process," which was dedicated "To Margaret Rose," his wife.

They named Terry Sanford High School in Fayetteville after Sanford. An ardent supporter of the Duke "Blue Devils," he wears a Duke jacket during his casual moments.

Sanford has served in many capacities and currently is on the board of Fuqua Industries, the International Telephone and Telegraph board, and the Prudential-Bache Mutual Fund Base.

He is also on several other boards, is vice president of the Municipal League, a trustee of Howard University in Washington, D. C., and a trustee of Methodist College.

A friendly, witty, well-knit man of 65 with a glint of adventure in his eyes, Sanford is a workhorse who accepts each day as a challenge. He has come a long way from a boyhood in Laurinburg, a place he still calls home.

7

City and County Government

No doubt about it, Lake Michie, our major source of city water, is the outstanding effort of all Durham city councils. The project was ram rodded by our first city manager, Radford W. Rigsby. Amazingly, the council's decision was carried by a single vote.

Durham first had a volunteer fire department. My father was a member and suffered a cut hand fighting Durham's most disastrous fire in 1914.

The City of Durham celebrated its centennial in April 1953. The county's centennial came twenty-eight years later.

Lake Michie Durham's Finest Deed, Says Former Councilman

Arthur M. Harris, 86, the only living member of Durham's first city council, insists that Durham's finest accomplishment was the construction of Lake Michie.

"I had two years left of my term as alderman when Durham adopted the city council form of government," he said in an interview. "I was on the committee to select a city manager."

Harris said that R. W. Rigsby of Washington state, a civil engineer and certified public accountant, applied for the job.

"He had plenty of brains to go along with both of these skills. At the time we had eight councilmen and the mayor, W. F. Carr. The vote for the big dam was four to four. My vote broke the tie in favor of the water basin. Then all of a sudden the other four members got enthused, changed their votes and made it unanimous for the lake," he said.

"That's how it happened. We couldn't do without this huge oasis today. In my opinion our water supply is what prompted the Research Triangle. There is no pollution in our watershed."

Before the lake was constructed Durham was getting its water from the old Nancy Hanks pond, about three miles west of West Durham. The old pump station site remains. "There were a lot of good picnics there."

Harris said that Rigsby was a great help in ramrodding the dam project across with the voters. "Lake Michie was named after old Captain Michie, who had been head of Durham's first water plant," he said.

Harris served on the council for 32 years and was mayor pro tem at least 10 times.

A native of Goldsboro, he was the son of the Rev. Junius Harris, a Methodist minister, and Lizzie Parnell Carr Harris. "We were living in Chapel Hill at the time I entered Bingham School, a junior college in Mebane. After a couple of years I decided I wanted to work. I came to Durham to see uncle Jule (Julian S. Carr, business tycoon and philanthropist)," Harris related.

"He had his office in the First National Bank Building, and when I told him I wanted a job, he called in his secretary, Tom Gorman," Harris said. "Uncle Jule asked Gorman to telephone Julian Carr Jr. at his Durham Hosiery Mill in Edgemont, and to tell him to give me a job. Gorman gave me a dime to get there and back on the street car. I got the job, one piddling around the office, checking invoices."

Harris said he was so jubilant at getting a job that he walked back to town.

About 1920 a new hosiery mill building was constructed on Corcoran Street and Harris said "I followed it there."

"In fact, that is the only job I ever had," he chuckled. "I was with the office for about 50 years before I retired."

Durham Hosiery Mill made only men's socks and women's stockings, and at first they were all cotton.

"We made a slew of socks for the Army, brother. I remember getting Herbert Kueffner (later director of public works with the city), manager of the mill dye house, to dye me some socks black while dying women's stockings. I was in between wars and I didn't fancy khaki socks," Harris laughed.

He said the mill's leading brand of sock was called "Tar Heel," and that women's stockings were named Queen Ann, Elizabeth, and Phyllis.

"The names were dug up by Marvin Carr, head salesman for the mill who lived in New York. My brother, Wesley Harris, was also a salesman for the mill living in New York," Harris said.

The mill changed over to lisle cotton, then to rayon, silk, and nylon. These hose have been manufactured at the mill's plant in Franklinton, since the Durham Hosiery Mill building on Corcoran Street was torn down five years ago.

"I was the first person to walk into the mill on Corcoran Street and the last person to leave when the building was torn down," Harris said.

Harris said he played on the Durham Hosiery Mill baseball team in 1910.

"We had a deaf mute battery in Kelly Biggerstaff and Dummy Woodell. It was a treat to watch those fellows give each other signals on their fingers. They didn't miss a trick, real competitors."

Harris said that the two best workers the mill ever had were deaf mutes, Roma Fortune, and his wife. Fortune later became a minister and was instrumental in the building of Durham's first church for the deaf mute.

Harris himself has been a member of Trinity Methodist Church here for about 67 years, since moving to Durham.

Harris said that the church was named Trinity Methodist Episcopal Church South, and that's the wording on the metal plaque in the church doorway. "As far as I am concerned that is still the name of the church, not Trinity United Methodist Church. They had no business changing the name."

Recalling Chapel Hill as a boy, he said bicycles were the favorite method of transportation, and the first bike in that city was owned by Frank Strowd.

"I was about 12 when Uncle Jule bought me and my brothers bicycles. We had bicycle races on downtown Franklin Street, and I played a lot of marbles and knucles on the sidewalk," Harris said.

Laughing, he said, "there were about 1,000 people living in Chapel Hill and I knew every one of them and they knew me. I knew their dogs by name."

Harris said he often went to a Mrs. Tenney's home to eat figs, and the next day would go to a Mrs. Strowd's home and feast on scruppernongs.

"I've never smoked, not even rabbit tobacco or corn silk. I never saw a drunk man in my life until I was well up as a boy. Old man Seaton Barbee who ran a grocery store on Franklin Street, and who had a marvelous voice, would usually get whisky from somewhere. But he didn't abuse it. I guess he thought about his store being across the street from a church. Anyway, he sang in the church quartet along with his married sister, Dell Tangersly; my sister Lida, and Clyde Eubanks."

Harris said a favorite drink at the drug store was sarsaparilla, and that the popular patent medicine for women was Lydia Pinkham's Compound. "Lydia was from Littleton, N.C."

Recalling his pea fowl or peacock, he said that the Tenney who lived a mile away, also had a peacock, and that late at night when things were still, the two fowls would call to each other in coaxing tones, keeping folks awake and laughing.

Harris, a sentimental man who fancies old letters, books, and pictures, has a beautiful music box, made in Switzerland, and an elegant, decorative, and dainty watch, both gifts to his mother by his father.

In 1918 Harris married Kate Lee Hundley, whose family had moved here in 1898. Her homeplace is the only house remaining on Liberty Street in the block between Roxboro Street and Dillard Street.

The Harrisses, who live at the Methodist Retirement Home on Erwin Road, have a daughter, Mrs. Kate Lee Adams of Houston, and a son, Thomas C. Harris of Greenville, S.C.

Another son, Arthur Harris Jr., was killed in the Battle of the Bulge during World War II, while serving in the Air Force.

You Wouldn't Get Rich Being a 'Bull'

In Good Old Days Chief Got $75 A Month

They've been called everything from "Bulls," and "John Law," to gestapo and fuzz. They've been treated with respect, awe, contempt, derision, and apprehension. The lot of a policeman certainly is not a thing of beauty and a joy forever.

Way back in 1897 before Durham's population exploded to 5,555, thanks to its fast growing fame for tobacco manufacturing, crime was primarily stealing, drunkenness, and street fighting.

Misbehavior of the multiplying people kept pace with the surge. Saloons sprang up almost overnight and milk pails did double duty—for milk and, much of the while, for the more effervescent liquid, beer.

Durham's main street knew no pavement, but it was studded with stepping stones to spare one's boots a bath in mud during inclement weather.

In 1904 the town of Durham boasted a police force of 14 men. The requirements for the job then were a pair of stout legs, a lot of nerve, and a billet.

Stepping stones also led to Durham's guardhouse just off Main Street. The miniature bastille mostly housed drunks, and they were few in number as the known sots usually were ignored until they, on occasion, waxed unruly.

When it became necessary to confine anyone, the prisoner was taken on the long journey to neighboring Hillsborough, at that time considered a more thriving community.

Inasmuch as travel was slow, what with poor roads and horse-drawn conveyances, a transgressor had to be a pretty sorry lot before he earned the trip into Orange County.

Durham's police department in 1904 was politically controlled and elections decided who would be police officers and chief. At this time Chief Jake Woodall had lost the ballot to Captain W. F. Freeland.

The pay of the chief was $75 a month, and he had to be satisfied with the prestige of the office.

The first sergeant's pay was $60 a month, and the second sergeant drew $5 less. Ten patrolmen were paid $50 a month.

The uniform enjoyed more respect than it does now, perhaps in no small way to the part played by the billet.

In 1905 Jake Woodall returned as chief as eight patrolmen also lost their jobs to bigger vote getters.

The police department was virtually rid of politics in 1909, when the Legislature passed an act creating the Police and Fire Commission Board. The Commission Board remained in power for 12 years.

Also in 1909 the patrolman's pay was boosted to $63 per month, and not long afterwards the pay went to $70 a month, where it remained until World War I.

In 1905 there were two shifts at the police department. One came at 12 o'clock noon and the other at midnight. This was a seven-day a week job. There was no grumbling because there was always somebody who envied the cops their jobs. Shifts were changed every month and there were 10 vacation days each year.

The late Thomas E. Rigsbee of West Chapel Hill Street, an early day policeman here, once said that he witnessed the only two hangings in Durham history and that he fetched the black hoods for the hanging.

Rigsbee said that when he was on the police force the magistrate who tried most of the criminal cases was the late Gabriel Barbee of Patterson Township.

If a man couldn't pay a fine he was made to work on the streets, with a ball and chain assuring that he didn't escape.

Few women were arrested at the time, but Rigsbee said that "when we did arrest them they were worse than a man to handle. They would fight, and we hated like everything to have to bother with them."

Besides long hours, the officers had to buy their own uniforms. Not unlike the Northwest Mounted Police who have been credited with always getting their man, Durham police had to stay on the trail of a criminal until the man was brought in.

Officers had to arrest and drag in drunks since there was no transportation in early days. There were no handcuffs, so the cops carried a small chain with a handle which was wrapped around the prisoner's wrists.

When there was a tough character to bring in, the officers would deputize citizens to help them. If they refused, they were threatened with billet and pistol.

A prohibition law was in effect in 1905 but officers searching places suspected of handling whisky were not allowed to seize any liquor found and to use it as evidence.

The law was an unpopular one, and thirsty citizens on occasion could find a hard drink in the very saloons barred from selling the liquor. Under cover of darkness, wagons whose loads were hidden with straw, managed to wheel in kegs of booze, and not long afterwards the "dry town" was counting more drunks than ever.

In 1913 police were given the choice of working an eight-hour day or receiving a pay increase. The men voted for the eight-hour day, and the three-platoon system was put into effect.

Just before trolley cars came along in 1910, the town bought two bicycles for the officers to use in answering calls. It was against the rules to use the bikes except on official business. Not long afterwards the bikes were eliminated and Durham purchased a patrol wagon with an open door at the rear and seats on each side.

The vehicle, cranked by hand, operated on a magneto, having no battery. After a few years this conveyance was discarded and Model T Fords placed into use.

Next came the establishment of a Recorder's Court, and the late R. H. Sykes became its first judge. At that time the city attorney served both as prosecutor and attorney.

Later the Legislature enacted a law whereby a person would be elected for the job of prosecuting attorney.

The city limits were extended and more officers had to be added to the police force.

When Hubert E. King, who was later chief of police, joined the force in 1919, the late George Proctor was chief and the force consisted of about 25 men. A rookie officer drew the same pay as an officer who had been on the force as long as 20 years, $105 a month, King once recalled. This was an exception to the chief and the sergeants. Everybody, including the chief, worked 10 hours a day, seven days a week. They had 10 days off a year.

At that time the department had a "Black Maria," an enclosed truck with two benches to carry violators of the law to police headquarters.

Only a few Durham streets were paved and the vehicle often mired up in mud, and officers and those in custody alike had to walk in to headquarters.

Officers were issued a pistol and a nightstick. Few men were given handcuffs because there were not enough to go around. They had to buy their own flashlights and uniforms. There was no regulation uniform, and the officers had different style uniforms purchased from different stores.

Chief King once recalled that late police Commissioner George Lyon had the police department as a hobby, and at Christmas would present each officer with a handsome pair of white gloves.

The gloves came in handy because police were often called on as pallbearers and white gloves were a must.

Bells Rang Often at 'Singing Fire Chief's' Home

Mrs. Valeria Shepherd Bennett, 91, widow of Durham's "Singing Fire Chief," Frank W. Bennett, heard the fire bell ring thousands of times in her home at 926 W. Markham Ave.

But she says the most exciting experience in her life was when she landed a 50-pound shark at Bogue Sound, "a long time ago."

With a youthful laugh and a twinkle in her eye, she exhibits a treasured message: "I pray that I may live to fish until my dying day. And when it comes to my last cast, I then most humbly pray, when in the Lord's great landing net and peacefully asleep, that in His mercy I be judged big enough to keep!"

Nodding, she followed: "You've got to keep the line tense, be patient, and very tenacious."

Mrs. Bennett is a neat, slender woman who bubbles over with enthusiasm. She was born in Six Forks of the Millbrook community near Raleigh on June 23, 1892, the daughter of the late Sidney and Ebraska Shepherd.

"My father was a farmer who believed in mules instead of horses. There were six of us children and we grew up in the feather-bed, hard-work era," Mrs. Bennett said. "But we had a rock-lined well with the best of water, and we all pulled together."

The Shepherd home, "except for a curve in the road," was in sight of an unpainted school which had one large room and a small office, she said.

"Yes, there was a pot-bellied stove and we had to learn the blue-back speller. The teacher was a Miss Penny who believed in discipline and keeping a pupil after school as corrective punishment," Mrs. Bennett said with a grin.

The Six Forks Christian Church, a little white frame sanctuary, was across the road from the school.

"The church had no cemetery at the time; families buried their dead on their own property," Mrs. Bennett said. "We were Baptists and attended Midway Baptist Church near Millgrove."

Chuckling, she said that she was the tomboy of the family and was a tree climber. "If I saw an apple or a plum that I couldn't reach, I'd shimmy up the tree and get it."

She rode mules, too. "Once I was riding one of our mules at a fast gallop between rows of cotton, when he stopped suddenly., I went sailing over that rascal's head. When I got myself together I looked straight at the mule. He was looking down at me as if to say, 'the ride is over.' It was, all right."

She recalled the time a neighbor's horse "committed suicide."

She said that one of Eugene Penny's horses caught a back leg under a sill at a barn. "In frantically trying to extract the trapped leg, he hit his head against the barn and killed himself."

In 1913 she came to Durham to visit her brother, Charles Shepherd. He and his family were living on Elizabeth Street, one block off Holloway. "I liked Durham very much. It was a city with things going on. Raleigh wasn't much in those days. It sure is now, though. I got a job as a sales clerk at the jewelry counter of Woolworth's 5-and-10-cent store. On Sundays we all would walk to Temple Baptist Church twice, attending morning and evening services. A Dr. Riddick was the preacher, a real good one."

"There were no picture shows or baseball games on Sundays, and of course there was no radio or television religious programs at the time. So, people went to church."

Mrs. Bennett recalled that everybody but the preacher used palm or folding hand fans to try to keep cool in hot weather. The fans were usually donated by furniture stores and funeral homes.

"The minister got pretty warm in the pulpit, what with his coat and no fan. I guess being uncomfortable was part of their job years ago."

Mrs. Bennett said that her husband-to-be, Frank Bennett, was a stock clerk in Woolworth's, and when the store manager was out he would be in charge. "Frank would talk with me while the boss was away, and pretty soon we were courting. About all there was to do at the time was to ride a street car to Lakewood Park, known as 'The Coney Island of the South.' I tried the roller coaster and was scared to death. Have they still got those terrible things around?"

Mrs. Bennett said she and Frank were married in 1913 at the home of her cousin, Mrs. Henry O'Neal, on East Main Street, with the Rev. Riddick performing the ceremony.

Lifting her head for a hearty laugh, she said: "Sometime later when our son, Frank Jr., was a toddler, Dr. Riddick, who had left Durham and returned as pastor at Watts Street Baptist Church, called on us. As the preacher was leaving our home, I told young Frank that was the man who married me. He looked up quizzically and said: 'I thought you married daddy.' I had to rephrase things."

After she left Woolworth's, Mrs. Bennett said, she worked for awhile at Kronheimer's, a fashionable store on Main Street. "They sold a lot of fine cut goods, including crepe de chine, pongee, velvet, silks, wool, cotton, lace, and ribbon. No synthetics."

Mrs. Bennett's husband also left Woolworth's and worked for awhile at Durham Book and Stationery, then joined the Durham Fire Department in 1921. Dennis C. Christian was chief at the time. Shortly afterward, Bennett was made chief.

"Frank was always at Station No. 1, which was at Mangum and Holloway Streets, facing old First Baptist Church. Fire horses were eliminated shortly after we were married," she said.

"I barely remember the big fire of 1914 which did so much havoc downtown, but I certainly recall the fire which destroyed old Trinity Methodist Church in 1923. That was some excitement."

Mrs. Bennett said her husband loved to sing. "He loved best of all to sing *Short'nin' Bread, When Irish Eyes are Smiling,* and *She's the Lass for Me.* Frank would come up our walk singing and leave the house singing. He sang in the choir at Watts Street Baptist, which we had joined, and sang at fire conventions, clubs, and especially at the schools during Fire Prevention Week."

Bennett was chief from 1922 until his death in November 1946. He was succeeded by one of his men, the late Cosmo Cox.

The Bennetts' only daughter, Edith, died at age 35 in 1960. She was not married.

The Bennetts only son, Frank Jr., lives on Driver Avenue and has long been a popular drummer of several bands. He has three sons. One, Frank III, of New Haven, Conn., also plays the drums for dances as a hobby.

Mrs. Bennett said that while her husband was chief there was a fire bell in their home that rang when the bell at the stations rang. "You could count the rings and tell in what area an alarm had been sounded. Three rings meant the fire was under control."

Laughing as if she knew something, she said: "I'm not going to get old. I don't worry about anything, and I've got peace of mind. The Lord takes care of his own."

8

Medicine

From maggots, leeches, and asafetida to penicillin, Neosporin, and transplants, Durham has played a chief role in the evolution of health services locally, earning the title "City of Medicine."

George W. Watts built and gave to Durham the Watts Hospital, which at the time as the state's finest.

John Sprunt Hill, Watts's son-in-law, who gave so generously in many ways in Durham and Chapel Hill, and Hill's son, George Watts Hill, through the years gave greatly to the hospital.

G. W. Hill, along with Dean Wilbert Davison of Duke Hospital, also initiated the Blue Cross—Blue Shield health insurance program in North Carolina.

The Durham County Health Department rose to prominence under the leadership of Director J. H. Epperson and Dr. O. L. Ader. It has gained renowned as one of the nation's leaders in the fight against venereal disease and infant mortality problems. It has helped to champion milk surveillance and nurse services, gaining the cooperation and assistance of Durham's hospitals and the dental officials of the University of North Carolina.

Blessed with excellent physicians, Durham has sparkled with the likes of Dr. Lenox D. Baker, for whom the Lenox Baker Children's Hospital here is named (also a wing of Duke Hospital); Dr. Bailey Webb, who has probably been physician to more children than any other woman or man in the state; and Dr. James Davis, past president of the American Medical Association.

Gift Of Hospital Inspired Warm Speeches On Wintry Day

Eloquent and flowery speeches flavored presentation of the new Watts Hospital to the people of Durham on a wintry day in 1909.

George W. Watts gave Durham its first hospital.

Appreciative city and county authorities praised the generosity and benevolence of the native son of Maryland, George W. Watts, founder and donor, in tones probably heretofore unheard in our little boom town.

But it was the business genius and philanthropist himself who best described the inspiration, seed, and birth of his magnificent gift.

Watts in his presentation remarks, referred to 15 years prior when he created and gave to Durham the 21-bed hospital on the northwest corner of Main

Street and Buchanan Boulevard, which cost $30,000, with an endowment of $20,000.

"For some three or four years afterward we were disappointed in the failure of the public in general to make use of the institution. Yet the reason now seems obvious. But few of the smaller cities and larger towns had hospitals and their uses were not only unknown, but misapprehended by the large majority of our citizens," he said.

"They were regarded as places where the sick were taken to die, and those in need of surgical attention to be mutilated. Time was required to correct this impression and educate the people as to the true intent and purpose of the hospital."

"Those in charge and our medical fraternity continued faithful in advocating the advantages to the sick of such a place. Those who had been patients were pleased and told others of their experiences. The hospital then began to grow in popular favor until there ceased to be room for the applicants," he said.

"This required in the spring of 1906 an additional two-story building containing eight wards, with the necessary baths, kitchens, etc. Even this, however, did not supply the demands, and the opportunity of doing the greatest amount of good, so we began to think of bigger and better things."

Watts said the matter was carefully considered for many months and discussed with his family. "We concluded that a new hospital to meet all the demands for years to come, and modern in every respect, might be erected for about $75,000

"The architect disapproved of an addition to the old hospital because of lack of room, as well as the noise and smoke from the streets and trains."

He said the location was selected after careful inspection of all of the available sites near Durham. At that time the population centered mostly about the downtown business area.

Work was started in May 1908, "And now, after 19 months, we bid you welcome the consummation of the first group of buildings . . . It is our desire to erect next year a nurses' home on the north side of the main building."

Watts promised to add other pavilions or wards to conform with a plan for a large group of buildings.

The speaker then gave a breakdown of the project cost, which totaled $217,000.

"And now Mr. Chairman, it is a great pleasure to hand to you, as a representative of the trustees and people the deed for this property, to be yours as long as it is used exclusively for a hospital for the sick, at which, board, attention, and nursing shall be free to the indigent sick of Durham city and county."

"May it ever be conducted in the true Christian or Christlike spirit, where all distinction of class or creed fade away in the one universal desire to bind up the wounds, to relieve the pains, and strengthen the courage of our common humanity," Watts said.

Then to the chairman, E. J. Parrish, a distinguished citizen and tobaccoman:

"In addition, I hand you securities amounting to $100,000 to be added to the endowment. At a convenient time I will increase the endowment to $200,000, and until this is done I shall contribute in cash sufficient to make the income from this source as if the amount of the endowment was already $200,000."

As a representative of the Board of Trustees, James H. Southgate, popular leader and insurance company founder, accepted the gift in the board's behalf.

Southgate began his talk saying, of Watts, "When I was an old man some 30 years ago, Durham had two places where its entire population assembled daily. One was the railroad station and the other was the post office. One day at the post office I saw a stranger. He was a young, citified man compared with us fellows, because he had on a tailormade suit, a necktie, and nobbly hat."

"He told me he had come to seek his fortune in this little manufacturing town of Durham, and I was glad. He had bought an interest in the tobacco factory of W. Duke and Sons, and thus began his successful business career."

"He was sober that day and still is, and it has been 30 years, I think, since we had one together. He wore the flush of manly youth upon his cheek; there was not a mark of dissipation upon him. Through the intervening years he has been an exemplar for energy untiring, and noted for his zeal in all things which his hands found to do."

Southgate said further: "We sometimes talk about the days of our good Commonwealth Club, when you were president and we were struggling for new railroads, streets, cotton mills, water supplies, electric lights, and all things that would go to make a modern city . . . "

The speaker continued, "He reached out a helping hand to the orphan children at Barium Springs, to the young men who would preach the gospel, in the enlargement of Theological Seminary at Richmond, Va."

"He gave of his strength to Elizabeth College, that young women might find an easier way to higher attainment in learning. For those who suffer a hospital was provided, and no one could relate a tithe of the blessing that has come to this community through Watts Hospital as it has been known to Durham since 1895."

Smiling at Watts, he added: "My dear sir, the Board of Trustees most gratefully accept this beautiful gift and from this day set it apart for the relief of man's estate."

Lawyer W. J. Brogden, later to become a justice of the N. C. Supreme Court, responded for the Board of County Commissioners.

He said that three forces, religion, science, and brotherhood, have been the three triumphant forces in life which "have rewritten human history, remade institutions, recast customs, and put new ideals, new meaning, new power, and new splendor in a man's life."

Brogden said they had "survived the shock of ignorance, the assault of crime, and the blindness of prejudice because they are redemptive forces."

"Because you have set upon the hilltop a great seer, I have the pleasure and honor of accepting this gift in the name of the County Commissioners of Durham County."

Mayor W. J. Griswold responded for the Board of Aldermen. He said, "In behalf of the City of Durham and its people I accept this beautiful philanthropic gift at your hands and pledge the hearty support of the City of Durham and its people. We love you, not for what you have, but for what you are. We love you because you have placed the man above the dollar. We shall never forget your good deeds . . ."

Dr. A. C. Jordan, as president and representative of the Durham County Medical Society, spoke of the time Watts gave to the need of a new high school building, and to the "crying need" for a YMCA building. "You need not be surprised with anything he might do to assuage suffering and beat back the death angel . . ."

"He conquers peak after peak and satisfies his Christlike desires . . . Mr. Watts, we the Medical Society of the Durham, with outstretched arms, open hands and hearts full of gratitude to you, do accept this hospital on our part, and pledge ourselves, as far as in us lie, to make it a joy to you in your day, and an ensign of your philanthropy, in coming days to generations yet unborn."

Dr. John C. Kilgo, president of Trinity College, accepted the hospital as a representative of the people of Durham.

He said: "The event which calls us together creates a new day in the calendar of Durham. These splendid buildings occupying the summit of this hill [the big tract located on the northwest corner of Broad Street, Club Boulevard, and Maryland Avenue] and overlooking our city, appeal to every noble impulse of our minds and inspire in us a gratitude which we cannot express."

Smiling, he said: "His quiet and steadfast faith in Christ has given us an inspiring example of our Christian living."

Dr. Lenox Baker: Many-Faceted Physician

Known for Tough, Yet Gentle Ways

Dr. Lenox Dial Baker describes himself as "an ultraconservative, an unreconstructed rebel," and that may well be.

He is also a no-punch-pulling maverick, a champion of the common man, a humanitarian, an orthopedic magician, an athlete's angel, and a fellow who at 72 cuts his own fireplace logs with vigor and tenderly kisses his wife when she least expects it.

And, as the late Mrs. William Preston Few (widow of Duke University's first president) put it, "He is a handsome devil."

Baker's listings in Who's Who in America requires two pages, and that doesn't include all of his endeavors and achievements.

"Doc" was born in 1902 in DeKalb, Tex., son of Doda and James D. Baker, a farmer, businessman, and county sheriff.

After graduating from high school where he played in three sports, Baker attended the Pierce School of Business and Banking in Philadelphia. Thereafter he was employed by the Chase National Bank in New York.

At age 23, Baker decided to follow his first inclination, that of becoming a doctor. He had made this his goal after his mother was badly injured in an accident.

He threw several straws in the wind and ended up at the University of Tennessee, where he remained for four years. During that time he served as trainer under Tennessee's famous football coach, Gen. Bob Neyland.

Attracted by Duke University's medical school plans, Baker came to Durham in 1929, one year before the school opened.

While waiting for the medical school to get in gear, he attended the University of North Carolina medical school as a special part-time student. Then in 1930 he transferred to Duke.

"I was the first student accepted at the Duke School of Medicine, and it was because my name was first in alphabetical order. I was the first four-year student to receive a diploma," he said.

That was in 1933. Baker then went to Johns Hopkins Hospital in Baltimore for orthopedic training.

On Dec. 20, 1932, Baker had written his grandmother: ". . . I gave Virginia her ring a few days ago and we both are very happy. . . . I . . . have an appointment at Johns Hopkins Hospital as an intern, beginning September, 1933. So you see, two of the great things in my life have come to me. My father has always been the influence of love, I think his love is the most beautiful love I have ever seen. Mother has been that of ambition, driving on, you can do anything! . . . you, my grandmother, have stood for purity, faith, and charity. If just one small part of these three virtues of yours can be incorporated in everyman's life, this will be a better life."

So, on Aug. 22, 1933, Dr. Lenox Baker married Virginia Flowers, the daughter of Robert L. Flowers, who was the president of Duke University.

Dr. George E. Bennett, renowned professor of orthopedic surgery at Johns Hopkins, upon learning that Baker had been paying for his education by serving as a trainer, took Baker under his wing. Little did he know at the time that the young doctor had long dreamed of training under him.

"Dr. Bennett's services were widely sought by athletes with bone and joint deficiencies and injuries so I considered it a feather in my cap when I found myself working at his side, operating on famous big league baseball players, professional football stars, and noted prize fighters," Baker said. "We also treated bench warmers as well as star college athletes. It didn't make any difference."

Dr. Lenox D. Baker at the Lenox Baker wing of Duke Hospital.

Baker's fame spread and soon he was treating such heroes as Babe Ruth, Jack Dempsey, Dizzy Dean, and Joe DiMaggio. And before he left Johns Hopkins in 1937 he had become an assistant instructor in orthopedics.

Later, at Duke Medical Center, he was to treat such college greats as Sonny Jurgenson, Ace Parker, Fred Crawford, Alex Webster, Art Weiner, and Bill George.

An injured athlete's team didn't matter to Baker.

Former Duke football coach Wallace Wade once recalled: "One year Wake Forest came to play us in a very big game. We got word that their star tailback was limping badly and probably wouldn't be able to play. The next thing I knew 'Doc' Baker was in the Wake Forest dressing room working on that player. He came out without a trace of a limp and was the star of the game."

Dr. Jim Urbaniak, a top orthopedic surgeon at Duke, said he came to Duke Medical School because of a similar incident which occurred during a football game between Duke and the University of Kentucky where both Urbaniak and his father played.

"My father told me that one of their players was injured and that suddenly a tall man, Duke's trainer, raced across the field to see what he could do to help. Dr. Baker was the trainer and he got the player in shape to return to the game. My father never forgot that, so when I expressed a desire to be a doctor, he told me I should first go to Duke and talk with Dr. Baker to see if he thought I could make it. Dr. Baker so impressed me that I came to Duke Medical School and decided to become an orthopedic surgeon."

And there was the time that Dr. Baker worked on the ankle of Wake Forest All-American Dickie Hemric during a Wake and Duke basketball game. He got Hemric back into the game and Hemric tossed in 35 points.

Wake Forest made Baker an "Honorary Deacon" and a member of the Wake Monogram Club.

After returning to Duke Hospital in 1937, Baker advanced to professor of orthopedics in 1947. He also became director of the Division of Physical Therapy, orthopedic surgeon for the crippled children's Division of the N.C. Board of Health, and medical director of the Lenox Baker Cerebral Palsy and Crippled Children's Hospital in Durham which he established in 1938 through the cooperation of and the gift of land by Duke University.

The Bakers had two sons, Robert F. Baker, who is now a Durham attorney, and Lenox D. Baker Jr., a heart surgeon. Both sons attended Episcopal High School in Alexandria, Va., and Davidson College.

Baker, talking about his sons, paused to laugh. "I remember Lenox Jr., when only four, insisted that he accompany me on my Sunday rounds at Duke Hospital. And he had to wear surgical garb when he stood at my side during some of my operations."

Young Lenox graduated from the School of Medicine at Johns Hopkins, and his brother Robert graduated from Duke Law School.

Baker's work with youngsters in various hospitals received national attention, and in 1958 he received the Physician's Award, presented by President

Dwight Eisenhower. The award is made to the physician who makes the greatest contribution to the physically handicapped.

Ironically, although he has worked on broken bones and joints most of his life, and played several sports, Baker has never had a broken bone.

Baker recalls seeing a football game between the New York Giants and the Philadelphia Eagles "and there were six players at one time on whom I had operated."

Excerpts from some of Baker's comments on various occasions and the remarks of others might give some insight into the man.

Speaking at the 1966 annual meeting of the N.C. Rehabilitation Association, Baker said, "Your work brings dignity, pride, and self-respect to those who had lost all happiness . . . I would say your program is as wide as the glory and love of God."

In a 1953 article in the publication "The State of North Carolina and its Physically Handicapped," Baker said, ". . . Society and industry are losing billions of work hours which are available through these well-trained, wise men. The loss, due to ill-conceived rules and regulations, and a compulsory retirement age pattern that has swept this country must be rectified."

In March 1973, as a member of the State Board of Health, Baker suggested that the board investigate the inspection methods of the State Department of Agriculture. "We've got some rules about barbecue which are going to run some of the small operators out of business. We've all got to die sometime. We might as well enjoy some barbecue while we're at it."

Once after listening to a patient complain that no matter how much insurance he carried he never had enough to pay the doctors, Baker said: "They have cut down the cost of getting sick more than people realize, but we do drive too many Cadillacs."

In a speech in the Duke Pre-Med Society in 1951, Baker said, "I don't like research as it is now done in medical schools. I think we should have a separate department of research instead of draining time from teaching due to excess administrative bureaucracy."

In an address in 1959 as president of the N.C. Medical Society, Dr. Baker said, "We must be kind. We must not forget the purpose of our profession. We must be courteous, but with abundant toughness of mind and spirit. Above all, may we be humble. We must feel that same thrill felt by a true christian when he sings, 'Onward Christian Soldiers Marching As to War.'"

After taking office as secretary of the state Human Resources Department in 1971, Baker was described by a Raleigh newsman as "tough as a drill sergeant, devout as a preacher, and a zealot for the discipline and dignity of work."

Jesse Helms in a 1964 television editorial after accompanying Baker on his rounds at the N.C. Cerebral Palsy Hospital, said: "He has demonstrated a love for children in need, and they see that love with a clarity that only a child's perception possesses. And there is nothing syrupy-sweet about Dr. Baker's relations with these young people."

Baker in 1962 was being presented as president-elect at the 75th annual meeting of the American Orthopedic Association in Bermuda. He said: "This is a great honor and I'm damned glad to get it. Like George Eggers (association president), I am a Texan . . . Two Texans named consecutively to the presidency of this organization is at least interesting and unusual but easily explained. George had Lyndon, Lady Bird and Billy Sol Estes, plus the 27½ per cent tax deduction going for him. And you must remember that the Duke Endowment is the world's largest such fund. And mister, that's a lot of gold behind you."

In February 1974 before the North Carolina General Assembly in behalf of the East Carolina University Medical School, Baker gave an impassioned plea for the construction of the school and sharply attacked the University of North Carolina Board of Governors, which opposed immediate ECU expansion.

"The Board of Governors is in deep water and they are having trouble navigating," Baker said. "They were never authorized to determine the needs and wants of the people. The General Assembly is recognized to do this . . . If we had listened to all the songs of 'It can't be done,' we would have no medical schools today."

Asked why he was at the session, Baker answered, "I'm lobbying for the people. I'm lobbying for a four-year medical school at ECU."

In December 1971, in a talk before the Pioneers Association at the 98th birthday of Texarkana, Tex., where he and his parents had once lived, Baker said, "I remember my first job, wearing a little page boy uniform and ushering for 50 cents a night at the old Sanger Theater. I was the envy of every boy in the village."

State Sen. " Monk" Harrington in introducing Baker at the dedication of a new hospital at Ahoskie on Jan. 12, 1975, said: "When Dr. Baker comes down the halls of the legislature with fire in his eyes, you know he's going to get what he wants if he can. We know he doesn't beat around the bushes. We can depend on him for the truth. He should have been a lobbyist, and maybe he is. If so, it's always with something good for the people."

In closing one of his speeches to the legislature two years ago in his efforts to remove architectural barriers to cripples, Baker said, "Ask yourself if Christ were serving on this committee how would you vote on this bill."

Baker is a Presbyterian, but he says he isn't active in church affairs.

Baker said that when his time came to leave Duke in 1972 (with the title professor emeritus), "I felt I had done my job well and that it was time for others to take over. I left with a great love and appreciation for those who gave me my opportunities. I was happy to leave orthopedics in the good hands of Dr. Leonard Goldner and his associates."

"If I had any particular pride in my work I feel that it was my interest in the state and what Duke contributed to it and my efforts toward that goal brought about by my connection with the State Board of Health by six different appointments by four different governors, and my work in establishing crippled children's clinics throughout the state which gave me my greatest joys.

My rewards have been my family, both past and present, and the love that I feel for North Carolina."

Doctor Has Seen Many Changes

"The reason I like pediatrics better than family practice is because the patients never get old. They get old and have babies and I just recycle them."

So says longtime Durham pediatrician Dr. Bailey Daniel Webb, the recipient of the first Ph.D. awarded by the University of North Carolina Medical School.

Dr. Webb, who has seen a lot of changes, "many for the better," in her 36 years of practice, says she thinks the practice of medicine "right now is at the crossroads, highly specialized and highly technical."

She said "people expect perfection and we simply can't do that. Maybe the threat of doing without vaccine will wake them up."

Lawsuits and threatened lawsuits against pharmaceutical firms manufacturing vaccines present a bleak picture, she said.

"We have a whole generation of people who have never seen a case of diphtheria, tetanus, whooping cough, polio, and measles. This is due to the vaccine. They're focusing on the rare reaction. The calculated risk of the disease far outweighs the risk of the vaccine," she said.

Dr. Webb was born in Granville County at Tally Ho, near Stem, on her Grandfather Webb's farm, the first of four little girls of William James Webb and Sue Daniel Webb. "Our cousins down the road substituted as our brothers."

"My mother was in her 30s when she started having children, and my father had become partly deaf at 16. There were no antibiotics back then. He was Granville County auditor for 30 years. During the Great Depression the county never missed a salary payment."

Smiling, Dr. Webb said: "I was not the easiest of children to raise—I was very mischievous."

She said the first crystal radio she heard was built in a tool shed by her first cousin, James Webb, who lived a block away in Oxford. He later became United States space administrator.

"We first heard radio station KDKA, Pittsburgh. We thought that a miracle. James, after finishing at UNC, joined the U.S. Marine Air Corps."

Laughing, she recalled that "he would come in in a nose dive between our two homes to alert his family to go out to the cow pasture and pick him up when he landed. There was no airport anywhere in the area."

Dr. Webb, who attended Oxford High School, recalled when everyone followed, by radio, Charles Lindbergh's historic airplane flight to Paris in 1927.

She remembers well the flu epidemic in 1918 on the heels of World War I. She recalls too what she said was "a lesson in loyalty by 'Uncle' Willis Doxey," an energetic and no-nonsense man who saw to it that everyone followed the rules established by his former employer, Dr Nelson Ferebee, grandfather of Ferebee Taylor, former chancellor at UNC.

" 'Uncle' Willis was one of the most gentlemanly men I have ever known. He was never a servant in our home, rather something of a guardian of the set ways of Dr. Ferebee. And it was just a mutual arrangement when our family took over the old Ferebee home."

Smiling, Dr. Webb said that Doxey, through the help of Dr. Ferebee, had the first legal divorce in the area, and thereby gained considerable status.

"Willis was self-supportive by the sale of a patent medicine, '7-11 Good Luck' tonic, put out by the Pan-American Drug Company."

She said that while she was in junior high school her father decided she was wasting her time in the study hall. "He sent me to an Oxford business school for a year. Then I went to Greensboro College and obtained an A.B. degree."

"I taught science in high school for three years. Then my father got me a job with Granville County Clerk of Court, August 'Gus' Graham, as secretary. I got to know many Superior Court judges and I found them all to be fine men, especially Judge Marshall T. Spears of Durham."

She recalled the time Judge R. Hunt Parker came to Granville to hold court. "He had all the slot machines rounded up and brought to the jail to be broken up."

In 1937 she entered UNC when there were about 4,000 students, all white and few women. "I lived in the Graduate Woman's Dorm, which was behind the home of President Frank Graham. His open house on Sundays for students was a fun time. He never forgot a face and would introduce students to each other."

Dr. Webb said she worked in the chemistry department as a lab assistant, along with Dr. Jim Davis and Dr Roy Parker, who later located in Durham.

As a graduate student in biochemistry with a Fels Foundation Scholarship, she took pharmacology in the medical school (MacNider Building).

"I did all the shorthand records of the lectures of Dr. William deBerniere MacNider, the late Kenan research professor of pharmacology, and took pictures," she said.

During World War II, she said, there was a search for chemists and Dr. MacNider offered her a teaching job, but instead, she went to Duke University Medical School as a freshman.

"I remember I was in the medical library at UNC on Dec. 7, 1941, when Jim Davis came in and said angrily: 'Those damn Japanese have bombed Pearl Harbor!' I've got the special pink newspaper issue describing the attack," she said.

She served her residency at St. Louis Children's Hospital. During her internship there were 800 cases of polio in St. Louis, producing an epidemic and hysteria. Then came the Salk vaccine and later the oral Sabine vaccine, a boon to mankind.

Dr. Webb said that while she was a student at Greensboro College, Dr. P. M. Ginnings predicted the splitting of the atom "in a class with a Japanese student and me."

While she was at UNC, Dr. MacNider told of the mold that had fallen on the culture plates and predicted the clinical use of pencillin made from that mold.

Duke Hospital at first used pencillin for treatment of syphilis only. The advent of the wax-oil type base pencillin was greeted with cheers by the Durham County Health Department's venereal clinic director, Dr. O. L. Ader, and by Supt. J. H. Epperson, who said it was a "godsend."

"Dr. Wilbert Davison, dean of Duke Medical School while I was there, was a great influence in the integration of Duke Hospital. The children's ward, he used to say, was integrated 22 out of 24 hours."

"Howland Ward, the children's ward, had the white children in front of the ward and the black children in the back. White visiting time was one hour and the black for one hour, so for 22 of the 24 hours the ward was integrated," she said.

Dr. Webb said that the polio situation at St. Louis hospital in 1946 also brought about integration.

"The black ward there was discontinued to make a polio ward. The black nurses agreed to nurse polio patients. They came into the white hospitals and stayed after the epidemic."

Dr. Webb says she has loved children ever since she was a child. "There was no decision to make as to my becoming a pediatrician—it was natural."

She said that the introduction of fluoride into water to prevent tooth decay "has made as much difference as the polio vaccination. It just doesn't show as much."

Flu Today Not Like Terror of 1918

Influenza, be it called A-Victoria, A-Texas, Russian (A-USSR) Hong Kong, or Asian is taking a toll across the country. It's mild in Durham they say, but try to convince a victim.

To thwart or to help soften its attack, medical science is hard put to come up with relief. And, ever since the government's 1977 program to fight flu fell on its face, there are probably more skeptics than enthusiasts for any new propagandized vaccine.

Though frightening indeed, the word flu does not carry the terror it did in 1918. Then there was no vaccine, only suffering and wholesale death.

The Durham County Board of Health, on Sept. 25 of that year, warned an alarmed public of the rapid spread of the disease in this country. No longer was ill health considered a refinement.

On Oct. 2, the board held a special meeting attended also by health Superintendent Arch Cheatham and J. H. Epperson, bacteriologist and milk inspector, and Mayor M. E. Newsom.

The group approved the following orders: "All children should be stopped from school when they show symptoms themselves. All moving picture shows, Sunday schools, and indoor public gatherings in the city and sanitary districts of East and West Durham will be closed. All soda fountains must use sanitary cups and sterilized spoons."

"Quarantine. Call on all teachers to inspect their pupils and all department heads of factories to have their operators inspected, and exclude from work those who show any signs of sickness. Physicians to be called on for prompt daily report."

Three days later, a new order included all schools, churches, and public gatherings whether indoors or outdoors. A relief bureau was established with Miss Jane Williams in charge.

On Oct. 9, the Red Cross executive committee met and agreed to unite its work with the board of health. The same day Cheatham met with black physicians and nurses and school officials and explained to them the situation. They agreed to organize and help.

The merchants and businessmen of Durham gathered on Oct. 12, and three days later Cheatham issued a call for 50 trained or untrained nurses.

Influenza infirmaries opened in East and West Durham for white victims, and in the southern area of the city for blacks.

World War I, which was raging in Europe, became secondary. Flu was a new disease, something the nation had never before experienced.

"It hit like a bolt of lightning," said the late Jesse Epperson, a Kentuckian whose family had been in the famous Oklahoma Run. "Overnight, entire families were made helpless. Many were too ill to eat or move the dead from their beds."

Morehead School on Jackson Street was converted into an emergency hospital; army cots set up in the halls and classrooms.

The health department's three sanitary inspectors were put in cars to haul in the badly sick to the school hospital.

"We were unloading them at the front door and the undertakers were taking them away at the back door," Epperson said.

Approximately three-fourths of the city's doctors were too ill to work. Cheatham turned his health duties over to Epperson and returned to the practice of medicine to care for the victims.

The City Council and county commissioners allocated money to the health department to spend any way it saw fit to deal with an unprecedented situation.

The board of health met daily to study the situation and to cope with it as best it could.

"We gave some relief, but as far as preventing the spread of the flu we weren't really doing anything, we made no headway against it," Epperson said.

Half-page advertisements ran two weeks in Durham's two newspapers, and 45,000 circulars on flu and its care were distributed.

Military camps of the United States were saturated with the disease and soldiers seen riding train cars out of Camp Polk at Raleigh looked strange and fearsome with masks over their faces, peering out of the windows.

Many of the city's older doctors were firm believers that whisky was needed as a stimulant to treat flu cases. Their influence induced Recorder's Court Judge Paul C. Graham to sign an order requesting internal revenue authorities at Raleigh to consign to the Durham Board of Health quantities of seized corn whisky.

The revenue men were astounded when Epperson presented them with Graham's order. It was during prohibition in North Carolina, and a judge was asking contraband spirits for the public. But the request was approved because of the emergency.

"They let us have a large quantity of liquor on several occasions," Epperson said. "We put it up in four-ounce bottles and it was distributed through doctors' prescriptions. Thousands of bottles were placed in the hands of the sick. I don't know that it helped them, but it was a popular remedy."

Dobell Solution, a potent antiseptic, was put up 10 to 12 gallons at a time at the health department for distribution to the public as a germ-killing gargle.

Epperson said it was learned later that many methods were worthless in coping with the flu, but that masks, corn whisky, and the gargle were all they had then.

During the months of October, November, and December in 1918, there were approximately 6,000 cases and 112 deaths from flu and pneumonia in Durham alone.

Health Department in Durham Started Off Small

The 1913 General Assembly ratified a bill and the Durham County Health Department came into being.

It was not the most glorious of starts. The department was housed in a one-room office above a store at East Main and Church streets across from the courthouse.

At the time, Durham was a bustling little city boasting textiles, tobacco, and timber as its main industries.

Durham would grow during the next 63 years and so would the health department. Three men would head the department during that time—Dr. Arch Cheatham, Jesse H. Epperson, and Dr. Ottis L. Ader—and one man had already set the groundwork for it—Dr. Thomas Mann.

Mann was the health officer for the city of Durham before the department was created. He was a persistent foe of tuberculosis and in 1908, he took the Durham Board of Aldermen to task because the law against promiscuous spitting was not being rigidly enforced.

"During some of the tobacco 'brakes' the warehouse floors are as bad as the floors of the courthouse," Mann told the board. "There is no telling how many people suffering with tuberculosis are expectorating on the floors, and it is impossible to tell exactly what results from this carelessness."

"When we take into consideration that over 15 million germs are discharged daily from the lungs of a consumptive, no public citizen can deny that the disposal of these discharges is a question of important social concern," Mann said.

He also opposed open toilets and pig pens in the same backyards and said the city stables should be properly cleaned and manure removed.

Cheatham headed the health department from its creation in 1913 until his death in 1922.

Epperson, Cheatham's assistant, was named to succeed him and headed the department for 36 years.

Ader was hired by the department in 1944 and became director when Epperson died in 1958.

Dr. John Fletcher became director last July when Ader retired.

In 1916, the department left its one-room office and moved to two rooms in the Geer Building at West Main and Corcoran streets.

After a year, it moved to larger quarters on the third floor of the courthouse and remained there until March 1942.

The health department next moved to a building at 300 E. Main St. which had been built by the Masonic Temple Corporation of Durham at a total cost of $162,000. The Masons lost the building during the Depression, and in 1938 it was bought by the city and county to house the health department.

In 1958 the county purchased the city's share in the health building property. They agreed to fully support the public health program on the condition that the county's ABC store profits, at a 70/30 rather than 50/50 proportion, go to the county.

In 1972 the county paid $609,000 for the vacant Sears, Roebuck & Co. store building and its huge parking lot, plus $85,000 for adjacent property owned by Alexander Motor Co.

Renovation began in July 1974 and cost nearly $1.5 million.

Ader noted that he had served with the health department for more than half of the years it has been in existence and said he could not recall when "there was anything other than an excellent working relationship" between the county commissioners, board of health, and the department.

He said that "someone has appropriately stated that no major disease has been controlled much less eradicated, by more hospital beds or clinics, more doctors, nurses, or better drugs. On the other hand, many diseases have been controlled through organized community effort."

Ader said that typhoid fever has been controlled by changing the environment of the community, the purification of water supplies, the pasteurization of milk, and the enforcement of food sanitation laws. Diphtheria, poliomyelitis, smallpox, and other communicable diseases have been controlled by immunization laws.

Public health, he said, "is soundly based in the legal and governmental structure of our country as a legitimate public function. Moreover, public health departments are secure in not having to win political approval, at least they were until some of the questionable health measures now being proposed came along."

Ader said public health programs are not static but undergo a continuous process of change and development. The programs must be flexible and designed in the terms of the community's health needs and its resources.

"The accepted concept of the responsibilities and services of the local health department has undergone considerable change during the past 30 years— when it was located in the attic or basement of the courthouse. The sharp decrease in communicable diseases, the marked changes in the age distribution of the population and in the widespread variety of today's health problems have resulted in markedly expanded public health programs. Fortunately or unfortunately, today public health programs are not only accepted but expected, and even demanded on some occasions," he said.

He said that whereas formerly public health services were provided free of charge, "now personal and third-party payments are legal and resulting in an ever-increasing source of reimbursement of county expenditures for health services ($187,500, 17 per cent of the department's proposed 1976-77 budget). This help was needed and will enable health departments to expand in primary care services."

Ader emphasized that the Durham public health program objectives remain the same: to reduce the amount of disease, premature death, and the discomfort and disability produced by disease.

Public health, Ader said, is now serving individuals for chronic diseases, providing bedside nursing care to homebound patients, and other services not confined to control of communicable diseases.

"The health department, in addition to proving routine public health services, is expected to keep the public informed on matters pertaining to health. Therefore, aside from adequate professional training, the public health worker's best tool is health education," he said.

Ader urged his staff to reach large numbers of people. "To reach people and effectively change their behavior to make for healthier living, we need to take the time and effort to understand what other people think and do, how they live and work, and what legal and other restrictions are involved in their work. Only then will we be in position to plan a way for working together to the benefit of our community, or to realize the most significant of the changing aspects of public health."

9

Sports

M. P. "Footsie" Knight, who was fondly and fairly called "Mr. YMCA," believed and followed the words of the triangle embedded in the tile floor of the old "Y" downtown: "Body, mind, and spirit." This code was his religion. Knight developed countless boys into fine athletes of character. They proved this in championship teams in junior and senior high schools and colleges.

In olden days Trinity College's baseball team for years played exhibition games against major league teams.

W. W. "Cap" Card of Trinity College, for whom a gym at Duke is named, staged the first college basketball matches in North Carolina at Trinity. He gained fame for his physical training programs for all students and for his fine calisthenics teams.

Duke football coach Wallace Wade's great team of 1941 was selected to play Oregon State in the Rose Bowl game at Pasadena, California. World War II was under way, there was a blackout on the West Coast, and it appeared the game would not be played.

Wade induced the Rose Bowl committee to have the game played at Duke Stadium—the first time it left Pasadena.

From Pasadena to Durham

After Pearl Harbor, Rose Bowl

It was eight days after the Japanese had ambushed Pearl Harbor, triggering war in the Pacific.

The football teams of Oregon State and Duke University, selected to meet in the Rose Bowl at Pasadena, were in the depths of despair. The government had canceled this game, along with the East-West contest in San Francisco, the horse races at Santa Anita, and all other bowl games west of Arizona. It was thought that the congestion of pedestrians and automobiles would be too great for safety in wartime. But about 75,000 of the 90,000 tickets available had already been sold for the famed Rose Bowl game.

Then out of the blue came the invitation from Duke's coach-athletic director Wallace Wade for the big game to be played in Durham.

Percy Locey, director of athletics at Oregon State, enthusiastically accepted. Thus was the 27th annual Tournament of Roses rescued in history-making fashion.

This grand gesture by Duke had a tremendous effect on civilian morale. And just three days after the announcement of the change of site, Wade reported that all the seats and bleacher space in Duke Stadium had been sold.

Coach Wade, a Tennesseean, had been to the Rose Bowl four times as a coach and once as a player. It was the Oregon State Beavers' first visit.

The University of North Carolina student body, in a great display of sportsmanship and patriotism, sent the Duke Blue Devils a congratulatory scroll seven feet long. UNC, along with Wake Forest and N.C. State College, also loaned its bleachers to boost Duke Stadium's seating capacity of 40,000 to about 56,000.

Made Historic Trip

At a press luncheon at the Washington Duke Hotel, Robert McCurdy, president of the Tournament of Roses, said: "We want you fellows to call this the 'Victory Bowl,' so that millions of fans will become national defense conscious."

More than 2,000 cheering fans were on hand at the Union Train Station at the foot of Church Street to welcome the Oregon Staters on Christmas Eve. Dapper Mayor W. F. Carr greeted the visitors, who appeared to relish the reception.

The Beavers paraded to the Washington Duke Hotel where they were the breakfast guests of manager George Serrett. Mayor Carr presented a plaque to Martin Chaves, Oregon State's captain for the game, naming him "Mayor of Durham" for the day. After this, the visitors boarded buses for their trip to the Carolina Inn in Chapel Hill, their official headquarters.

Durham could not compete with Pasadena's traditional parade and flowers, but southern hospitality was evident in other ways. There was a Christmas dinner at Duke, a polo match at Pinehurst, a barbecue at Josh Turnage's Place on Morreene Road, a press luncheon sponsored by Herald-Sun Papers, a kick-off luncheon sponsored by the Durham Kiwanis Club (at which comedian Joe E. Brown stole the show), tours, and other features. The media, through the courtesy of proprietor George Whitted of The Little Acorn, made this eatery their headquarters for off-duty hours. And all of this was done in just 15 days.

All hotel rooms were full and restaurants crowded. There was a carnival air throughout the city. In hotel lobbies Duke was quoted at 3-1 odds to win the game. The Blue Devils had won all nine of its games in 1941 while Oregon State had a 7-2 record. In fact, Duke had lost only three games in nine years on its field. Its 311 points for 1941 was a school record. The rankers had given Duke second place in the national standings for 1941, while the Beavers were 22nd.

Because of the war, the Mexican Government couldn't send the 400,000 gardenias and 100,000 orchids previously ordered for Pasadena to Durham. But it did send a bunch of roses to Tournament of Roses president McCurdy in Durham.

The price of game tickets was $4.40, but some scalpers were getting $15.

Details of handling traffic and crowds was worked out by Duke's W. E. Whitford, State Highway Patrol Sgt. R. S. Harris, Durham police Capt. Norman Hardee, and Safety Director Roy Bishop. C. E. Vandiver, transportation engineer for Durham Public Service Co., said that 28 special buses would be assigned for the game.

Sheriff E. G. "Cat" Belvin reported that he had a squad of about 50 deputies and volunteers to keep gate-crashers out of the stadium.

Ted Mann, former Duke publicist, as a lieutenant j.g. in the U.S. Naval Reserve, was fortunate to get assigned to duty in Durham and was able to see the game.

Coach Wade's assistants were Eddie Cameron, who was also basketball coach; Ellis "Dumpy" Hagler, Hershell Caldwell, Dennis "Dutch" Stanley, and Robert L. Chambers.

Wade at 33 was the youngest coach ever to take a football team (Alabama) to the Rose Bowl. That was in 1926. Oregon State Coach Lon Stiner, 38 in 1942, was the second youngest coach to participate in this bowl.

Duke had a squad of 48 players and had yielded but 41 points in 1941, while the orange and black-clad Beavers had only 32 players, but they were known as the "Iron Men," and the "Cinderella Team of the Pacific Coast."

Quarterbacking Duke was Thompson Prothro, a great blocker, who later became a professional football coach. Duke halfbacks included the spectacular Steve Lach, an exceptional runner, blocker, and pass receiver, Tom Davis, Moffat Storer, and Bill Wartman.

Winston Siegfried, Leo Long, and James Wolfe were fullbacks. Ends included Alex Piasecky, Bob Gantt of Durham, James Smith, Luther Dempsey, and Herman Smith. The tackles were led by Bob McDonough, Mike Karmazin, Bob Nanni, and Clyde Redding. Top guards were Tom Burns, Jimmy Lipscomb, and Pete Goddard, who at 168 pounds was opposed by Beaver Bill Halverson at 230 pounds.

Durham boys on the squad included Gantt, Ralph Morgan, and Charles Haynes. Art Vann, now a veteran Durham lawyer, a native of Dunn, was a Duke half-back.

Coach Stiner, who didn't like the 3-1 odds, expressed confidence before the game. Conservative Coach Wade said: "You can't tell what a team will do once it breaks training and resumes its practice sessions."

Came the day of the game and cold rain fell. Scalpers took a beating, many parting with a ticket for $1.50, while one, disgusted, sold a boy a ticket for just a quarter.

A composite band composed of musicians from Duke, UNC, Wake Forest, Davidson, N.C. State, and Durham High School furnished the music for the game.

Before the game the crowd stood for a moment's silence in tribute to the men in armed services, and with note of Lt. Foy Roberson Jr. of Durham, a basketball player at UNC, who died in a plane crash.

Five hundred officers and enlisted men from Fort Bragg who had bought game tickets days before were unable to attend. Their tickets were sold quickly long before the game.

News cameramen from Fox, Movietone, Pathe, News of the Day, and Universal, were on hand, along with 200 sportswriters and newspaper photographers from all over.

Duke's publicist, Add Penfield, was in charge of the west side of the field, and sportswriter Dick Herbert handled the east side in covering the game for Duke.,

Don Durdan of Oregon State, a triple-threat lefthander who passed, kicked, and ran with the ball, and Duke's do-everything Lach, were the two players being watched. Oregon State scored first with a touchdown and the extra point. Duke came back to tie the score in the second quarter and then knotted the score again at 14-all in the third period. But the Beavers racked up another six points in the third to assure the victory. Duke got a safety in the fourth period but it wasn't enough. Fumbles and interceptions killed the Blue Devils, leading to a stunning 20-16 upset.

Durdan and Lach averaged nearly 50 yards on their punts and Duke had 15 first downs to Oregon State's 14, but the Beavers had the best of the offense and the defense and capitalized on mistakes.

Pickpockets were active throughout the game and car thieves prospered. One fan from Richmond lost his wife and didn't see her until the next day.

Thus was the mighty battle that was moved from the purple mountains of Pasadena to the green pines of Carolina.

Duke President Robert L. Flowers opened his home on the campus for an informal gathering after the game. The university also gave a buffet supper for distinguished guests at the Washington Duke Hotel. The Red Cross-Senior Hadassah held a dance in the hotel in honor of the occasion. There were also many other private dinners and breakfasts in honor of the game a war couldn't stop.

Old Durham 'Y' Was World of Its Own

It was a kaleidoscopic world of its own, the dirty-face old Durham YMCA at Main and Roxboro streets back in the early 1930s.

In the little game room on the right, just inside the big front door, two figures sat hunched over a checker board. Expressionless, they seemed transfixed, dedicated to the task at hand.

Spectators stood quietly by, almost reverent toward the determined contestants.

"Cap" W. W. Card and Claude Luquire were involved in one of their classic matchups, masterminding the moves of the little red and black wooden discs on a battlefield of squares.

In another corner of the room Ben "Banjo" Elliott was locked in deadly joust on the chess board with a game-skilled Duke professor.

Standing, and ready for a go with the checkers, were George Moore and Walter Lamb.

Imbedded in the tile floor of the "Y" lobby was that familiar, almost sacred circle with the symbolic triangle and the words: "Body, Mind, and Spirit."

In the reading room on the left side of the lobby a high schooler made notes from his textbook. A chair away an elderly man slept with his eyes open, his liver-spotted, bulging purple-veined hands gripping the arm rests.

At the big office desk Arnold E. Jenny, "Y" secretary, was engrossed in describing his trip to Vladivostok. His voice, penetrating, was accustomed to rising above the din from the nearby tables where paddles slapped pingpong balls and cue sticks jabbed multi-colored pool balls.

From a small stairway door behind the tables came a thundering herd of chattering, clean-looking youths who, having just quit the swimming pool and showers in the basement, were once again ready for sunlight.

From a far corner of the lobby several older men talked politics while a knot of teen-agers joked and clutched their school books almost disdainfully, as if they were crosses to bear.

On the gymnasium floor, barrel-chested M. P. "Footsie" Knight, the director of physical education, was putting a class through calisthenics.

In a corner there was a piano badly in need of tuning. The keys were being thumped vigorously by Henry Brewer, a blind man who roomed at the "Y."

On the second and third floors of the "Y" were the dormitories, and in the hallways of these floors were drinking fountains. Brewer, who had a short fuse, had the habit of almost swallowing the faucet when he drank at the fountain. The habit was broken when a nettled guest rubbed red soap on the spigot. Brewer made the discovery. Then he demonstrated his purple vocabulary.

There was once a South Atlantic swimming match at the "Y." Knight, an advocate of clean living, constantly warned his swimmers that smoking would shorten their breath and make them losers.

One of the visiting swimmers kept a lighted cigarette in his mouth, and Knight reminded his swimmers of his warning. "That fellow has no business in this match. He won't even be able to complete a race," he growled.

At the conclusion of the match, which included diving, the fellow with the cigarette had won more contests than anyone else. Knight, disgusted and fuming, had to strain to keep from exploding.

There was a window in the west end of the hallway on the third floor of the "Y" from which for a long time some of the boys would stare into the rooms of the Lochmoor Hotel, just a few feet away.

Finally, when word reached Knight about the Peeping Toms, he lowered the boom. He collared several boys and led them out of the building. But he first pointed to the emblem in the tile floor of the lobby. "YMCA stands for Young Men's Christian Association!" he blasted.

Knight had a weekly radio Sunday school program which was very popular, particularly so because of his booming, authoritative voice. In later years at the old "Y" W. L. Hampton, an official who also became a tradition, sometimes taught the lessons.

Once Hampton was relaxing in a chair in the reading room, his eyes closed, when one of the boys placed a note near Hampton's feet and slid a firecracker under the chair. When the cracker exploded, Hampton did too. Then he saw the note. It read: "Make a joyful noise unto the Lord." He shook his head. Then he smiled.

The "Y" had great basketball teams and frequently whipped college teams with ease. The younger boys learned so much about the game from Knight, and with keen competition, that when they reached high school they were accomplished players.

Volleyball was also popular as was the health club where tired and flabby bodies were steamed, slapped, and massaged with wintergreen, rubbing alcohol, and liniment, by efficient masseurs.

Working out on the trapeze rings and the "horse," were favorites of many "Y" members. Some preferred the wall pulls, the punching bag, and tumbling mats.

During calisthenics medicine balls were sometimes used, and if a fellow had difficulty in picking up and throwing the heavy, leather-stuffed balls, Knight would tell him to sit on it for a while and rest.

Knight had a number of baseball and softball teams in the "Y" league. I thought it strange when he once asked me, just a youth, to umpire a championship baseball game with cross-town rivals at the old hosiery mill diamond in Edgemont. But I was flattered and agreed.

The game was extremely close and exciting, with a large, noisy crowd on hand. In the ninth inning with one team leading by a run, but with the other team at bat, a player hit the ball a country mile. It sailed over the center fielder's head. The happy hitter practically waltzed around the bases to a bedlam of cheers.

Then the fielder retrieved the ball and tossed it to the shortstop who promptly stepped on second base. "How about it, Mr. Ump? He didn't tag second base, did he?"

"No, he didn't," I agreed. I called the batter out. They came running toward me, two or three on bicycles. Instead of a tie game, it was all over and the "other" side had won.

One guy drew back a soft drink bottle as if to throw it. But fate was kind to me. "Footsie" Knight, unbeknown to me, had driven up to the field a minute or so earlier and sized up the situation. He blocked off the would-be lynchers and shielded me with his big body. "Stand back!" he thundered. "The batter didn't touch second base. The game is over. Behave yourself!"

In the safety of Knight's car en route to the "Y" it dawned on me. " 'Footsie,' you asked me to umpire because you couldn't get anybody else to go down there. That's right, isn't it?"

"Footsie" never answered. He started humming and talking about what a busy, trying day he had had.

What a man. The head honcho of the "Y" for many years, no one who ever knew "Footsie" could forget him. And when the old "Y" which had been built in 1908 was eliminated and the big and handsome "Y" on Trinity Avenue was dedicated in 1957, he said it this way: "It is the answer to a long dream I've had."

He Brought Basketball to the State

The YMCA code: "Body, Mind, and Spirit," which was embedded in the tile floor of the lobby at the old "Y" on Main Street, was specified, glorified, and exemplified by a modest Durham man who perhaps had no equal in the world of physical fitness. He was Wilbur Wade "Cap" Card, for whom Duke University in 1953 designated its men's gymnasium.

Card, who introduced basketball to North Carolina in 1905, was known as the grand old man of sports at Duke, and upon his death in 1948 another beloved "Mr. Chips" passed from the scene.

Born in nearby Franklinton, the son of Sabert H. and Cecilia Fuller Card, he attended Franklinton Classical and Military Institute and the Raleigh Male Academy, where his grades averaged above 96.

He entered Trinity College (now Duke University), in the fall of 1895, with plans for becoming a Methodist minister. His maternal grandfather and great grandfather had been Christian ministers. Later he changed his program and concentrated on athletics as a profession, and graduated with a bachelor's degree.

In the fall of 1900, with the endorsement and aid of three leading Durham citizens: Benjamin N. Duke, Thomas J. Lambe, and James H. Southgate, Card was admitted to Harvard University.

There he took special courses in hygiene and was a student in physical education, graduating in 1902. Card returned to Harvard every summer through 1913, and during two of those summers was a gym instructor.

As a student at Trinity, Card competed on the track and baseball teams and was captain of the 1899 baseball team. From then on he was known as "Cap." He set and broke numerous baseball records. At Harvard he distinguished himself for his athletic prowess and strength.

During the 1901 and 1902 session, Card was director of physical education at the YMCA at Mobile, Ala.

In the fall of 1902 he received an invitation from Trinity President Dr. John C. Kilgo, and returned to Trinity as director of physical education at the Angier Duke Gymnasium, a connection that continued for the rest of his life.

In the summers of 1914 and 1915, Card worked in Baltimore and Boston in the recreation programs there. During World War I he was physical training secretary at Camp Sevier, S.C., and received certificates of commendation.

Baseball was Card's favorite sport, and in addition to playing for Trinity he played semi-pro baseball at Tarboro in 1898, and at Concord the following year.

The Boston National baseball team offered him a contract to play professional ball in 1900, but he went to Harvard instead. During the regular and summer sessions at Harvard, Card acquainted himself with all types of sports. These sports included: gymnastics, association football, track, field hockey, bowling, swimming, fencing, volley ball, and basketball.

The first collegiate game of basketball in North Carolina was played at Trinity College in March 1906, with the score Wake Forest 8, Trinity 6.

Beginning in 1902, Card kept meticulous records of every entering freshman's physical condition. These records, written in pen and ink in large ledgers, are still at Duke.

A medical history of each student was entered in the ledger, along with thorough physical measurements which included such confidential items as "9th rib expansion." A space was also used to record the examiner's observations such as "flat chest," "near-sighted," or just "needs developing."

The years 1902 through 1913 provide the most complete statistical evidence. During this period the average age of entering freshmen was 18 years and 4 months; the average height, 5 feet, 6 inches; and the average weight, 130.1 pounds.

Today, freshmen have larger feet, are heavier, and taller. The freshman who comes to Duke to participate in intercollegiate athletics is more proficient in his particular sport than athletes were at Trinity College. The athletic department no longer places its sole emphasis upon exercises that increase the physical development of the individual.

Card was widely recognized in his field. Beginning in 1921, he served as state chairman of the American Physical Education Association, and his reports were published in the *American Physical Education Review.*

His staged gymnasium exhibitions were popular attractions through the years, especially so during the halves of basketball games. He initiated physical education in North Carolina, and an instructor's course, which was novel in this state.

Before 1910, he worked successfully to get money for physical education in all schools of the state through the State Legislature.

Card was the marshal for the collegiate division of the first annual Olympic games held in Durham, May 4-6, 1922.

Card was an active churchman, and from 1891 to 1899, was a member of Mrs. W. H. Bobbitt's Sunday School class of Edenton Street Methodist Church in Raleigh. For 46 years he was a member of Duke Memorial Methodist Church in Durham, where he taught a Bible class for 35 years.

Card was married on Dec. 30, 1902, to Anna Luella Waldo, in Wyoming, Ohio. She was a prize-winning graduate of Detroit Training School of Elocution and English Literature, and a popular vocalist.

The Cards had two children: Elizabeth Cecelia Card, who is married to Wortham C. Lyon of Durham; and Helen Kendrick Card, who is married to Oliver W. Upchurch, also of Durham.

In commencement exercises at Duke in 1942, a portrait of Card, painted by one of his former students, Paul Whitener of Hickory, was presented to the university. It hangs in the lobby of Cameron Indoor Stadium.

A. C. Jordan, retired Duke professor, who recently made comments at the Wilbur W. "Cap" Card Lecture program in the Bryan University Center, said that he was on Card's freshman handball team which played in the "Ark" on the east Duke campus.

"Cap himself played," Jordan said. "He always tried to keep his boys from smoking—he preached against the evils of cigarettes."

Jordan said he was also in Card's calisthenics class. "It was in the curriculum, and required. He was really a fine fellow, and nationally known."

In the Card portrait presentation, the late Duke Professor H. E. Spence, a member of the first basketball team at Trinity, said, among other things: "Cap's greatest contribution is in the realm of the intangible and the immeasurable. He has been a personal friend to thousands of discouraged young students. My most vivid recollection of him is his tireless attempt to teach a crippled boy the use of his helpless limbs. And many a man throughout the world today owes his healthy body and fine frame of mind to the efforts of this man who cheered them on to success."

Many oldtimers who frequented the old "Y" on Main Street will remember

Cap sitting quietly and studiously poring over a checker or chess board with one of his favorite, friendly adversaries.

This sports immortal died at age 74, five years after suffering a stroke. Officiating at the funeral held in Duke Memorial Methodist Church was Dr. Frank S. Hickman, dean of Duke University Chapel, assisted by Dr. H. E. Myers.

Pallbearers were all Duke athletic officials: Wallace Wade, Eddie Cameron, Walter "Jack" Persons, Mike Karmazin, Bob Chambers, Herbert Lewis, Dan Hill Jr., and John Henemier.

Among the tributes at that time were those of Duke President Robert L. Flowers, who said: "Cap Card befriended and encouraged the discouraged, cheering them with his kindly attention, and setting an unforgettable example for them through his own fine character."

A Runner

At 80, He Says He's Never Lost A Race

Randolph Moore Shears is no less a fixture at Duke University than the wall around the east campus and the horseshoe stadium on the west campus.

And at 80 years old, Shears, better known as "Nurmi" after the great Finnish runner Paavo Nurmi of the 1930s, says he will still accept a challenge to a foot race.

A tall, plodding man with thick shock of white hair. Shears is rarely seen without his briefcase, pocketwatch, and broad smile.

He has tutored students, particularly Duke athletes, in French, German and Spanish for many years but his first love is walking and running.

Just for kicks and exercise, Shears used to deliver telegrams between Duke's two campuses. Often mistaken by strangers as a professor late to class, Shears, in street clothes and hanging on to his briefcase, would burn the pavement dispatching the messages.

About three years ago he gave an impromptu exhibition of running for the fans between halves at a Duke football game.

In April 1971, the Duke Chronicle ran his picture with the title "Everyone's Friend, 'Nurmi.' "

The Duke Chanticleer of 1969 carried a full page photograph of "Nurmi" facing Colonel Sanders of 'finger lickin' good" ' fame.

Shears, who lives at 1405 Woodland Drive with his wife Mable, a Durham native, was born in New York City.

He attended Berkeley, a private school in New York, and was a student at Columbia University.

"My mother and I came to Durham about 45 years ago to see my brother Lambert, a Duke University professor. We liked it here and stayed," he said.

He said he became interested in athletics and when not tutoring, ran around the Duke track for hours. "I became such a regular on the track that a lot of the students began calling me 'Nurmi' and I accepted it as a compliment and a challenge."

Asked if he ever pitted his speed against Duke trackmen, he looked as if the question were elementary or foolish.

"Of course I did," he answered quickly. "I can't recall losing a race and even at my advanced age of 80, I believe I can still beat some of the Duke runners. I figure my stamina and endurance will help me live to be 95."

Asked if he thought the Duke students permitted him to win the races with them, Shears scoffed. "I hardly think so," he said. "Nobody likes to lose a race."

Correct time, he insisted, has long been one of his hobbies. "I'd say I am a precisionist. I carry a Hamilton Railway Special pocketwatch I've had for years. It won't vary as much as a second in 24 hours."

Fingering his heavy gold watch chain, he lamented, "It's hard to find a pair of trousers with a watch pocket."

Shears doesn't do much tutoring now but he says it is not because of his advanced years.

"I'm not too old, my mind is clear as a bell with the languages. But I don't get many requests for help. Maybe students have less trouble with their studies, I hope that is true."

Shears says he never smoked more than three or four cigarettes in his life. He sleeps and eats well, and takes exercise by walking and walking. He has never owned or cared to own a car.

As to correspondence, he disdains writing letters. He writes small and clear on a postal card, sometimes putting as many as 200 words on a card.

Shears and his wife have never had children and a lot of their affection is poured upon a yellow-red tomcat named "Chubby."

Shears says that he believes his life has been prolonged because he never becomes angry, "When you lose your self-control it's easy to become a fool."

Although he professes to be a Republican, Shears said he has not voted in 40 years. "It's not lack of patriotism, I've just been plain disgusted with politics."

Back to the subject of running, Shears said he was like television's Perry Mason, his favorite character. "He has never lost a case and I've never lost a race."

10

Religion

Durham has been fortunate in having through the years outstanding ministers. These would include Father William F. O'Brien, Durham's first Catholic priest; W. W. Peele; and Duke University Chapel Ministers Dr. James T. Cleland and Dr. Frank S. Hickman.

Years ago the evangelists of fame came to Durham, including Billy Sunday, "Cyclone" Mack Ham, Ramsey "Gypsy" Smith, and "Daddy" Grace.

Many run-of-the mill tent preachers have held forth here, at least one of whom had his tent burned, and not accidentally.

River baptisms were popular in some areas and oftentime a head was held underwater what I thought was too long a time. Singing and food and yelling made it all a good show.

He Captured Hearts From Chapel Pulpit

Dr. James T. Cleland, the bonny Scotch clergyman who came to Duke University in 1945 and captivated the hearts of campus and town alike, says the school treasurer is the only one who knows he is retired. "I don't get any more checks," the 72-year-old Cleland shrugs with his patented impish grin, "But they keep using me."

Dr. Cleland, who prefers that his old friends call him "Jim." is struggling to remove his shackles of a "workaholic."

Although he lives in a modest apartment in sedate Croasdaile, removed from the huge Duke complex where activities and emotions are as vibrant as the waves of the Atlantic, the minister retains an office a stone's throw from his magnificent Duke Chapel. And that is where they seek him out, incessantly.

Two women, like bookends sheltering the prized volume, all but manipulate Dr. Cleland's exhaustive day-in-and-day-out schedule of events. They are his wife, Alice, who he met in New York two weeks after coming to America, and Mrs. Marie Smith, his secretary. "Good secretaries are pearls of great price," he says.

He was born in Glasgow to the Rev. James Cleland, who had been a master carpenter, and Margaret Curdie Cleland. Dr. Cleland said his father died at age 47 when he was 12. "My father walked alone where other preachers walked in pairs. No one touched him. When he passed drunkards they'd always stagger to their feet and say, 'Hello, minister,' and sometimes they'd immediately pass out," Dr. Cleland chuckled. "He had a gold watch and a chain across his waistcoat and they lent an air of distinction."

Dr. Cleland was the oldest of three children. His sister Margaret married three years ago at the age of 60, to a man 70. "They had known each other 11 years, so you see we Clelands don't dash into matrimony. She calls him 'My Yorkshire laddie.' They live in Yorkshire."

Asked how he happened to wend his way to Durham, Dr. Cleland smiled. "I was teaching Bible at Amherst and preaching at Harvard, Yale, Princeton, and Columbia when I received a call from Harvey Branscomb at Duke. He told me that Duke needed a pulpiteer and that he would make me an associate professor if I would accept."

Grinning, he said that when he told Branscomb that Amhurst was offering him a full professorship, Branscomb told him, "Cleland, the job is yours on any term you want."

"I accepted. We had a Chevrolet, my first car, and gas ration coupons. But then the war ended about the same time. Alice loved New England and really didn't want to leave, but we drove down," Cleland said.

"A tire blew out near Sweetbriar in Virginia, but a big black man in a truck stopped, changed the car's tire, and refused to accept pay for it."

"That was my first meeting with a black in the south," Cleland said. "I had taught Albert Whiting (president of North Carolina Central University) at Amherst."

Asked why he came to the United States, the minister said he had earned his degree at Glasgow University, and that the school annually sent three of its graduates to Union Seminary in New York. "I was thrilled. We loved New York. It was safe in those days. We called the seminary 'the Yankee team of theology,' the faculty was so good," Cleland said. "It was the No. 1 seminary. The Catholics and the Jews would admit it."

Shrugging he added, "I came to Duke because Branscomb was a gambler and so was I. I had never had a parish. When we arrived at Duke we were given the home just vacated by Duke Dean of Divinity Paul Neff Garber."

Laughing, Dr. Cleland recalled that when he was invited to Glasgow to preach at Wellington, he wrote his mother in Scotland to tell her about it. "She wrote back, saying, 'It is a great honor. Accept, but don't come. You're not

Rev. James T. Cleland, Dean of Duke University Chapel, was awarded the game ball from a 1970 match.

good enough.' But I did go, and after the service she told me I did well, but not to risk it again. She was a superb sermon critic, a great little lady," he said.

"At least 75 percent of those who attended her funeral were men and boys, she was so well liked."

The class of 1949 requested that he preach their baccalaureate, making Dr. Cleland the first member at the Duke Faculty to do so. "The students said that if I didn't, they wouldn't attend, because I preached them in and they wanted me to preach them out," he chuckled.

"When I 'preached them in' it was my first sermon, and I told the freshmen that I couldn't welcome them to Duke because I was a stranger, too. It was their first time in the chapel."

When Cleland arrived at Duke, soccer was not an official sport at the school. It was a club sport, with the basketball coach, Gerry Gerard, coaching soccer out of a book. He had never played the game. "As a Scot, it was my game. Wallace Wade, Duke's football coach, coaxed me into coaching soccer at Duke," the minister recalled. "I was teaching a full load in the Divinity School Monday through Friday and some Saturday mornings, and preaching somewhere, if not here. I'd take the train in Durham on Friday night and go either to Princeton or Yale, or a prep school, and preach on Sunday. Alice didn't see much of me and I don't see how she stayed with me."

Shaking his head, he said, "I don't know how to relax. That's why I am glad to take a rest now and then. The doctors at Duke Hospital say I'm a wonderful patient. It's so good to have a hospital bed. I don't play. I don't take any exercise. That's why my wife has gone along with my books. I wear old clothes and buy new books. Yes, she's great. She's for real. Until recently I've followed Duke sports, accompanied the team on many distant trips."

Laughing, Dr. Cleland said, "The late Donald McCadie, the Scotchman stonemason who helped build this great university, was the only man who ever called me Jimmy. He wanted a Scotch funeral for his wife. He didn't tell me she was so sick. I asked him if she died happy, and he said she did. He said, 'She heard you preach over the radio that morning and saw the Baltimore Colts win on television in the afternoon.' "

Win or lose, on Sunday afternoon following Duke's ball games on Saturday, Cleland said, he mentioned something about the game in his talks.

"Once I asked Duke's great baseball coach Jack Coombs why he never protested to the umpires. He said, 'I've been in baseball too long. They are incompetently honest, but they're incompetent for me as much as against me.' "

Conceding that he has had great affection for Duke coaches, Cleland said, "I loved Gerry Gerard. He was a brave man, never complained, even in his dying days. Yes, we've had gentlemen for coaches at Duke."

Frowning, Dr. Cleland said, "A lot of students today are boisterous and nasty, and even some of the other students are up in arms about it."

The minister said that sports have made a "bigger dent" on racial relations than the church.

When Dr. Cleland was 66 two of the top men from the Duke Medical School went to the Duke president to say that he was a teacher in the pulpit, and that they wanted him to be dean of the Chapel. And so it came to pass. He gave up the classroom and stayed in the pulpit, two Sundays in the month.

"I've been in the classroom since I was six. I have to teach, never had a parish, never wanted one," he said. "You can learn so much from your students, if you listen." Shrugging his shoulders, Cleland said, "I hate committees. I never wanted to run anything. Thank God for those who do. My interest has been in the classroom. If you've heard me preach, you know that I have been a classroom teacher. I love to talk to a class. It's an interpretation of the Bible, not the Bible."

Pointing to a paperback production of an Agatha Christie yarn, Cleland said, "I love detective stories. I always keep one at bedside. Agatha has a beautiful style."

"I have a list of all the books I've read since I was 12, except for one year when I tried to stop it. I couldn't. I read plays and I'm fond of the theater. I read everything. I pick up a textbook now and then."

Asked about golf, the game of Scotland, he said, "I think golf is a good way of spoiling a walk. I have no hobbies unless it's this: I collect people and stories. I read, smoke my pipe. I'm beginning to experiment with tobacco, I smoke what people give me. I walk instead of riding elevators. That's my exercise."

Cleland said he has never smoked a cigar. "My wife forbids cigars in this house. She said cigar smoke goes into the drapes. A pipe is a baby's pacifier. The smoke doesn't go up through my nose."

He said he had never played a bagpipe or a piano. "It has been work, work, work at the desk."

Conceding that his once-robust figure was now thin, maybe wiry, he said, "I try to put on weight. The doctors put me on three cans of beer a day. I have a collection of beer cans and bottles. I wonder if I could deduct it from my income. But I'll tell you this. I've never had a corn or blister. My wife says if I die first she wants Dr. Leonard Goldner to transplant my feet to hers."

Dr. Cleland still drives a car. "I wish I could walk over three miles, although I do get a headache. If walking three miles for a purpose, though, I don't get a headache. The one thing that keeps me going is the funnybone. It's very important. It's not a question of being a comic in the pulpit; I'm whimsical. You know, a beagle was named after me, 'Dr. Jim.' I said I made a dog happy, and I am glad."

Commenting on his usual full agenda, he said, "I have too many engagements. The Army wants me in Germany to preach and lecture for four weeks. Plans are too uncertain at this time."

As to his retirement, Dr. Cleland snickered. "I keep hopping, but I do go to bed early. Like I said, I don't watch TV much. I suffer for the Duke teams. I don't listen to radio except for the news because I get tired of the announcers."

Nodding, he said, "Duke has been very good to me, they've done great things for me. Some of the girls on the East Campus renamed Brown House, a dormitory, 'Cleland House.' That is really something, isn't it?"

Smiling, he added, "We like Durham very much. We've made good friends. This is our home."

A modest man, Dr. Cleland conceded that now and then he does book reviews, and has written several books on preaching. These include "The True and Lively Word," "Preaching to Be Understood," "He Died as He Lived," and "Wherefore Art Thou Come."

"I've written 82 articles on worship, preaching and liturgics for the magazine 'The Chaplain,' for the military chaplains; and I've been consultant at different times, the three chiefs of chaplains, the Army, Navy and the Air Force," he said. Many of his sermons have been published.

In the spring of 1973, after 28 years of service to Duke University, Dr. Cleland retired. As James B. Duke professor of preaching and as dean of the chapel, he served as teacher, preacher, counselor, guide, friend, and inspiration to students and faculty, "town and gown"—to everyone who came in contact with his keen mind, piercing wit, and unfailing kindness.

That same year countless friends, eager to honor Dr. Cleland, established the James T. Cleland Chapel Endowment Fund as a living memorial to provide funds for distinguished visiting preachers and musicians, for development of the choral programs and for general enrichment of Chapel worship. Within a short time the sum of $100,000 was realized, and more money was soon to come.

On April 21, 1974, a service of celebration and thanksgiving for the ministry of Dr. Cleland was held in the Duke Chapel. Six years earlier he retired from the teaching faculty, but continued to serve as dean of the Chapel, with the title of James B. Duke professor emeritus. He was honored on May 16, 1968, at a retirement dinner attended by colleagues and friends.

A sermon by Dr. Cleland was named one of the best sermons of the year and appears in the "Best Sermons of 1949–50." The anthology represents a cross-section of the best preaching throughout the world, including 52 sermons by men of Protestant, Catholic, and Jewish faiths, chosen from 6,585 sermons that were submitted.

Dr. Cleland's sermon was selected as the "lead" or first sermon in the book. His work, entitled "A Religion that Sings," was based on Verse 54 of the 119th Psalm.

The editor said of the sermon, "James T. Cleland has a glow in his preaching that captures the imagination and the heart. . . . His preaching has a fine understanding of the problems of man, a kindly sense of humor and an ability to say the exact word in the right place."

In 1953, Dr. Cleland was among the nation's outstanding preachers, Biblical scholars, and teachers who contributed to the then new 12-volume "Interpreter's Bible." He wrote three expositions for the work, which was the first full-scale commentary to appear in English in more than 50 years.

In 1954 Dr. Cleland probed deeply at the psyche of America in a speech to the N.C. Press Association in Durham. A Greensboro newspaper editor said of the speech. "He found three significant traits in the 'average American'. 1. A pragmatic assurance ("The American lives in a country which is remarkably sure of itself. He can evidently do anything he has a mind to do; if it is impossible, it just seems to take longer'). 2. A general neighborliness ('This is a country of joiners. . . . It is no wonder that group discussion is an American phenomenon. The American is unwilling to be left alone. If, by mischance, he is forced to solitariness, on goes the radio or the television'). 3. Ultimate anxiety ("There is an underlying uneasiness of mind respecting the meaning of life and the outcome of individual existence. . . . It is partly due to the fact of international responsibility. It is ultimately due to certainty of death. Therefore this average American has a sense of futility of transience, of personal insignificance.)

Dr. Cleland is frequently invited to preach and lecture in many pulpits of this country and abroad. He has also conducted worship services during Christmas at main bases and outposts of the U.S. Air Force. He has conducted seminaries for the Army in Germany.

He has held a teaching fellow in Glasgow University, and has been visiting professor of preaching in New York City and at Berkeley, Calif. He was given honorary degrees at Duke and Davidson College and is an honor member of the Red Friars at Duke, the Alpha Omega Alphon, of the Duke Medical Society, the Duke Nursing School Alumni, and the Duke Medical School Alumni.

Dr. Cleland gave the invocation at the North Carolina Sports Hall of Fame banquet here last February. In part the invocation read, "Almighty and eternal God, who hast, the good providence, set us in a world of struggles, which demand of us competition and cooperation, conflict and time-out, and stamina of body and keenness of mind; we offer to thee this sports banquet, in which we honor four athletes of distinction. We are glad that thy servant St. Paul, spoke in athletic terms. Help us all to hear again, and to take heart his words, that we run the straight race, that we box as one who does not beat the air, that we stay in training for the contest that is set before us, and so receive the prize of thy high calling."

Durham's First Priest Took Shine to Town and Left Lasting Glow

Perhaps it was the bustling nature of the town, the heady aroma of the golden leaf, or the feeling that here was a cocoon with interesting possibilities. Or just that the young Irish Catholic born in Washington, D.C., wanted to be Durham's first priest.

William F. O'Brien, son of William J. O'Brien and Mary Ann Conway O'Brien, was 16 when he first came through Durham en route to Belmont Abbey College in 1889 to take a theological course for the priesthood. He took note of the town, which was booming and drawing widespread attention. After serving as a priest, first at New Bern and then Fayetteville, he was sent to Durham in 1907.

Father O'Brien struck his first roots here when he adopted a 2-year-old Durham orphan. He cared for the youth and educated him through the years and saw his adopted son grow into manhood and marry.

But he struck roots elsewhere in Durham soil. Through his work with the people and children of this then swashbuckling town—Catholics, Protestants, and Jews alike—Father O'Brien made his indelible mark in Durham's history.

"My first thought," he once said, recalling the early days of his priesthood in Durham, "was to work to get a school. But the idea of working for a school did not meet the heart of approval of my little flock."

"As they looked at it, it wasn't the practical thing to do. The children weren't here. I didn't have a home. It would be folly to bring the sisters. There was no place for them to stay."

Durham was a community of little more than 100 Catholics in 1907. "It certainly looked like a foolish thing to do to start such a project. We didn't even have any money."

But in 1909 Father O'Brien started his school. Nine children came the first day. When the year closed there were 23, not only Catholic but "also the children of our good neighbors."

Times were hard. Money had to be solicited and Father O'Brien made trips around the state and country, "begging and borrowing" so that his school could continue. Through the years "his" school has been housed in four different locations, the most recent a $125,000 (original cost) structure on Burch Avenue, where about 200 students are enrolled.

Why, in the face of opposition from his flock and neighbors, did he set out to build a school? "A school is a crying need of every Catholic mission. I consider aid given for schools in the Southland when the population is chiefly non-Catholic, practical missionary work directed in the right channel," Father O'Brien once explained.

The young priest, fresh from his work as a chaplain of Nazareth, the Catholic orphanage near Raleigh, had other work too. He had his church newly dedicated in 1906, and his duties as first priest in Durham's small Catholic community. He had Mass and confessional responsibilities. He had the 101 duties that go together to make up the daily work of the man of God. He had his children.

"I always hoped I would be sent to Durham if I were ever called away from the Nazareth," he said. "Not because Durham has more religion than any other place, but because it seemed that everybody was working in Durham."

And Father O'Brien hustled and bustled with the town. He worked at expanding his school and church membership. He traveled to nearby communities to help and advise scattered Catholic families. He met people and made friends for his church and friends for Durham.

Wherever he went, the energetic priest, with the trace of an Irish brogue, radiated a warmth of friendship that drew people to him. He was a goodwill ambassador for God and man, with the unforgettable accent, the twinkling eyes, and the taste for blarney.

Laughing, he once said: "I'll tell ye, I've been told many times that I really came from the other side. Even the people of Ireland when I visited there many years ago, told me I had a Cary accent. I can't say where I got it unless it came from the Cherokee Indians I've known since my father was a government agent in Arkansas."

Monsignor O'Brien never had reason to stem his easy facility for warm friendship. His faith in people never faltered, but there were occasions when he had to be firm, tough, even fiery. He called it "necessary chastizing."

Father O'Brien and his pastorate, the Church of the Immaculate Conception, became inseparably linked in the memories of Durham generations. His good works brought him respect, not only from his community and state, but the country, and even in 1938, from His Holiness, the Pope.

That year Father O'Brien was elevated to the rank of domestic prelate with the title Right Reverend Monsignor, in a papal bull by Pius XII. His work and efforts in Durham were recognized by Catholic and non-Catholics throughout the area.

Beginning in 1925 he was consultor of the Diocese of Raleigh and remained in this capacity for years. Monsignor O'Brien stepped down from his official capacities in 1951, but acted as pastor emeritus of the church until his death in March, 1960, at the age of 87. His retirement hadn't been retirement in the full sense of the word, for he was too energetic. He visited his school and each day accepted friends and visitors in his home next door to the new school.

Father O'Brien wrote two books, *Early Catholicity in North Carolina,* and *Memoirs.*

Though somewhat slowed down by age, he still liked to travel. It was a part of his life. He once said, chuckling, "I have so many friends in Canada and Mexico, I feel I should get around to seeing them now that I'm a man of leisure."

He said when he decided to become a priest he felt he had a calling and answered it. "It was a response I never regretted. As a priest I know I have found happiness, happiness in people and in the confidence of the people. You must realize that the greatest suffering a priest can experience is to lose the confidence of his people. For then he has failed God and his people."

The Right Reverend Monsignor O'Brien became ill in July 1959, and was a patient at St. Joseph's Hospital in Southern Pines when he died. The Most Reverend Vincent S. Waters, bishop of the Raleigh Diocese, conducted the impressive service at the Church of the Immaculate Conception in Durham. Interment was in Maplewood Cemetery.

It was a long time ago that this reporter had the privilege of becoming a friend of Father O'Brien, a modern day Pied Piper whose kindness and smiling benevolence attracted children and youth in wholesale numbers.

Truly, this was a man for all seasons.

11

Duke and Trinity

Julian S. Carr, who with the family of Washington Duke put up the money and induced Trinity College in Randolph County to move to Durham, gave the land for the site of Trinity, now the site of the East Duke campus. This tract had been the ground of Blackwell's horse race track.

Durham almost lost Duke University to Charlotte years ago. Duke family members and pleas of Durham leaders won a change of heart.

Old Hanes Field on the Trinity campus was becoming smaller, so then football coach Jimmy DeHart in 1929 played the first game in the new Duke West campus stadium.

DeHart induced his old football teammate, Jock Sutherland, to play Duke in the first game in the new stadium. But the "Pitt Panthers" were too tough.

A Look At Old Trinity College

Trinity College (now Duke University) boasted a student enrollment of 280 in November of 1905. In making this enthusiastically received report, board of trustees President James H. Southgate also disclosed a student body of 170 in Trinity Park School, an affiliate.

Trinity College, a Methodist institution, moved to Durham from Randolph County in 1892 when Benjamin N. Duke and Julian S. Carr donated a site comprising 73.2 acres of land.

The grounds surrounding the college were known as Trinity College Park, featuring walks and drives and a race track.

The late Mrs. William Preston Few, wife of the late president of Trinity College and succeeding Duke University, was a student at Trinity in the year 1905. Her husband-to-be was a professor at the time.

When we talked in 1966, she recalled with pleasure her student days in the

Mary Duke Building, the woman's dormitory, and recalls looking out of a window to see Josephus Daniels hung and burned in effigy.

She explained that this came as a result of Daniels running in his newspaper, the News & Observer, a statement by Trinity professor Dr. John Spencer Bassett to the effect that Booker T. Washington ranked with Gen. Robert E. Lee as the greatest men the South had ever produced.

Mrs. Few recalled the dedication for the library which was given to the school by Benjamin N. Duke.

"The dedicatory speech was made by Walter Hines Page, the literary genius who later was ambassador to England. He told his audience that before coming to Durham he went by Mr. Duke's office in New York to ask what he should tell Trinity students. 'Tell them that each one of them should think for himself,' he quoted Mr. Duke as saying."

A two-story white house at the left rear of the Mary Duke Building was the home of Trinity president, Dr. John Kilgo.

When Dr. Few succeeded Dr. Kilgo as president he moved into this house and here he and wife Mary Few raised their sons.

A two-story white house northwest of the president's home was the home of Prof. Robert L. Flowers who later was to become president of Duke University.

Dr. Flowers built the home for his five brothers and himself, in the sake of education. The brothers were to become successful in the world of business and its affairs. They were: Claude, Will, Charles, Fred, and Horace. Dr. Few also roomed in the Flowers home until he became Trinity president.

The year 1905 was momentous for Durham and Trinity. Here are a few highlights of yesteryear, November 1905.

Nov. 1; George W. Watts donated $10,000 for an addition at Watts Hospital, which when constructed a few years earlier cost approximately $50,000. Watts gave the hospital "to the people of Durham." The addition included wards and nurses' quarters.

On the same day a lesser event but of more painful significance took place in the basement of the courthouse.

Mayor's Court had convicted a boy on a charge of "boarding a moving train." Punishment ordered was a whipping meted out by the offender's grandmother, a grim-faced woman who knew her task well.

Nov. 3; Trinity's tennis team was beaten by Wake Forest College, although "Trinity fought like mad men." Umpire was W. W. "Cap" Card, referee was L. L. Herndon, and scorer, W. S. Lockhart.

Nov. 6 saw train cars wrecked by several boys who were seen loosening the brakes in the Norfolk & Western Railroad yard near Duke Factory. On the same day Col. E. J. Parrish bought from Durham & Southern Railroad, property next to the courthouse and fronting on Main Street, for $15,000.

Nov. 9 was a redletter day at Trinity College. Crowds attended a free gymnastic exhibition in the Angier Duke gym under the supervision of director W. W. Card.

Arthur B. Bradsher, for years a star pitcher on the Trinity baseball team, delivered an address at the YMCA, entitled "The Toning of College Life."

Nov. 10; University of North Carolina alumni staged a gala banquet at Hotel Carrolina (so named after Carr, the owner).

Nov. 11; Three whisky stills were captured by the sheriff and his deputies. Two were uncovered in Lebanon Township and the third near University Station.

Unidentified persons burned the home and barns of widow Mrs. D. L. Belvin. Law enforcement officers searched for "incendiaries."

Nov. 16; W. W. Fuller of New York wrote Trinity's president, Dr. John Kilgo, that he had bought and was shipping to the college a small statue of Cicero to be placed in the school library.

On the same day D. T. Sasser of Durham presented to the Trinity library a bronze plaster bust of President McKinley.

Nov. 17; Z. Hinohara, a Japanese student who had received his A.B. and A.M. degrees at Trinity, delivered an address at the YMCA, entitled "The New Japan."

Nov. 21; The Kennedy Stock Co. opened at the Durham Opera House, drawing good crowds with the plays "Midnight Express" and "A Dash for Liberty."

Nov. 23 saw a "first in the South" come to Trinity in the form of "Association Football," introduced by W. W. Card.

This is a game styled after the old English rugby, with an elimination of the brutal part of football. There is no piling on, eliminating brutal force by the players, and kicking, tripping and holding are strictly taboo.

The quick and the nimble rather than the rough and brawny men of standard football, can win at this game. The ball can be thrown and kicked or knocked, but not run with. The game already is popular in the North and West.

Nov. 27; R. J. Ferrell of Red Wood, fishing in the Neuse River, caught a German carp weighing 17½ pounds. It has been on display for non-believers.

Nov. 28; a preacher is charged with carrying a pistol into the church.

Nov. 29; Durham people are generous with food gifts for orphans and the poor. Services are held in churches and merchants close their stores.

Also on that day, a large crowd from Durham and Chapel Hill went on two special trains to Norfolk to see the University of North Carolina football team wallop Virginia 17 to 0.

Those more religious bent went by train to nearby Red Wood to witness presentation of a Bible and flag, and to have dinner on church grounds.

The Durham Lodge of Masons surprised its first Worshipful Master of Lodge, James Southgate, with a silver loving cup. It was presented by W. J. Brogden, Junior Deacon of the club.

Durham Almost Lost Duke to Land Costs

Mrs. Marian Noell Williams, who at 88 is still full of ginger and enthusiasm despite the burden of a wheelchair, helped persuade the late James Buchanan Duke to establish Duke University in Durham instead of Charlotte.

"That was back in 1924 when 'Uncle Buck' became incensed because land value went sky-high as soon as it became known that he was interested in purchasing a huge tract as a university site," she said.

Chuckling, Mrs. Williams said Buck Duke virtually exploded, declaring that he could buy land at a reasonable price in Charlotte where he lived.

"I told him that putting Duke University in Charlotte would be simply awful, that his father, brothers, and sisters were born in Durham and that his father, Washington Duke, had given about $85,000 to get Trinity College moved from Randolph County to Durham."

Mrs. Williams said she didn't know whether Duke's threats to build the university in Charlotte were just a ruse to get prices down, but he finally decided to locate in Durham. Born in Danville, Mrs. Williams was 16 when she came to Durham in 1908 to visit the family of Capt. Joe Renn, Durham's train stationmaster. She was introduced to Edwin Buchanan Lyon, the first cousin of Angier Duke who at the time was living in the home of Washington Duke. They were later married.

"I met 'Buck' Lyon at a banquet of Kappa Sigma held at 'Wash' Duke's home which was located on the present site of Liggett & Myers Tobacco Co. The lilies that decorated the long table came from Loch Lilly at Roxboro, and since they bloomed only during the day, we sat with bloomless lilies that night," Mrs. Williams laughed.

"My husband, who was named for his uncle Buck Duke, used to come to Danville to court me. He had a Reo automobile and in Durham we would ride to Christian Mill, which was on the only macadamized road outside of town," she said. "Back in those days courting couples didn't kiss or hug even though they wanted to."

Mrs. Williams said she wouldn't marry Lyon until he was 21. That came on New Year's Day, 1910, and nine days later the young couple repeated the holy vows in a Methodist church in Danville. George Lyon was best man, and Angier Duke, Claiborne Carr, and Eric Johnson, her brother-in-law, were ushers.

After the wedding in Danville they went by train to New Orleans and stayed at the old St. Francis Hotel.

"Then we went to California by way of Danville, and next to New York City, where Buck's cousins Angier and Mary Duke Biddle, entertained us at the Plaza Hotel. When we returned to Durham we were met at the train station by Eric Johnson, who was driving a Reo limousine," Mrs. Williams said. "Buck Duke didn't attend the wedding but he sent me a gift, a Pierce Arrow car."

Reminiscing further, she recalled that she and her husband were in Raleigh at the time Gov. William W. Kitchen invited them to lead the grand march at the ball in Raleigh which opened the N.C. State Fair.

"I was three months pregnant at the time, but nobody knew it. I was supposed to walk with the governor but I didn't want to walk with anybody but my husband. I called the governor's wife and told her about it. The governor had to walk with his own wife."

"Nobody had ever told me the facts of life or anything like that. For years I thought maybe you had babies through your elbow. I wasn't sure."

"Buck proposed to me at George Lyon's house, in the front living room where they had a pool table. Afterward I lived in that house for 40 years. We were sitting on the pool table, and I said, 'All right. I'll wait until I get home and then ask my mother and daddy, then I'll let you know.'"

"Nowadays that sounds just crazy, but that is the way those things went on at one time. I think we were engaged about a year until I finished Randolph-Macon Institute. The school, which is now Stratford College, adjoined our home in Danville. Buck had gone to Poughkeepsie and Trinity College."

"Buck got into the automobile business and he and Bill Bryan, a wizard in mechanics, built a car in the basement of what is now the North Carolina National Bank."

Tilting her head and laughing, Mrs. Williams said, "They had to dismantle the car to get it out of the building."

Buck and Marian's first home was on W. Chapel Hill Street almost across from Duke Memorial Methodist Church on one side, and the Ben Duke home on the other.

"Chapel Hill Street was a brick street at the time and I remember when it was paved. My friend Nello Teer with a mule pulled a scoop in preparing the ground for the pavement," Mrs. Williams said.

Recalling the street cars that passed her home, she said, "Children had a lot of fun soaping the street car tracks on the incline. The conductors had to stop the car and put sand on the tracks to make the inclines when the rails were soaped."

Lakewood Amusement Park on Chapel Hill Road, the site of which is now occupied by Lakewood Shopping Center, was the most popular place in town. Mrs. Williams recalls that on one occasion a prominent Durham businessman who dealt in stocks and bonds removed his clothes in the men's dressing room at the park pool, and walked out on the springboard wearing only his hat, with a Wall Street Journal rolled up under his arm.

"He calmly jumped into the pool, unmindful of the screams of an old maid who was in the pool along with a married woman who seemed to care less,"

Mrs. Williams chuckled. "Someone summoned the park manager who ordered the naked swimmer to come out of the pool. This he did, retaining his composure."

Buck Lyon's business was in the building that is now the site of the Five Points Restaurant, and he was dealer for the Reo, Thomas Flyer, and Stanley Steamer.

"We once drove to Charlotte in a Stanley Steamer and we had to stop wherever we found water, in creeks or rivers, to put more water in our car. The Stanley Steamer burned kerosene oil, and it had to be fired up a half hour before driving," Mrs. Williams said. "The engine's odors went all over the house."

The Buck Lyons later moved to 803 South Duke St. into the home of his brother, George, and Snowden Lyon, who had died a year apart.

"We bought the home from the estate, and that is where our fourth child, Washington Duke Lyons, was born. He was a pilot and was killed in World War II," Mrs. Williams said. "Earlier, we had three children: Buck Jr., Marian, and Laura."

She said her husband was in the Navy and served aboard a submarine chaser during World War I.

"I remember going to New York City to visit him at the time the great flu epidemic was raging. Buck became very ill while we were in the Waldorf-Astoria Hotel. When he didn't report back on time one of the top brass telephoned to say that if he didn't return at once they'd come and get him," Mrs. Williams said. "I told him, 'Over my dead body.' Aunt Sally, Ben Duke's wife, who lived in New York, finally located a nurse in Canada and sent her to the hotel to look after Buck. She and the hotel doctor pulled him through."

She said that when her husband reported back for duty he was punished. "He was a regular doughboy with no rank. They thought I was a floozie because they didn't think he could afford a room in a hotel."

Mrs. Williams said that on her return train trip to Durham there were coffins "stacked as high as this room" at every station stop, all victims of the flu."

She said this affected her so strongly that she went to Raleigh to wrap bandages with Mrs. George Watts of Durham, a trained nurse who had volunteered for the war effort.

"My husband and Jones Fuller had gone to New York City in 1921 to see the world champion boxing match between Jack Dempsey and Georges Carpentier, when Buck became seriously ill and died in a hospital there."

"I went to New York at once and Uncle Buck Duke brought us back to Durham on his private train for the burial," Mrs. Williams said.

In 1924 she married John Kuntz, who operated Carolina Sales Co., a Studebaker sales agency located on Chapel Hill Street at the site last occupied by Lyon Hardware Store. The Kuntzes later separated and he died several years afterward.

"In 1934 I married John W. Williams who was associated with the American

Tobacco Co. We were happily married and he was congenial to my children," she said.

Two years later the couple bought Mrs. Williams' ancestral home, Melrose Plantation, in Yanceyville, where her mother had lived, and remodeled it. Wooden pegs instead of nails were used in the construction, and the home actually was two houses that had been joined. Her great grandfather built Melrose in the Revolutionary war days.

"My father, Charles Noell, was a tobacconist and warehouseman in Danville, and we raised tobacco on our farm. All my life I've been messed up with tobacco," Mrs. Williams laughed. "And of course I've seen a lot of changes in the tobacco business."

Williams died in 1974.

Mrs. Williams hates a wheelchair which became necessary due to a serious operation. She is frequently permitted to sit in a chair and to ride in a car.

"I have nine grandchildren, seventeen great-grandchildren, and two great-great-grandchildren," she beamed. "I am an ancestor and I am not hanging on a wall just yet."

Mrs. Williams lives in her home at 3304 Devon Road, along with her son Buck and his wife, and her two pedigreed dogs.

Fifty Years Ago: A New Stadium, But Blue Devils

Fifty years ago Duke University christened its big horseshoe, acclaimed "the finest and largest football stadium in the South." And the Blue Devils received the customary shellacking that goes along with a dedication. The ruthless Pitt Panthers, coached by Dr. John Bain "Jock" Sutherland, mauled the less-talented team of Coach Jimmy DeHart, a former teammate at Pitt, by the humiliating score of 52-7.

But all was not disappointment that October day in 1929. Props of the gala production included the handsomely virgin 35,000-seat stadium, the antics of the Eastern football power, spirited brass bands, colorful uniforms, and dignitaries and boisterous fans riding into the very campus by special trains.

And there was North Carolina Gov. O. Max Gardner's impressive motorcade with screaming sirens and fanfare.

It was the beginning of a new and promising era, despite the approach of the Great Depression. The Hill Directory reported Durham's population as 51,966. Hill also said that Durham was the second largest tobacco manufacturing city in the world. It was an electrifying occasion, and I am glad I was there.

On a rainy Thursday two days before the game, it was announced that all highways into Durham were open and all hotels in the area booked to capacity. The fire department put 1,000 flags on the whiteway standards in the downtown business district, with Pitt's colors, blue and old gold, festooning one side of the street, and Duke's royal blue and white the other. The flags were flanked by Old Glory.

City Manager Bob Flack announced that downtown parking regulations would be suspended Saturday, and Police Chief Walter Doby warned "impatient" motorists to take special care to avoid accidents Saturday. Some businesses, including banks, said they would close early for the game, while others said they wouldn't open until 6 p.m. because of the Jewish New Year.

Pitt arrived Friday morning, then bused to Chapel Hill for practice at the University of North Carolina.

At 7:30 p.m. the Duke band under the direction of Jelly Leftwich gave a concert in front of the Washington Duke Hotel. Exuberant Duke students paraded and yelled cheers along Main Street.

Saturday morning there was a breakfast at the Washington Duke Hotel in honor of Pitt's and Duke's brass bands. A concert by the bands followed. More than 100 police officers from Durham and neighboring cities, and state highway patrolmen on motorcycles directed traffic downtown and to the stadium.

The parking fields of the stadium had been given a thorough test by heavy trucks and found to be firm and level. The campus roads had been gravelled and packed down. Special trains from Pittsburgh, New York City, and points in North Carolina were carried directly into the new west campus to stand only a short distance from the stadium.

The governor, members and officials of the Duke Endowment, trustees of Duke and various other officials were on hand. It was described as the largest gathering of nationally known figures ever to assemble in the state.

On Friday night in Raleigh, North Carolina State College (North Carolina State University) played Washington and Lee and lost, 27–6. The game, like others in the state, had been scheduled so that Duke would have a clear field Saturday.

The Duke press box counted 64 sports writers, including the *Durham Morning Herald's* Fred Haney. The day was cloudy and a few drops of rain fell, which was blamed for holding the crowd to 20,000. But even then it was a terrific turnout a half century ago.

The dedicatory ceremony was very brief, but the game was very long to Duke fans, especially when they learned later that arch-rival UNC had beaten Maryland in College Park. Panther halfbacks Jim Rooney and Tony Uansa ran roughshod over the Durham dandies, and Pitt's Williams scored the first two touchdowns. Duke managed to get the football to Pitt's eight-yard line when the first half ended with the enemy leading, 26-0. The Blue Devils scored near the end of the game on a pass from Sam Buie to Flop Beaver, good for 55 yards. Buie kicked the extra point.

A bright light was Buie's leap-into-the-air passing. He threw 42 times and completed 16 for 368 total yards. But his team rushed for only 57 yards. Pitt gained 70 yards on six passes and amassed 558 yards rushing. Strangely, Duke had 17 first downs, just three less than Pitt, but a touchdown run doesn't count as a first down. Duke punted six times and Pitt just five.

Sports writers agreed that Pittsburgh was the best team ever to play in North Carolina. Certainly no alibi, Duke fans pointed out that injuries kept captain Henry Kistler, a tackle, and fullback John Jankowski out of the game.

Bill Murray, a rampaging back who later was to become Duke's football coach, and Weldon "Pap" Harton and Nick Warren, both of Durham, did play. Kidd Brewer, who was to become a great all-around Duke athlete, didn't play. He was fullback in 1930. Duke's initial lineup for the opening game included Don Hyatt, Warren, Thorne, Friedman, Taylor, Carpenter, Peeler, Rosky, Buie, Murray, and Godfrey. A displeased DeHart put six new men in his lineup for the next game, which was a 45-13 loss to Navy.

Duke's football fortunes took a sweet turn less than a decade later, when Coach Wallace Wade's Blue Devils upset a mighty Pittsburgh team here in a game featuring snow, superb Duke defense, and brilliant kicking by "Eric the Red" Tipton. That in itself was reason enough to name the stadium for Wade after he had concluded a brilliant coaching career and retired to his farm on Snow Hill Road.

Duke Chapel—A Dream and a Magnet

Duke University Chapel, towering over Durham like the Statue of Liberty over New York Harbor, still carries popular magnetism after half a century. Truly, James Buchanan Duke envisioned a sanctuary of unsurpassed greatness when, in planning Duke University, he insisted on a church as the central building. He envisioned it as "a great towering church which is bound to have a profound influence on the spiritual life of the young men and women who come here."

And it came to pass. Not only does the stately Duke Chapel pervade campus life, its Gothic architecture and atmosphere have long capitvated millions of visitors.

Chapel hostesses say that many visitors are so awestruck at the beauty of the chapel that they don't hear the greetings. Visitors to the chapel are now signing the 65th registration book. Approximately 2 million persons have signed since the chapel was completed. It was formally dedicated at the university's 83rd commencement on June 2, 1935.

Hostesses say that only about one out of four visitors sign the book. Oftentimes a school group will enter the chapel and only their teachers and several students will sign, the others being preoccupied with the elegant surroundings. In springtime there have been as many as seven or eight busloads of youths at a time to visit the chapel. As you may suspect, some of the visitors have signed such names as Kilroy, Adolf Hitler, Winston Churchill, Jack Dempsey, Shirley Temple, and Babe Ruth.

All of the countries of the world, it is believed, have been represented by signers. The first volume of visitors to the chapel contains the names of nearly every person who figured prominently in the life of the university. First to sign the book on June 6, 1932, was George G. Allen of New York, a member of the executive committee of the university. The second signature was that of a trustee, W. R. Perkins of New Jersey. These two trustees jointly donated the carillon to Duke Chapel. Third to sign was W. S. Lee, engineer, of Charlotte, whose construction firm built the chapel. These were followed by other executives, trustees, and governors of the university.

Durham persons represented on the first page in the registration book were: Harper Erwin, B. Rose, C. T. Poe, Dr. R. L. Flowers, Henry Dwire, M. E. Newsom, Madeline Knight, and Margaret McGary. The first out-of-state person to register in the chapel, on Jan. 2, 1933, was Mrs. M. Thurber of Shelburne Falls, Mass. The first visitor from out of the country was Capt. Joseph Duncan Grant of London, who gave as his New York address, the Explorers Club. Eleanor Roosevelt signed in 1936.

Hostesses say that weather is no deterrent to visitors. An example was an icy February day while snow was falling and very few chapel employees were on hand. "We found that visitors from seven foreign countries and 10 states braved the elements that day to enjoy the beauty of the chapel and sign the registration book," a hostess said.

Upon completion of the books they are stored in the Duke University archives in Perkins Library. Some signers add messages behind their names, such as a visitor from Norway who wrote that he was a "conductor of a symphony orchestra."

Early last Tuesday morning signers were from North Carolina, New York, Oklahoma, Pennsylvania, Arkansas, Florida, Colorado, and Germany.

Although the chapel was planned first, in 1923, it was the last building to be completed in the quadrangle. The cornerstone was laid in 1930, and the chapel first used at commencement in 1932 when President Few spoke. Like most buildings on Duke's West campus, the chapel is constructed of stone from Duke's own quarry, just 12 miles west, near Hillsborough.

Railroad tracks were laid like steel parallel bars through a dense forest. Then came Europe's best stonemasons, artisans from Italy and Scotland to erect the crowning joy of Mr. Duke's dream.

The chapel was designed by Horace Trumbaur, university architect for all buildings erected from 1924 to the completion of the chapel. It took two years to build and cost more than $2 million.

In the Memorial Chapel behind the altar are three limewood figures: St. Paul (book and sword), Jesus, and St. Peter. The three sarcophagi here are those of Benjamin and Washington Duke (trustees and benefactors of Trinity College before it became Duke University in 1924), and James B. Duke, founder of the university.

Between the Memorial Chapel and the chancel is a flight of steps descending to a crypt. Here is buried William Preston Few, first president of Duke University, and Mrs. Nanaline Holt Duke, wife of James B. Duke.

Famous ministers have preached from the chapel pulpit, including Billy Graham, twice; the Right Rev. Edwin Anderson Penick, The Right Rev. Ralph Washington Sockman, the Rev. Lynn Harold Hough, the Right Rev. John Kenneth Pfahl, E. Stanley Jones, noted missionary, and the Rev. Martin Niemuller, of Germany, who had been a U-boat commander in World War I but changed his career when Hitler came into power.

According to William A. Kale of Durham, professor of christian life in the Duke divinity faculty, 1952-73, "We waited a long time before a woman minister filled our pulpit. She was Dr. Georgia Harkness, a teacher in a seminary in California, about 25 years ago."

Professor Kale, a 1925 graduate of Trinity College, whose diploma read Duke University commencement, Fall 1924, recalls that famed Rabbi Stephen Wise once spoke in Duke's Page Auditorium, years ago.

"Rabbi Wise said, as I recall it, 'The president of this university (Dr. Few) and I have something in common, we both look like Jews,' " He was referring to their beards.

Duke Chapel has had two deans: Dr. Frank S. Hickman, 1938-48, and Dr. James T. Cleland, 1956-73. Titles were to be changed. Dr. Hickman was preacher to the university from 1933-37, and 1949-53. Dr. Cleland was preacher to the university 1949-55.

Other Preachers to the University were: Dr. Elbert Russell, 1933-37, and Dr. Harold A. Bosley, 1949-50.

Chaplains to the university have been ministers: James H. Phillips, Barney L. Jones, Howard C. Wilkinson, and acting chaplain W. Harvey Floyd, who was also director of religious life. Robert T. Young was minister to the university from 1974-83.

The Duke Chapel choir in the beginning had representatives of the Durham community as well as Duke students. Then the choir's noted director, J. Foster "Bishop" Barnes, molded an outstanding choir of Duke students.

Edward Hall Broadhead was the early day organist, followed by Ms. Mildred Hendrix. Anton Brees, famed carilloneur of Florida, gave several recitals at the chapel. The splendid chapel organs, the Mary Duke Biddle organ, and now the Flentrop organ, have carried prestige of their own.

On the bleak side of the chapel's past were the two occasions lightning struck the tower in the late 1930s, and the suicide of a Durham woman who leaped to her death from the tower after pretending to go there to paint the skyline.

A. C. Jordan Jr. Makes Good Grammar a Way of Life

Archibald Currie Jordan Jr., who taught English at Trinity Park School and Duke University for 45 years, thinks poor grammar is worse than smallpox and baldness. He has done his part to make good word usage a habit and not an accident. He has written numerous books and handbooks on English composition and writing.

"I've enjoyed teaching and I always made a point of making friends with my students," Jordan said. He estimates he taught over 8,000 students at all levels at Duke.

Jordan is an Orange County native, but has lived in Durham since 1905. He and his wife have four daughters, the youngest a student at East Carolina University.

Jordan quit teaching when he reached retirement age in 1969. "I've had many offers to teach in colleges throughout the country, but I preferred retirement," he said. "I have a law degree but have never given thought to the practice of law."

"But retirement doesn't mean becoming a homebody and spending a lot of time with relatives. I have a 315-acre farm on Wilkins Road bordering Flat River, a few saddle horses, cattle, and two houses on the river. And I've just completed my second cutting of hay this season."

Jordan prefers the comfort of a bare head and work clothes over the baggy tweeds and cap of fellow retirees from the campus. He walks with the jaunty gait of an athlete. He was born in the Caldwell section of Orange County, son of Dr. A. C. Jordan, a country doctor who covered a 10-mile area, carrying his medical supplies in saddlebags on one of his four Texas cow ponies.

"In 1905 my father was invited to take over the practice of a Dr. Young who lived in East Durham over Crabtree Drug Store," Jordan said. "So our family, three boys and three girls, moved to Durham." After completing his public schooling, Jordan attended Trinity College, earning a major in English and minors in Greek and Latin.

"I was scheduled to go to Plattsburg, N.Y., in 1918 for military training for officers, but Dr. William Preston Few, president of Trinity, wanted me to teach at Trinity Park School, a top prep school operated by the college. And that's what I did," Jordan said.

"The war ended that same year but I continued teaching at Trinity Park for three more years. I also took a law course while teaching and during the summer taught classes for Trinity students at Oriental," he said. Meanwhile, Jordan turned down the offer of a scholarship to Dartmouth, passed the state bar, went to Columbia University in New York on a Rockefeller Foundation grant, and took residential requirements for his Ph.D. Next came offers of scholarships to the University of North Carolina and Yale which he also declined.

During a visit to Durham on vacation from Columbia Graduate School, Jordan was met by President Few and Dr. R. L. Flowers, Trinity vice president, "and given quite a bundle of information concerning the plans for Duke University. They asked me to deliver the material to Arthur Brisbane, a brilliant New York newspaperman and a friend of James Buchanan Duke. So, Mr. Brisbane published the facts about Duke." Jordan returned to Durham in 1925 intending to practice law. He had an offer with a law firm in Graham and also a new offer to teach at UNC.

Jordan decided to think things over so he went to High Point to visit a sister for a few days. "I was on a ladder nailing roofers at a tabernacle when I received a telegram from Dr. Few, offering me a teaching job at Duke in the department of English. I accepted."

Anna Jane Myers of Toronto, Ohio, was a student in one of Jordan's classes and he soon found that she was more to him than a student. Jordan recalled that he was at home writing his third book on English composition when Anna Jane's parents came to see their daughter's beau-professor. Three years later the professor and the student were married.

In 1941 Jordan and George Gregory of Bucknell collaborated to publish a handbook entitled "How to Write Correctly." Five years later Jordan published "The Writer's Manual."

Since his retirement, Jordan has been editorially assisting several departments in the Duke University Medical Center "in the preparation of individual scholarly papers and journals."

On one occasion he rewrote the entire Duke catalog when asked to check to see if there were errors in grammar and spelling. "It's second nature to me to automatically detect a flaw in grammar spoken and written," Jordan said. "And I will tell you that educated people are worse in this respect than anybody else."

Jordan showed a letter from the late U.S. Justice Felix Frankfurter which read in part: "Let me say compendiously and emphatically that one of the great shortcomings of our bar, speaking generally, of course, is the poor respect it pays to the English language . . . I have no doubt that the shortcomings in this regard are due to the failure to inculcate habits of writing decent English in high schools and colleges. And the failure to do this is due in part to the fact that the habit of life-long reading of good writers is, I am convinced, far below what is desirable—I should say necessary—for a truly well-trained bar."

Jordan said that schools of religion concede that their students have poor basic training in grammar. "There has been too much of a tendency in the past 25 years to get away from the fundamentals of English usage. It's the age of permissiveness," Jordan said. "The pendulum won't swing back until the people realize that when they go into a business, they find there is an obstacle to promotion because of inadequate training."

Jordan quoted two authorities who back his contentions. "Dr. Charles H. Wende of Dupont once said: 'The person who doesn't understand grammar doesn't understand punctuation, and the person who doesn't understand punctuation doesn't understand his own thought.' "

"Thomas F. Woodlock of the Wall Street Journal said: 'It was not by chance that grammar, logic, and rhetoric, in that order, preceded music, literature, geometry, and astronomy, in the scheme of the seven liberal arts in an age noted for the clarity of its thinking and its exactness of its expression.' "

Jordan said, "Accuracy in grammatical constructions is essential for clarity." He said the most frequent mistakes made in writing include the misuse of pronouns, the disagreement of the subject and predicate, the misuse of collective nouns with plural words, the lack of parallel construction for parallel ideas, and the use of incomplete comparisons and misplaced modifiers.

Even more mistakes are made in speech than in writing, he said. "A person who is careful will reread what he writes and usually see the errors. I wouldn't dare write a letter and mail it before rereading it," Jordan said.

Bad use of grammar "is serious even among college faculties because of the very careless use of words," he said.

Jordan says he became a Republican when the late John F. Kennedy ran for office. "He was the first Democrat I didn't vote for," he said. Asked who he considers excellent and grammatically precise speakers, Jordan didn't hesitate for answers. "I think Spiro Agnew has been one of the most careful, dignified, logical and accurate users of the English language in public for a long, long time."

Jordan said President Nixon "speaks out accurately and forcefully without fundamental language errors," and said Congressman Jesse Helms "is a user of excellent English." Edward Kennedy, Billy Graham, and Ronald Reagan also came in for praise for their use of language.

Jordan has four large bound books of letters from many learned people and government officials, including Gerald Ford, but he probably prizes most those from former students, and two from an inmate of a prison in Colorado, who was interested in improving his grammar. Of course the professor mailed his book on English composition to the inmate.

12

Education and Music

Back in the days of discipline, prayer, patriotism, reading, writing, arithmetic, health, homework, geography, dress codes, and parent-teacher associations, tardiness and poor attendance brought apprehension to pupils and students in grammar and high schools in Durham, and parents too were concerned.

Teachers made you stay in after school—they stayed too. Dedication to the tasks at hand was the lesson they taught.

Music abounded in the Durham of yesteryear. There were high school and college bands, the Durham orchestra and band, the Durham Auction Co. Band, the Durham Post Seven Drum and Bugle Corps of the American Legion, the Southern Conservatory of Music, the Academy of Music, and several music stores, and many music teachers. W. P. Twaddell of Durham High School trained students for the Julliard School of Music and onward to professional opera and orchestras and bands.

The Old School

Hobnail Shoes, Ink Wells And Bibles

"The boy stood on the burning deck. . . ." eating peanuts by the peck. The beginning was a famous verse in early school until it lost credence after a pupil introduced the tomfoolery of other rhyming words.

North Durham School, built in 1905 on North Street, was an unforgettable place, what with its high front steps of curbstone, a heavy creaking door, and the peculiar musty-antiseptic odors as you entered.

Teachers and principal Lilly Jones attempted, foolishly, to have things library quiet. They scrutinized snickerers and heavy feet with penetrating looks, possibly for future discipline. Or so we thought.

On the left side of the building outside was an ugly fire escape whose platform was supported by heavy black iron poles down which daredevil boys slithered on occasion.

Inside the classroom was the teacher's desk, an imposing heavy oak which held a clock with its back always to the class, a vase for a rose, daisy, pussy willow, or ivy. There was a ruler which was to come into prominence for palm or hand-burning for corrective purposes; a Bible or Testament, a dictionary, ink, a quill pen, note pad, subject books, smelling salts and miscellany.

The blackboard, massive and vital, with its ledge holding chalk and dusty felt erasers, was like a dark and menancing thing, especially if you were called on to write upon it words or numbers.

The pencil sharpener was a sure hand-dirtier, and almost always had dull blades which ravenously chewed up pencils.

The desk, scarred and faded, held an ink well which had a trapped agate or ball to keep the ink from splashing. The initials of previous captives were also scratched somewhere on the desk.

The teachers, all female, were primly dressed and mostly wore their hair in buns or ungodly bobs. There were brooches, mother of pearl pins, gold-plated clasps, and cameos.

Dresses were usually long and mostly severely dark, with sometimes a white collar. Needless to say, low-cut collars were taboo. Hose was of fairly dark hue and of cotton, sometimes rayon, and rarely silk. Shoes were plain and black.

Makeup consisted of powder, with little or no rouge, and lipstick. Mascara and false eyebrows, of course, were forbidden. School marms followed the tradition.

One suspected that a wig covered a certain teacher's head.

Gum chewing, talking, and note passing brought instant censure and sometimes a stand in the corner for discipline. This usually produced subdued snickering, rarely sympathy, unless it was your secret heartthrob.

Book bags carried by boys were usually those khaki-colored, heavily woven canvas, and strangely constructed things which originally were made by the United States government as gas mask containers for World War I soldiers.

Most book sacks carried by girls were homemade, although fancier satchels were available at Durham Book & Stationery store.

Prayers were said in school and Bible verses recited. The American flag was sacred, and right behind were Christmas, George Washington, Robert E. Lee, Thomas Jefferson, Abraham Lincoln, Black Beauty, Rebecca of Sunnybrook Farm, Horatio Alger, Tom Swift, the Rover Boys, Tarzan, William S. Hart, Ruth Roland, Pearl White, Mary Pickford, Douglas Fairbanks, Fatty Arbuckle, William Farnum, Rosa Ponselle, Mme. Shumman Heink, Caruso, John McCormack, licorice, jaw breakers, candy kisses, washington pies, root beer, tutti-frutti and caramel ice cream, licking the dasher, eskimo pie, taffy pulls, bobbing for apples, jackrocks, mumbly peg, mudball and snowball fights, fireworks, circus parades, train rides, streetcars, tom walkers, spugging tops, hay rides, picnics, recess, vacation, barefeet, rabbit tobacco, kites, doodle-bugging, trapping junebugs, hunting arrowheads, watching fire horses run, Katzenjammer Kids, Happy Hooligan, river baptisms, holy-roller watching, throwing at flying bats, rabbit gums, locust and persimmon beer, watching your brother get his mouth washed out with Octagon soap for using bad words, listening to workers sing spirituals while they worked in the Liggett & Myers stemmery on Main Street, hayrides to General Julian S. Carr's Oconee-chee Farm, the roller coaster at Lakewood Park, watching Gypsies, shooting rats at the city dump heap at now the city garage's parking lot and fire training tower, Whizz Bang, Chic Sale, the Police Gazette, Boys' Life, crystal radios, staying up late, minstrel shows, and playing hooky.

Boys loved hobnail shoes which were also of World War I vintage, but they were soon banned for floor damage and noise.

For the heck of it, some boys peroxided their hair. They wore knee britches, long stockings, Buster Brown shoes, blouses, ties, jackets or sweaters, and most carried buckeyes in their pockets for good luck, pocket knives for whit-tling and mumbly peg, a spinning top, dabs for ring shooting, a hidden bit of forbidden licorice, and sometimes a jews harp or harmonica. Daredevils some-times carried a toad frog until warned by the ignorant that toads would cause warts.

Hell raisers would sometimes sneakily rip a quarantine sign (smallpox, whooping cough, measles) from its posted place on the victim's house, and place it secretly on somebody else's house.

In front of the school was a flag pole around which a May dance would be held annually, with girls dressed in white, lacy crepe-de-chines, pongee, or crepe paper dresses.

The boys would have tumbling exhibits on canvas mats on the front lawn.

The janitors had so many duties that boy pupils took turns policing the school grounds, picking up trash (there was a rule against dropping it on the ground), pointing out poison ivy or oak, and cleaning blackboards and erasers.

Chapel period, almost without fail, opened with an old hand-cranked Vic-trola playing John Philip Sousa's immortal Stars and Stripes Forever. One of the school bullies once stole the needle-scratched record, smashed it, and bur-ied the pieces. But you guessed it, the school promptly replaced the record with an exact duplicate.

Whenever the first case of "pink eyes" appeared in the school, we all had to line up to get eyedrops which had the color of tobacco juice. Throats were examined regularly in school when winter came and somebody coughed or talked hoarse. And many a morning at about 10 o'clock, there were lines to inspect hands and fingernails for dirt. Octagon soap and water were readily available and used. Pupils had collapsible aluminum cups, and teachers induced their owners to clean their teeth, even if no paste was around.

The Zaner and Palmer methods of penmanship or handwriting were requisites and writing inspections were strict. The three Rs were strenuously taught.

Staying in after school was almost as bad as sitting on the front row, but teachers enforced this when rules were broken.

Boys who satanically wrote with chalk so as to make flesh-crawling shrieks on the blackboard made a mistake if they repeated the excruciating act, because the teacher would pound the palm of his hand with that cat-of-nine-tails ruler with unbelievable force.

Tattle-tales were scorned and sometimes came up one book short.

Most pupils carried their own lunches to school, but if you didn't, the lunchroom (no cafeteria) supplied for a nickel each a big bowl of vegetable soup or white beans, both with crackers. What could be better?

If a pupil wasn't behaving or wouldn't study, he or she had to carry home a note written by the teacher to the parents. And the teacher always knew if you failed to perform this dreaded mission.

Thanksgiving in school was always a joyous occasion. Harvest Home, and America the Beautiful were sung, classrooms were decorated with pumpkins, cornstalks and persimmons, and crayon drawings were made and exhibited. Stories were read and told of the Indians, the Pilgrims, and John Smith and Pocahontas.

I always dreaded report cards, staying in after school, and recitations, but I later discovered they were necessary evils. And I never carried flowers or apples to a teacher, and neither did I kiss one until I started dating Duke summer school teachers about 100 years ago.

She Recalls When, and Why, Southern Conservatory Moved

She was a student at the Southern Conservatory of Music in 1924 when the popular school was moved from Main Street "to the country" to avoid flirting between its girls and the boys of Trinity College.

Mrs. Mary Blackwell Pridgen Martin of 1029 Buckingham Road is one of the few people in Durham who knows why the school moved. She also can recall Ben Duke's Four Acres mansion and other homes of Durham's old tobacco families. She was growing up, after all, when Durham was growing along with the fortunes of tobacco.

In a 1984 interview, she told about the conservatory's move. The school's operator, Gilmore Ward Bryant, "a really strict but gifted man, was furious when 'his girls' leaned out of the second-floor dormitory windows and waved, giggled, and carried on with the Trinity students on the sidewalk below."

Mrs. Martin, who "grew up with the piano and kept at it for years and years," said that the conservatory at the time was located on the southeast corner of Main and Duke streets, now occupied by one of Brightleaf Square's parking lots.

"Mr. Bryant moved the school to a building on Alston Avenue. I believe it was later occupied by the Salvation Army's home for young, unwed mothers-to-be," she said.

The conservatory had a bus and it transported students who didn't live at the school to and from downtown Five Points (now Muirhead Plaza).

Mrs. Martin is the daughter of the late Joseph Davis Pridgen and Lavinia Blackwell Pridgen, the youngest of 12 children. Her uncle, William Thomas "Buck" Blackwell, who early historian Hiram V. Paul called "world-famed and the father of Durham," was the oldest of the dozen. Blackwell was a Durham tobacco magnate and a philanthropist.

Boyd's history of Durham gives Blackwell the distinction of being "in a material sense, the builder of the town . . . When laborers came to Durham but found no house wherein they might live, he financed the construction of cottages and based the rent on cost plus 10%. He was no profiteer. By meeting such demands he once owned 336 houses in the town."

Mrs. Martin's father, Joe Pridgen, and Thomas Jones operated Pridgen and Jones Shoe Store on Main Street, now the site of Baldwin's store.

The Pridgen home was on the northeast corner of Chapel Hill and Duke streets where Rutledge College is now.

Mrs. Martin, who was born on Thanksgiving Day 1905, said that in 1906 her uncle "Buck" Blackwell moved his home from the northwest corner of Chapel Hill and Duke streets "to right behind our home. His vacated site became that of Duke Memorial Methodist Church."

She said that the Ben Duke home, located where famed Four Acres was to be, was moved across the street and later was occupied by the N. E. Green family, also prominent in tobacco operations.

"Then the magnificent Four Acres mansion of Ben Duke was built. What a great shame it was in later years to be torn down. It was beautiful and a showplace. I remember it well."

A yet vivacious woman who while a student at Southern Conservatory of Music was named "the prettiest," Mrs. Martin recalled a summer of long ago when a violent storm brought down telephone poles from Five Points to Milton Avenue. "It was some sight."

Laughing, she said that riding a buggy, a Model-T Ford, the train, and a streetcar were exciting experiences. "My aunt, Mrs. Lucy Ruffin Blackwell Holloway who lived with her daughter Maggie on Driver Avenue, used to regularly ride the streetcar from East Durham to our home and spend the entire day. Then she'd ride back home on the streetcar."

13

Disasters

The flu epidemic of 1918 saw mass burials of families in Durham. World War I was tragic enough, and then came the flu and isolation of victims and stringent regulations by the County Health Department.

When Hurricane Hazel hit Durham on Oct. 15, 1954, it caused more damage than all of Nature's lashings together in our city and county.

Hazel

Hurricane Hammered Durham

She was a terrifying combination of Typhoid Mary, Calamity Jane, Carrie Nation, Bonnie Parker, and Belle Starr.

She was Hurricane Hazel, the most devastating storm ever to hit Durham. She rode in with ferocious winds that reached 90 to 130 miles per hour and heavy rains that ended a prolonged drought. She punished the Carolinas on Friday, Oct. 15, 1954.

On Thursday, Oct. 14, Miami had reported a monster hurricane speeding toward Wilmington. At West Palm Beach, Fla., the ocean under Hurricane Hazel had been described as "a phenomenal sea, a sheer white rippled sheet as far as you can see."

But there was little apprehension in Durham.

A record high of 89 degrees had been set here on Wednesday and farmers and city folk alike were fretting about the unseasonable heat.

Durham High School's football team was preparing to play Fayetteville here on Friday night, and the U.S. Army football team was to arrive Friday to play Duke. At least 42,500 fans were anticipated for the Saturday contest. J. W. Posey, meteorologist at Raleigh-Durham Airport, was predicting that Hazel might end the dry spell. His forecast for the Triangle area: "A bit windy with showers and scattered thunderstorms followed by clearing, windy and cooler late Friday." Still no dire forecast.

The rain began Friday morning, and by early Friday afternoon winds of more than 60 miles per hour hit Durham. It was big-league stuff and we felt the onslaught. WDNC was the only radio station in the area not forced off the air by the storm. Announcers kept giving the progress of the femme fatale, Hazel.

The roof of the Colonial Linoleum and Tile Co. at 519 Morgan St. was blown off, and the fourth floor west wall caved in.

The Center Bowling Alley and the Rolling Pin Bakery reported heavy damage. In the blown-out window of one downtown store someone put up the sign: "Hazel was here."

Meanwhile, winds were wreaking havoc along 120 miles of the Carolina coast. The Red Cross was calling for help at Myrtle Beach. Gov. William B. Umstead called out three units of the National Guard to aid the stricken Wilmington.

Highways east of Raleigh were blocked by fallen trees. The Perquimans River flooded Highway 17 and roads were booby-trapped by debris.

At Atlantic Beach, waves crashed into the ground floor of the Ocean King Hotel. The 300 residents of Salter Path were evacuated to Morehead City. And, farther north, the highest winds in history battered the nation's capital.

Trees were being blown down throughout Durham. Cars overturned, and garbage cans, chairs, signs, and television antennas were hurled crazily about.

Metal trim from Huntley-Stockton-Hill Furniture Store was yanked from the building and propelled like javelins into the air. A huge tree toppled onto the display pavillion of Weeks Motor Co. The ice-freezing unit atop City Ice Co. on Peabody Street was blown down.

The roof of the penthouse of the Washington Duke Hotel was ripped loose, and the roof of Thomas Book Store across the street from the hotel was pounded apart. A portion of the roof of the Virginia-Carolina Chemical Co. plant on Angier Avenue went sailing. Garages and sheds in East Durham were yanked from their bases.

The weather bureau warned that even stronger winds were on the way. The city and county schools closed. As of noon, about two inches of rain had fallen in the area.

Sixteen school buses slid into ditches and were mired by mud.

Crews evacuated about 37 aircraft from Norfolk Naval Air Station to Raleigh-Durham Airport where they waited out the storm.

The hurricane delayed the arrival of the Army football team, and the Durham High game was postponed until Saturday.

This writer, wrapped tightly in his best rain gear, left home on foot Friday afternoon to cover his beat at the old courthouse. Just two blocks from home, having dodged downed live electric wires, climbed over tree limbs, and sidestepped debris on the vehicleless streets, I found myself rain-soaked.

Back home I changed clothes, and saw from the kitchen window that the winds had knocked down our dwarf cherry trees in the backyard.

Down Mangum Street south to Main Street, I found things in great disarray. There were no other pedestrians and the old police department was all but deserted. A few telephone wires were open and switchboard operators were being driven almost frantic.

The *Morning Herald* force, accustomed to the unexpected, got out the Saturday morning edition while at the same time feeling a bit sorry for the fellows who would deliver the newspaper.

Mayor E. J. Evans went on the air at WDNC to reassure the public and to say: "The people of Durham should be thankful for the fact that as terrible as the damage is here, it is not as great as in other areas nearby."

City work crews began clearing the streets of debris, and the city advised private property owners to move fallen trees from their own property. Storm damage was more than $1 million here.

By Saturday, 18 deaths in North Carolina and 114 in the nation had been blamed on Hazel. Hundreds of Durham homes were without lights or telephone.

At Duke Stadium, Colonel "Red" Blake's "Black Knights" of West Point, a strong outfit, whipped Coach Bill Murray's Blue Devils 28-14 before 40,000 hurricane-weary fans. Durham High School's "Bulldogs" trimmed Fayetteville 14 to 13.

Then came "hurricane sales" throughout Durham and memories of Hazel that would last for generations.

14

Civil War and World War II

Durham was well represented in the War between the States, probably the cruelest conflict of them all. It was a case of David versus Goliath, but that time Goliath had too many weapons.

Civil War widows, many of them young girls when they married the old veterans after the war, provided sad and interesting tales when I wrote of them.

Julian S. Carr of Durham was honored in 1922 in Richmond, Va., at perhaps the greatest reunion of the Confederate Army. He was reelected commanding general of the Confederate forces. This was 57 years after the end of the war.

Durham lost many warriors during World War II. Company D machine gunners of the National Guard suffered at least 50 percent of their number as casualties.

World War I saw great local patriotism, as did World War II. Then patriotism waned with the Korean and Vietnam wars. The latter two wars were political, with no all out-to-win plan. Thus these vets suffered outrageous verbal abuse in many quarters.

Vietnam vets have their own monument in Raleigh, while another monument there represents the memory of the vets of World War I, World War II, and Korea.

There are also monuments representing those who fought in the Civil War and the Revolutionary War.

'The Devil's Own Agent'

Victor Bryant's Grandma Hated Yankees, Especially Sherman

Native son and dean of the Durham County bar, Victor S. Bryant recently recalled his first train ride and his grandmother's hatred of yankees.

A man of many seasons, Bryant said that he was only 5 when he was permitted to ride the Southern Railway train from Durham to Raleigh to visit his grandparents, Leo and Nannie Heartt. Heartt, a banker, later moved to Durham and was a member of the first board of Watts Hospital in 1895.

"I learned later that I was supervised more than I thought," Bryant said. "I was carried to the Union Train Station at the foot of Church Street by one of my parents. After being given the amount of the round-trip ticket to Raleigh, I was left in charge of Capt. Joe Wrenn, the stationmaster and a friend of the family."

"I boarded the coach, having been told in advance to find a seat and not get out of it. I sat looking out the window as the world rolled by. I was a travelling man on my own, and was seeing the world. I tried to think I was grown up, even though my chubby little legs reached only halfway to the floor," Bryant said.

He said the conductor called East Durham, Brassfield, Morrisville, Cary, and Method. When the train ran through a deep cut with red banks, he knew he would be coming into the Raleigh station.

"A young man with a Union News name on his cap and a wicker basket filled with peanuts, bananas, oranges, newspapers, and other goodies, including a glass pistol filled with small red candy balls came by at regular intervals. He was what was known as a 'candy butcher,' and he kept calling out his wares."

"But these things were luxuries and I had been told I could do without luxuries, as tempting as they were," Bryant said.

He began to look upon himself as an experienced world traveler. When the train reached Raleigh, Grandma Heartt was waiting for him.

"I was a big man in her house. In my home I was not permitted to drink tea. At her home I could drink 'kettle tea.' This showed I was growing up. I learned later that 'kettle tea' was made of hot water, milk, plenty of sugar, and a dash of tea," Bryant laughed.

Bryant said that his grandparents Nannie and "Pa" were devout Presbyterians. "When visiting them I made myself ready for bed, omitting to wash my face and ears, however much they needed it, if I could get by with the omission. Putting on my nightshirt (this was in the days before I knew about pajamas), I said my prayers at her knee."

Bryant said he remembers many of the stories she told him, particularly those that related to the Civil War and Reconstruction.

"As the war dragged out, she said it became a belt-tightening process in which her family as well as others, came to learn the many things they had to do without: sugar, coffee, medicines, clothes, silks, ribbons, and many other things. There was little money to buy them with, even if they could get by the Federal blockade."

"The awful casualty lists grew. The fields were largely unworked. Cotton sheets were cut into strips and rolled for bandages to be sent to the Army. Food was scarce."

Bryant's grandmother also said that after Atlanta was burned and Sherman's army was headed north, she with other children and women were sent to Salisbury until the war was over.

On the morning of April 17, 1865, Sherman, then in Raleigh, ordered a car and a locomotive to carry him to Durham Station. The dispatcher held the train until the telegram telling of Lincoln's assassination the night before had been decoded. Sherman then came to Durham and at a house just west of there (Bennett Place), met Confederate Gen. Joseph Johnston, and the surrender terms were soon agreed upon and the war was over. Sherman's terms were considered generous by many Southern officers.

"The legend still persists that Sherman poured himself a drink from his flask and then poured one and handed it to Johnston. Later, Sherman took another drink without offering Johnston a second. Johnston is reputed to have said later that Sherman's manners were bad. He should have handed the flask and turned his back while Johnston poured his own drink."

Bryant said that his grandmother told him that when she got home from Salisbury, empty coffins were piled high in her home, which had been used as a kind of Yankee headquarters. The china was broken and scattered, the portraits slashed, and the furniture broken. Food was very scarce.

Bryant said that "it would be a mistake to think Nannie was all bitterness. No one ever had in their heart the loyalty and kindness she had for her family. She was a devoted mother and grandmother."

Madge: A Genuine Angel

She had a face like a bruised cabbage and a figure like a pregnant cat. When she walked it was with the labored stride of a workman pushing a wheelbarrow of cement up a narrow plank. Her voice was somewhere between a carnival barker's and a wagonmaster's.

But I soon learned that this waitress-cashier-cook was quite a humanitarian, given to a kindness nigh indescribable.

That was way back in World War II days when hordes of Camp Butner khaki and Duke Army finance and Carolina pre-flight GIs gave the Bull City quite a population boost and made cash registers light up like pinball machines.

And just before the military boom in this area, there were British sailors coming into town, surprising a lot of folks who didn't know they preferred their beer "right out of the case, if you don't mind, mate."

The Limey gobs were living in temporary quarters at Crabtree Creek (William B. Umstead Park) while their battle-battered ships were being repaired at Wilmington and Newport News.

I first met Madge—that wasn't her real name—when I visited a Durham cafe-oasis after being discharged from a military hospital while the war still went on. "What're you having, sport?" she asked from behind a counter almost saturated with soldiers. "If it's beer, we got lots of off-brand stuff, not much good suds."

Canned beer hadn't come in then and 12-ounce bottles ranged from 22 cents to 25 cents at most places.

I noticed a small bulletin board on one wall. Curious, I got close enough to see that it held messages to and from GIs, a soldier's cap that had been found. "This is kind of a clearing house for the military," Madge said, grinning.

A young soldier came in and whispered to Madge. She nodded. "Take off your coat, soldier," she said, "I think I got a button I can sew on for you." She did the sewing with practiced speed.

Another soldier came in took a long swallow of beer and asked, "Madge, you still got the shoeshine kit? I stepped in a mudhole at the bus station. Somebody's gonna break a leg around there."

The waitress nodded toward a small corner near the men's john. "It's still there," she said. "Just don't take too long, buddy."

A Marine, strangely out of place, it seemed, in the crowd of Army men, came into the establishment. He shook hands with Madge and hugged her neck. "I got your letter at the hospital," he said. "Only letter I received. Thanks, it meant a lot to me."

"Sure," Madge beamed. She pretended not to notice his limp, the cane and how loosely his uniform hung. "Now I'm gonna cook you up something," she said, motioning to a table.

Madge first served a couple of beers to loud soldiers seated at a table nearby. One of them sounded off with a string of oaths and Madge walked back to the table and said, "Soldiers, this must be the first time you've been in this place. We don't have profanity in here. I know you have to blow off steam sometimes, but do it on the outside, okay? We're just a big family here, and I'm crazy about GIs, but there will be no cussing, understand?"

"Yes, ma'am!" one of the soldiers responded. The other one mumbled, "Sorry."

"It's okay," she grinned, and returned to the Marine who was eating and smiling.

Days later I returned to the watering hole, and Madge recognized me. "Well, civilian, I see you again. You okay?"

I nodded. She opened a Budweiser. "I had a few cases of Bud to come in, glad you're getting one. You have been in the service?"

I told her I had and showed her my discharge paper.

"Shake, fellow," she said, thrusting out a ham-size hand. "I've seen those discharge pins, too, the ones some call a 'ruptured duck.' "

A slightly inebriated soldier wobbled into the cafe, sat down at the counter and asked "for a beer, any brand."

"Well, well, soldier," Madge said. "Just one more and you'll be paralyzed. I have a good cup of coffee for you. It's on the house."

The soldier looked up to see commanding, smiling faces and a woman he realized could handle most any situation. "Okay" he said, "you're the boss."

"That's right, when he's not around I am the boss. I am a friend, too."

One rainy day I was surprised to see only one other civilian and no soldiers when I visited the place for a couple of hotdogs.

"There's been a ship-out at Butner," Madge explained. "But there'll be a new bunch of men in soon."

"Madge," I said, "you have quite a personality and the soldiers seem devoted to you." She turned on a big grin. "That's true," she said. "I'm a regular house mother. Like one fellow said, a mother away from home."

She sat down beside me and pulled a snapshot from a billfold. The picture was that of a Marine with spectacles, a studious-looking chap.

"He was my real love," she said quietly. "A polite, soft-spoken man. Not young, mind you. He got into service a long time ago. I met him at Cherry Point where I worked in a cafe. I had just moved there from the Navy shipyards in Virginia. Anyway, he was a tall, wiry, kind, but tough man. You couldn't believe I'd fall for that type, could you? Well, I was trimmer then, and had a few looks." She showed another snap shot to back up her claim.

"I don't show these pictures to everybody and I don't talk about it, but today, this cold rain and dark clouds makes me remember. It was that kind of a day that I received word from the War Department that he had been killed in the South Pacific. I just let myself go, just about turned into a sloppy drunk. I lost my job. Before I moved on to Newport News I heard again from Uncle Sam. My love had made his GI insurance to me. He insisted, said he had no folks and that I was his best friend. I also got a few other personal things he had."

Madge found me to be a good listener, so she continued. "But it broke me up, I tell you." Tears welled in her eyes. She went back behind the counter and produced a partially filled bottle of Old Rocking Chair whiskey, really cheap booze.

I shook my head when she offered me a glass. Madge poured herself a big drink, slugged it down. She returned the bottle to its hiding place.

"The last time I saw him this was the only brand of liquor we could find," she said. "I can buy good stuff now, but it's only when I get moody that I take a drink, and that's not often."

I nodded, understandingly. She got up to wait on a customer.

About a week later I dropped by the joint. I didn't see Madge. The bulletin board was gone, so was the shoeshine kit.

"Where's Madge?" I asked the new and skinny waitress.

"She's not here anymore, she's gone," the waitress said. "She took everything she had with her. God, she must have been a real doll. And I know she had a lot of friends, because a lot of soldiers have asked about her. Some of them left without buying anything when they didn't find her here. One soldier cried, said he owed her some money. She didn't leave no forwarding address, just took flat off. The boss said that I might fill in, but that nobody could possibly take her place."

Realizing that she had rattled on without coming up for air, she paused and asked, "Mister, just what kind of person was she?"

"An angel," I said. "A genuine angel."

Bittersweet Memories of a Fallen Comrade

I passed your home today, oh departed comrade, and all of the ghosts of yesteryear paraded before me and my heart was glad.

Fred Anthony Edwards, a handsome, devil-may-care, fun-loving friend, predicted his own death during his Army Air Corps stint in World War II.

A radioman on a C–47 transport carrier, Staff Sgt. Edwards was one of 10 men on the plane on a September 1944 mission when it was lost in flight in the treacherous, ice-winded Aleutian Islands in Alaska.

As a student at Durham High School, Fred, with lifted eyebrows, sometimes referred to himself as "Sir Anthony Edwards." Not only was he a ham actor, he was an athlete, played in the school band, and was a vocalist in a little Durham orchestra.

As a songster he received as a songster lots of fan mail from the female sex, some of the letters being perfumed and bearing a lipstick kiss.

His older brother, Abe, a real jokester too, would sometimes intercept these letters, and secrete them until he was in a gathering of cronies at Abe's little house in the backyard of the Edwardses' big home at 818 Cleveland St.

There, in the presence of Fred, of course, Abe would read the fan letters in plaintive tone while his howling audience held back a protesting, fuming Fred.

Abe's house was called the shack. The gang, often consisting of Joe Umstead, Bob Cunningham, "Hunk" Munday, "Spec" Ferrell, Joe Donohue, Travers Putnam, Howard Basile, and this writer, usually played a game of "Spank Tail Hearts" there. It was played with a pack of poker cards.

The loser had the choice of walking the gauntlet of fiercely swung rolled-up magazines or coat hangers, or to hie forth by foot to Moss Bakery on Peabody Street to fetch jelly doughnuts.

After several sessions of Abe reading Fred's fan mail, Fred finally found a way to stop it. Late at night, after the gang had left Abe to become the sole occupant of his part-time manor, Fred would slip out of the big house and lower his mother's backyard clotheslines.

When Abe had to go into the big home, he'd have to duck several clotheslines. You can guess what happened, Abe's yells awakened his mother's roomers and boarders.

"Miss Nellie," and "T.G.," were the parents of the Edwards boys, Once T.G. accompanied Fred, Abe, and me on a fishing venture at Flat River, where we plied hook in waters just below the dam and amid rocks where we would stand.

At a certain time of day dam employees would open the gates to allow some water to flow into the area below the dam where anglers sometimes tried their luck. We knew this, but T. G. didn't.

He was busily engaged in fishing, standing on a large rock which was reached by several smaller stepping stones.

We watched as the rising water covered T.G.'s rock. When it reached the calves of his legs he realized something was amiss. Not finding any rock visible, T.G. yelled: "Get me out of here!"

Abe was doubled up in laughter. Fred called: "Hey, T.G., what happened to your stepping stones?"

Apprehensive that T.G. would fall and be injured, I called to him to grab my hand, that the water wasn't more than three or four feet deep.

Floundering, and his false teeth clicking in rage, T.G. reached the bank, his face livid. Besides, he hadn't caught a single fish.

On the way back home I had visions of T.G. cutting off his sons' allowance.

Fred's first job, I believe, was as a shoe clerk for the Greenbergs, who had opened a shop on Main Street.

A sharp dresser and smooth operator, Fred soon became popular with the lady customers who fawned on flattery and oily talk from the tall clerk.

Fred was a proofreader at Seeman Printery when the attack on Pearl Harbor shook the world and awakened this country. He volunteered for military duty and soon was an Army Air Corps cadet at Shepard Field, Wichita Falls, Texas.

A year or so before this war Fred and I attended a movie at the Paris Theater. The movie house was always dark except for the light of the film, and ushers with flashlights would seat patrons.

As Fred and I went down the aisle, ahead of the usher, Fred spied a pair of women's shoes which had been removed and placed near the aisle. As if groping in the dark, he kicked the shoes far down the aisle.

It was one of those sad pictures, and seated in front of us were two women who soon were crying, softly but openly. It had been raining outside so old Fred leaned over the seat, holding his slicker (raincoat), and asked the women ever so sweetly and understandingly: "Would you ladies like to protect your dresses while you are crying?"

One irate woman cut off the tears and snarled to Fred: "Have you no sense of decency?" We moved our seats.

Then Fred mockingly loosed exaggerated sobs until I, between laughs, threatened to leave.

Fred loved good music and his favorite song was *Smoke Gets in Your Eyes*. He hummed and sang this ditty quite often.

Fred, besides being adept at playing the Sousa, or big horn, decided to learn the more sophisticated violin.

Once, upon coming home from a late date during the hot summer, Fred decided on a cool tub bath. A roomer awakened to weird, animal-like noises coming from a hallway bathroom.

He grabbed a heavy bookend and jerked open the door of the bath. There in the tub and playing his violin, Fred looked up and calmly asked: "What's up, Vernon?"

Fred married pretty Helen Pleasants, also of Cleveland Street, beforer entering the military. They were to have a son, Fred Jr.

Once, while here on a rare furlough, Fred was called back for a second span of duty in the Aleutians.

One leaving Durham by train, Fred was accompanied to the Union Station by T. G. and myself. He said he didn't want anyone else along, that it was sad enough as it was.

T. G., who was afraid to show his emotion, stood back as I walked with Fred to the step for boarding the train. Fred looked at me seriously and whispered. He said he had a feeling which wouldn't leave, that he wouldn't be one of the lucky ones coming back after the war.

"We are losing men in the Aleutians because the weather is our worst enemy, but even at that, I worry less about my own safety than about whether little Fred will accept the 'old man.' "

Shaking my hand for the last time I ever saw Fred, he asked me to promise that I would see that Helen and his boy were doing all right, and to keep an eye on Nellie and T.G. I nodded and said nothing. Then I slipped him a pint of bourbon.

On the way back to the car with T.G. I told him I thought it only fair, even though I knew he detested alcoholic drink, that he should know that I gave Fred a bottle of whisky at the train.

T.G., with tears in his eyes, shook my hand and placed an arm about my shoulder. "I'm glad you did, boy, I'm glad you did."

After the U.S. War Department sent word that Fred's plane was lost in the Aleutians and he and his companions were presumed dead after a long and fruitless search, one of the men in Fred's outfit, another radioman named "Rosey" Rosenbloom, wrote to Helen.

He poured out his heart in the letter and told how close he and Fred and the entire group were. In paying tribute he said, "Fred was very much in love with you both and so proud of you. He treasured the pictures you sent."

So, when I pass Fred's old home on Cleveland Street, smoke gets in my eyes.

Legion Post 7 Keeps Patriotic Fires Burning for Durham War Veterans

The raucous bellow of American Tobacco Company's "bull," and the shrill screams of other steam whistles at Durham's factories and textile plants, led the mighty outburst.

There were ear-splitting horns, fireworks, shotguns, and unfettered cheers from an excited populace.

Thus was greeted the signing of the armistice that November 11 morning in 1918, signifying the end of World War I.

The Kaiser had been kicked, and good. Germany was defeated. Now our town awaited the return home of its sons in khaki and navy blue, its daughters in hospital white who had nursed the wounded, its doctors, and the men of the cloth who served as chaplains.

And there were those stalwart workers of the Salvation Army, the Red Cross, and the Knights of Columbus volunteers.

Tobacco factories were commended for donating millions of cigarettes to our expeditionary forces. Hats were off to the war savings bonds and savings stamps programs that helped finance the conflict. And don't forget such groups as the senior girls of Durham High School's class of 1918, whose colors were red, white, and blue, in assembling and donating ditty bags of toilet articles.

The returning military brought home oft grimy uniforms that included cloth wrap leggings, knapsacks, and gas mask bags that were to become school booksacks.

The victors brought also such strange names as "doughboys," "cooties," "trench rats" and "40 and 8" (40 men and 8 horses or mules to a boxcar).

And there was that French-inspired risque song, *Mademoiselle of Armentiers;* the British song, *It's a Long Way to Tipperary;* and our own *Keep the Home Fires Burning,* and George M. Cohan's famous *Over There.*

The men said that the rousing marches of Sousa, and James Montgomery Flagg's poster of a stern Uncle Sam pointing a finger and saying "I want you!" kept them determined.

But the greatest sight of those returning from Europe was the "Lady With the Torch," the Statue of Liberty in New York Harbor, bidding them welcome.

In 1919 the veterans of World War I formed the American Legion, an organization dedicated to the glory of God, freedom, and country.

White Durham veterans organized Post 7 of the Legion, meeting in the basement of old Durham High School on Morris Street. Black veterans organized the Weaver-McLean Post.

According to Bill Isaacs of Carolina Avenue, who twice served as Post 7 commander and as chaplain, "we soon decided we needed a post of our own. We bought stock at $10 a share and made outright donations for the project."

A simple log cabin house with porch, featuring a huge fireplace, became Post 7's home, one almost camouflaged by trees and shrub. The place was called "Hut," a name borrowed from the French "hutte," in 17th-century military usage.

The Hut was in the 200 block of north Queen Street, across from the old Beth-El Synagogue. Both are long-since razed, replaced by larger buildings at different sites.

With veterans of World War II, the Korean War, and the Vietnam War returning, the post membership began to bulge.

Through the sale of the Hut on Queen Street the post bought a tract of 20 acres on Fay Street. The parcel included land to be occupied by the Durham County Fair, under sponsorship of the post.

The land and new building cost about $60,000, and the mortgage was burned in special ceremony on Aug. 10, 1976, with post finance officer Zack Long applying the match.

In the infancy of the post, World War I veterans organized "Barracks 707." An auxiliary was to follow.

Isaacs said in a 1986 interview that this organization hadn't met since its last commander, Luther H. Barbour, died several years ago.

"There are so few of us left. At one time we had 444 members," he said.

The post organized early a 40 and 8 unit, the honor society of the Legion. Jake Nurkin organized the Durham unit of the "Cooties," the highest branch of the Veterans of Foreign Wars. He also organized the local order of the "Trench Rats," the highest branch of the Disabled American Veterans.

In 1945-46 Nurkin had the distinction of being commander of five military organizations simultaneously, including the "Purple Heart."

Several of the old post boys organized "The Last Man's Club," which was originated by the 113th Field Artillery. The group joined hands and pledged that the last man alive in the order would receive a $12 bottle of bourbon bearing their names, plus a $1,000 government bond.

Although the post 7 roster today lists only about a dozen of its WWI vets, with several no longer living in Durham, a few of the old guard, health permitting, still visit the post.

Harvey Everitt, a veteran of WWII, and current post service officer, who keeps tab of members, especially the charters, lists the old veterans as follows: Isaacs, Mack Winberry, Z. V. Waller, Earl Wrenn, W. D. Murray, Norman Reeves (Broken Arrow, Okla.), John P. Gunter, Bryant W. Bobbitt, Henry Davis, Paul Ligon, Garland McBroom, Frank E. Moore, and E. H. Monroe.

Some of these men have been members of the post since or soon after its inception.

Winberry recalled recently that "we once had over 1,000 members in this post. But today, people are not as appreciative of our country, they're just not as patriotic."

Meredith W. "Bishop" Cannon was elected commander of the post for 1949-50, succeeding Egbert Haywood. Other officers then were: first vice commander, Mack Winberry; second vice commander, Marion Long; adjutant, Hugo Walker; finance officer, W. C. Alexander; chaplain, John Rowell; sergeant-at-arms, George L. Coleman; service officer, Paul G. Noell; and chairman of the memorial committee, W. L. Hampton.

Cannon kept records of post activities during this regime, and some of the events from his scrapbook are herewith related.

The post organized a burial group made up of members of the 40 and 8, "to lay away to rest with full military honors" Durham County veterans, including those brought home from military cemeteries in foreign countries.

Members of the team were: John C. Allers Jr., commander; and George Coleman, Herbert Whitfield, Arthur Allers, John Taylor, S. O. Blalock, M. W. Cannon, Sam Hancock, Lee Warren, Bill Josephs, Mack Winberry, Mallie Ellis, Marion Long, George Upchurch, W. C. Alexander, W. R. House, and Henry Davis. The Rev. Leon Hall was chaplain. The men were neatly uniformed and in drill condition.

Local observance of Armistice Day saw flags flown throughout the city, especially downtown. Veterans met at the American Legion fairgrounds for a barbecue supper and a speech by former U.S. Senator William B. Umstead, a Post 7 member. Mayor Dan K. Edwards was master of ceremonies.

Umstead, branding communism a threat to the democracy of the United States, called the United Nations "the greatest hope on the face of the earth in which we can find some hope of peace."

Post 7 elected to participate in the nationwide "Junior Marshall Plan" of the American Legion to collect and send toys to the needy children of the world.

Post 7 honored the Durham High School state championship football team at a banquet. Dr. D. R. Perry, post athletic head, presided.

Rain-drenched ground-breaking ceremonies were held for the 500-bed Veterans Administration General Hospital on Erwin Road.

Because of the weather the program was changed, with most of the talks by distinguished visitors being delivered at the Washington Duke Hotel. J. D. Pridgen represented Post 7 and was arrangements chairman.

Included among the dignitaries were Dr. W. C. Davison, dean of Duke Medical School; Congressman Carl T. Durham, Governor Kerr Scott, Mayor Dan Edwards, Col. B. L. Robinson, division engineer, Army Engineer Corps of Wilmington; and Col. J. D. Deramus, manager of the Veterans Administration regional office, Winston-Salem.

Post 7's Junior Legion baseball team was coached by Glenn Bunting, The Legion's team included: Clifton Walker, Louis McDaniel, Millard Oakley, Worth Lutz, Robert Hazelgrove, Wade Jones, Odell Rhodes, Billy Chestnut, Bill Perry, Connie Rigsbee and Bobby Burns.

The American Legion departmental headquarters in Raleigh released a membership report which ranked Post 7 as among the top 10 in the state, with 487 members.

Post 7 again sponsored an annual Durham Golden Gloves boxing tournament, with Al Mann Jr., as chairman.

Ike Harris and Lewis McKee were tournament ringside doctors, and Matt Raymond and Glenn Penland of Durham and Bob Harden of Burlington were ring officials. Cecil Cates and Jim Hursey were coaches of the Durham team.

Post 7 made arrangements to care for 107 visiting boxers. Contestants were given rooms, meals, and tickets to the Center, Carolina, and Rialto Theaters.

Trophies were presented to the winners by Add Warren, "Choo Choo" Justice, Art Weiner, and Eddie Cameron.

Durham entrants included: Gene Crawford, Curtis Ennis, Sonnie Rochelle, Chester Britt, W. T. White, Clyde Carter, Mac Elvington, Charles "Snag" Cole, Billy Rorie, Amnren Hassen, Bobby Dye, Benny Deaton, Hubert Lassiter, Jimmy Pearson, Wade Toler, and Doyle Cates.

Dr. D. R. Perry of Post 7, national vice commander of the Legion, delivered a "Pearl Harbor Day" address in Savannah.

Teddy Stone of Durham High School was first place winner in the annual American Legion countywide oratorical contest at the post "Hut" on Queen Street.

Legion members on May 28, 1950, attended Memorial Day worship services at Carr Methodist Church. The program included a salute to the flag with the hymns: *My Country 'Tis of Thee,* and *My Soul Be On Thy Guard.*

A tribute to veterans of all wars was made by program chairman W. W. Green, and a sermon, "Lest We Forget," was given by the church pastor, the Rev. Millard C. Dunn.

Post 7, led by W. W. Green, launched a church attendance program as part of a nationwide effort to get families to attend church together.

Jake Nurkin was named by the post to head the planning committee for Durham's first observance of "Armed Forces Day."

Isaacs recalled that in 1962 the post sold 168 American flags to downtown Durham merchants for display on certain occasions, at a cost of $19.95 a flag. Post 7 also put holes or sockets in the sidewalks along the curb for the flags.

Today the post sponsors junior softball and baseball teams, Boys State and Girls State, and gives Christmas baskets and donates money to the Veterans Administration Hospital. About three years ago it gave a new van to the hospital. The post also assists needy veterans and families, participates in the 4-H Club scholarship program, and participates in high school oratorical contests.

Post 7 officers this year are: commander, Bill Helms; vice commander, Bill Robinson; finance officer, Zack Long, service officer, Harvey Everitt; adjutant, Wade Copeland; and sergeant-at-arms, Tony Mederious. Long and Copeland have served in their offices for many years.

Post Auxiliary officers are: commander, Elizabeth Fisher; vice commander, Martha Isaacs; Girls State chairman, Lucille Cranford; secretary, Mary McSorley; and treasurer, Barbara Powell.

He Fought 'The Desert Fox'

When Tom Gallagher got off the Greyhound bus at the Durham terminal Nov. 1, 1944, he was wearing a Canadian beret and uniform and walking laboriously with the aid of two stout canes. His once-raven hair was shot with gray and his shrapnel-torn jaw was scarred, but the wiry ex-prizefighter's grin was as wide as ever.

Thomas Malloy Gallagher, Irish aplenty, had left Durham in the late 1930s, first to box and then to work for Bethlehem Steel in Baltimore. But things were popping in Europe and he was itching to be a part of the argument. That's why he and several of his buddies gave up their jobs and went to Canada to enlist in the Canadian armed forces. The men were readily accepted and soon Gallagher became a tail gunner in the 319th Bomb Squadron. From there his war history parallels that of a storybook hero.

In 1940 his squadron pelted the Germans with the big bombs and then turned tail through heavy ack-ack to head home. "We are over Brest, France, when hot lead exploded one of our bombs that didn't release from the ship," he once said. "The explosion ripped our crate apart over the (English) channel. I automatically pulled the rip cord. The dark waters came up like a protecting shroud. Shadows and schoolday memories played tricks on my numbed brain."

A Royal Air Force patrol boat darted through flying missiles and rescued the nigh-frozen survivors from a watery grave. Months later Gallagher was discharged from a Canadian hospital. His was deaf in his left ear. His flying days were over, so he was transferred to the First Canadian Armored Division. After a 30-day sick leave, he left England for the battle of Crete.

"The Jerries came after us from every quarter and we were trapped like rats. Their heavy guns and dive bombers annihilated nearly everything we threw at them. Outnumbered by far, a few of us were lucky to get back," Gallagher said.

In July 1942, the memorable Dieppe conflict found him again in the thick of the action. A German machinegun nest was blocking his group's progress and spewing death. Gallagher went up to close range and with a direct burst of fire, knocked out the entire displacement, killing 12 of the enemy. Then a German shell landed in his open-top armored gun carrier, some of the exploding fragments tearing into his body.

Three months later he lay in an English hospital. Then-Princess Elizabeth in Horsham, England, pinned on Gallagher's breast the Distinguished Service Medal. A month later he went to Africa and was placed under the command of "the spit and polish" Gen. Bernard Montgomery in the 8th Army.

Rommel, the German "Desert Fox" tank commander, was giving the British tank forces a royal battle and, according to Gallagher, was employing the

Tom Gallagher, war hero.

most strategic maneuvering system ever demonstrated in desert warfare. "America sent us those great Sherman tanks and then it happened. The fight turned into a rout of Rommel's tanks."

Grinning, Gallagher said that Rommel was not only a beautiful broken field runner, but he also used a sidestepping change of pace while being chased to Algiers.

Near Antonio, Italy, came more fireworks. "We met unusually heavy resistance as the Germans fought to stem our advance. The citizens of the town had hidden in their cellars, huddling together and shivering as the big guns roared, shook the buildings, and tore structures into bits. We came to grips with the enemy at close range. There was street fighting and firing from rooftops and any cover left," Gallagher said.

Crawling through the smoking and charred rubble of an ancient, beautiful cathedral, he said, he and several other soldiers sneaked between plaster, stone, brick, and broken glass, firing all the while. One of the walls of the church remained standing and as he hugged its bricks for protection, Gallagher saw a handsome crucifix hanging on the wall. He placed the sacred emblem in his pack after giving up the idea of attaching it to his body with wire. Then he dodged back into the open.

"It was almost Christmas in 1943 and the crucifix meant much to me," Gallagher said. A short time later shrapnel caught him in the head, leg, and spine. He was taken to a Canadian hospital set up in Naples.

He said that it was touch-and-go for a time and school memories cropped out again. Durham High School had won the state basketball championship and he climbed atop the school to paint the class colors. Somebody jerked away the ladder, leaving him stranded on the building for hours. He was transferred to an English hospital where he remained until June 1944. There was another sick leave and on Oct. 25 he was given a service discharge at the hospital.

Gallagher once coached football out of the state and he was something of a Duke fan, although his brother, Father Patrick Gallagher, retired priest at St. Thomas More Catholic Church in Chapel Hill, remains a died-in-the-wool Tar Heel, having been a member of the University of North Carolina boxing team. Tom also boxed on this team before leaving school.

Despite his physical handicaps, Tom Gallagher worked for a while as an automobile mechanic in Durham. Then he went north, where a few years later he died of his war wounds.

War's End at Durham Station—
Johnston's Surrender to Sherman

The cause was lost. Out-manned, supplies depleted, and its proud cities facing devastation, the Confederacy reluctantly conceded further resistance was futile.

Northern Gen. William Tecumseh Sherman was encamped in a rain-logged Raleigh when on April 14, 1865 he received word from Gen. Joseph Eggleston Johnston at Greenboro that his southern armies were prepared to lay down arms.

Only days earlier Sherman learned at Smithfield of Gen. Robert E. Lee's surrender to Gen. Ulysses Grant at Appomattox Courthouse, Va.

Elated with the turn of affairs, Sherman agreed to meet with Johnston at a point intermediate between pickets at noon on the 17th.

The meeting place selected was Durham's Station, a hamlet of perhaps 200 people.

Sherman was climbing aboard a train for Durham's Station when he received from Morehead City a telegram telling of President Lincoln's assassination in Washington.

The shaken general pledged the telegrapher to secrecy. With sadness and apprehension he rode to Durham's Station, a rustic village destined because of the meeting to become a bustling tobacco manufacturing city.

Gen. Johnston, a native of Farmville, Va., and a grand-nephew of Patrick Henry, had served in the Black Hawk, Seminole, and Mexican wars. He had resigned from the U. S. Army to enter the Confederate service.

Gen. Sherman, who like Johnston was a graduate of West Point, was a native of Lancaster, Pa.

They were meeting now for the first time at close quarters and with undrawn guns.

Johnston, at 58, wore a graying beard and well groomed mustache. He was neatly dressed in gray uniform coat buttoned to his chin and carried his slight frame with military bearing.

The 45-year-old Sherman, a taller man with unruly red hair and straggly beard, in mussed clothing appeared more the fighting private than conquering general.

At Bennett House

Following handshaking and introductions, the general retired to the inside of the small and unpainted frame dwelling of Lucy Bennett and her four children. Her husband and their father, Lee Lerenzo Bennett, had fallen in battle.

Mrs. Bennett and the children retired to one of the two outhouses on the premises to permit privacy for the history-making consultation.

While the chieftains conferred, their subordinates outside swapped horses, ran foot races, spun yarns, and talked of the future.

As soon as they were alone, Sherman showed Johnston the dispatch announcing Lincoln's assassination.

Prespiration came to Johnston's forehead and he made no attempt to conceal his distress. He said with feeling that the murder was a disgrace to the age.

Johnston stated simply that further war on the part of the Confederacy was folly, and that every life sacrificed after the surrender of Lee's army was the highest possible crime.

Agreeing that Grant's surrender terms to Lee were honest and fair, Johnston said he desired to embrace in the same general proposition the fate of all Confederate armies in existence.

Johnston conceded that slavery was dead. Then he asked for concessions that would enable him to maintain complete control over his followers until they could get back to their homes.

Sherman readily agreed to give it consideration.

Terms for Amnesty

On April 18, Sherman and Johnston met again at the Bennett house and Johnston satisfied Sherman of his powers to disband all rebel armies.

Sherman agreed that Lincoln's proclamation of amnesty, of Dec. 8, 1863, was still in effect, enabling every Confederate soldier and officer below the rank of colonel to obtain an absolute pardon by simply laying down his arms and taking the common oath of allegiance.

Such a pardon, Sherman understood, would restore them all their rights of citizenship.

The sidearms, private horses, and baggage of the Southern officers also were to go untouched in the surrender terms.

Sherman told Johnston that he would get the memorandum of the surrender terms to new President Andrew Johnson, a native of Raleigh, for official confirmation. An armistice was ordered.

Gen. Grant, who had moved into Raleigh, approved the memorandum and it was forwarded to Washington.

Washington Disapproves

Sherman soon learned to his consternation that the memorandum was disapproved without reasons assigned. He received orders to give 48 hours notice and to resume hostilities at the close of that time.

Within an hour a courier was on his way to notify Johnston of the truce suspension.

On the night of April 25, Gen. Johnston asked Sherman for another meeting at the Bennett house at noon on the 26th.

Shortly after the generals entered the house, Sherman stepped to the door of the dwelling and asked for his saddlebags. A bottle of whisky was taken therefrom and the two leaders renewed their discussion in more sociable manner.

Sherman apologetically explained that surrender terms had to be altered. He said that Washington was not recognizing state government in the south and that he could offer no concessions other than those allowed Lee by Grant. Sherman emphasized it was not to his liking.

A historian one day was to write: "If the terms he (Sherman) sketched had been accepted our country might have been readily united. But the politicians would not have it thus."

Johnston accepted the new arrangements and the two men amicably departed, Sherman once more to report his actions to Washington.

"It Does Seem Strange"

Soon afterward Sherman saw an April 24 copy of a New York newspaper containing military news under the signature of Secretary of State Edwin Stanton.

The article gave full report of a March 3 dispatch of instructions from Lincoln to Grant, instructions of which Sherman never had knowledge, and providing the public with what Sherman considered erroneous impressions.

Sherman read on. He burned at the report.

"It does seem strange," he commented, "that every barroom loafer in New York can read in the morning journal 'official' matter that is withheld from a general whose command extends from Kentucky to North Carolina . . . When an officer pledges the faith of his government he is bound to defend it. . . . "

On April 28, Sherman met with his commanders at Raleigh and completed orders for the future. The next day he left by rail for Wilmington and thence to Washington.

On May 22, in Washington, at a Committee on the Conduct of the War, Gen. Sherman testified in full. He felt content to abide by the judgment of the country on the patriotism and wisdom of his conduct in this connection.

A grand review of the military was staged in Washington on May 24, and Sherman was later in placed in charge of Army headquarters at St. Louis.

On May 28, 1884, he wrote from that city his expression of a move to nominate him to the Presidency: "Any senator can step from his chair at the Capitol into the White House and fulfill the office of President with more skill and success than a Grant, Sherman, or Sheridan, who were soldiers by education and nature."

At an honorary dinner on Feb. 8, 1890, his 70th birthday, Sherman said:

"But the way to reform the community is to reform yourselves. But you have to take the world as it is. It is a good world. It is the best you have now. I don't see any who are anxious to depart from it."

Johnston's Last Ceremony

Sherman died of the effects of asthma just six days after his next birthday, at his home in New York.

At his request his remains were taken to St. Louis, to rest beside those of his wife, Ellen Boyle Ewing Sherman, and "the infant son whose brief span of existence did not bridge the interval of one campaign in the life of his great father."

Johnston was an honorary pallbearer.

Standing bare of head in the chilling February air, Johnston, the one-time Confederate, fell victim to pneumonia. He died of its effects the following month.

Bennett Place Memorial

Morgan's Dreams Realized 58 Years Ago

"I'm not here to join in celebrating the surrender of my father and his comrades in the Confederate Army by General Johnston to General Sherman, but to participate in helping North Carolina assume responsibility for the care and preservation of this historic spot."

Thus spoke Gov. Cameron Morrison at the unveiling and dedication of the Bennett Memorial in November 1923.

Many eyes in the nation were focused upon Durham that Thursday afternoon 58 years ago, at a place hallowed by the memory of the men in gray and their northern foes in blue during their meeting there in April 1865.

Bennett Place, a little unpainted frame house on a 36-acre piece of ground off Hillsborough Road on the edge of Durham, was occupied by Lee and Lucy Bennett and their four children.

But on April 26, 1865, the Bennetts retired to one of their two outbuildings on the premises while Confederate Gen. Joseph E. Johnston and the North's Gen. William T. Sherman discussed terms of the surrender while they toasted each other with a bottle of whiskey that Sherman procured from his saddlebag. The surrender at Bennett Place ended the Civil War.

Gen. Johnson, at 84, was honorary pallbearer at the funeral of Sherman, 71, and bare of head in the chilling February cold, developed pneumonia and died the following month.

The years rolled by after the surrender, and finally only the chimney of old Bennett Place remained. Then came Samuel Tate Morgan, founder of the Durham Fertilizer Co. and the Virginia-Carolina Chemical Co. after much dickering, he purchased the entire Bennett tract as a park and a fitting memorial for the Confederacy and the re-United States.

Morgan died before his dream was realized, but his heirs, just as loyal as he was to North Carolina, carried out his plans. They offered the grounds and a suitable monument to the state on condition the state maintain Bennett Place as a park and memorial.

The General Assembly accepted the property and created the Bennett Place Memorial Commission, which was headed by Col. Benehan Cameron, a close friend of Samuel Morgan. Then came the day of the unveiling and dedication, and a crowd of about 3,000 persons, many from other states, was on hand.

Through the cooperation of the Durham Public Service Co., double street car service was provided for the event. The cars discharged passengers at the Country Club on West Club Boulevard where buses and jittneys took them to Bennett Place. There was ample parking space, too, for automobile owners who drove to the grounds.

For the occasion, Trinity College loaned bleachers, which were quickly filled. All of the growth of weeds and underbrush had been removed from the area and the ground leveled. Walkways were laid throughout the park to the memorial and to the no-longer-lonesome old chimney.

A number of Confederate veterans in their gray uniforms were present. The presence of a gray-haired black man on the edge of the speakers' platform was significant in that the event which transpired nearby, and for which the exercises were held, meant the freedom of the black race from slavery.

Dr. D. H. Hill, a former president of N. C. State College, whose father was a Confederate Army commander, filled in for Col. Herbert M. Hughes of Virginia, nephew of Gen. Johnston, who was unable to attend.

Famed evangelist M. H. Ham, who was preaching in Durham, offered prayer at the beginning of the ceremony, and Dr. A. D. Wilcox, pastor of Trinity Methodist Church gave the closing prayer.

The monument was unveiled by Samuel Morgan's only grandson, 17-year-old Morgan Ayres Reynolds of Charlotte, who had the chimney rebuilt. Durham's Gen. Julian S. Carr, who served under Gen. Robert E. Lee in the Army of Virginia, presented the memorial to the state in behalf of the Morgan family. His spirited talk was on the Confederate soldier and the Civil War.

Gov. Morrison accepted the memorial in behalf of the state.

But the principal speaker was U.S. Sen. Burton K. Wheeler of Montana, representing the north. He said that the economic and civic war remained to be fought by the people of the nation. Then, he added:

"Who in America can begrudge North Carolina the splendid progress that it has made in the last quarter of a century? Who can question your love and fidelity to these great United States? Who can fail to glory in your pride that your fathers were 'First at Bethel, furthermost at Gettysburg, and last at Appomattox?' . . . It is a no longer undeniable fact that America is a great united nation, moving forward in the light of God's smile."

Life Of Contradictions Led By Old Slave

A lot of people liked old Jerry Markham, but he was a man of contradictions. He was a slave when he was a boy, but he always flew the Confederate flag in front of his little house along the railroad near the Duke Street crossing.

Markham was a philosopher and looked upon life as an optimist, but as he got older he began to feel that the world was gradually degenerating in its morals. He blamed automobiles for that.

A lot of people in Durham knew Markham before he died in 1940 at the age of 91. One of them was Mrs. C. B. Martin, whose grandfather Blackwell owned much of the land on Duke Street and along the railroad.

Markham, Mrs. Martin said, was "a good old soul. He took care of a lot of hoboes. He let them sleep in his house, fed them. But he was a man of no foolishness, she said. "He was humble and nice, always working, but he'd raise sand with the hoboes who wanted everything for nothing. He tried to keep them straight."

Markham came to Durham a few years after the Civil War. He had been born at Patterson's Mill in 1849. Despite his years he was clear of mind and he could recite much of the early history of Durham. Adults and youth in early Durham held him in high esteem.

Markham lived on a site loaned him by the Southern Railroad. His modest little one-room home filled his every need and as he put it, "No king on his throne gets more real enjoyment in his modern convenience palace than I do in my home."

Markham tilled the soil in season, coaxing from what was once barren soil unfit for anything but weeds which lined the property—vegetables sufficient for his own use, with plenty to spare for his friends. He also had three cows, a horse and chickens, and an orchard in which he took great pride.

Markham's home was probably the most interesting feature of all his possessions. It was on the south side of the Southern Railway on Duke Street. He bragged that the Confederate flag, the south side and the Southern Railway all proved that he was a loyal Southerner.

The grave of Jerry Markham, former slave.

The house was not much higher than six feet. The first step towards erecting the structure was to employ a brickmason to build the chimney. Markham did the carpentry himself, and with skill. He plied two coats of paint to the house and then moved in with his wordly possessions, which didn't take long.

He was able to sit in his own home and view the passing show of life about him with the lordly air of a homeowner. A hearty welcome awaited any of his friends until evening, when he closed the door for the night. The door wouldn't be opened under any consideration unless it was a matter of life or death, or a train wreck, so he said.

As custodian of the Southern Railway's Duke Street crossing at the time the long wooden bars were lowered to hold back traffic, he was interested in anything pertaining to the railroad.

His home didn't have a wooden floor. The cot on which he slept was an old one abused by wear. It rested upon boxes and other things but he said it gave him a comfortable sleep. He said he was forced to drink milk since liquor had been hard to come by. One of his cows, his pride, gave one and a half gallons of milk a day. This was more than enough for his needs so he divided it with his chickens and his friends.

As to the chickens, he boasted that he had named them and each responded to his call, apparently knowing their own names. A little peach orchard, consisting of live trees, afforded Markham both fruit and pride. There were also flowers and shrubbery about the premises which earned him considerable praise.

Markham was born the slave of Daniel Carlton. He said he was a boy of tender age when his first master died. There were several heirs to Carlton's estate, and the property was divided.

At the time slaves were drawn for by the heirs, with the result that Jerry, his mother, and two other members of his family were drawn by Miss Nannie Lee Carlton. Jerry's mother brought 15 children into the world, but only two of them were alive when the Civil War broke out. At the time the war began Jerry was almost 13.

After he was freed, Markham worked for several men, including Anderson Couch, Sam Patterson and Henry Markham. He adopted Markham's name. At one time he owned considerable real estate. He said he lost it through his operations in the sale of whisky.

But Markham's adversity of fortune failed to dampen his enthusiasm and love of life. He became mascot of the Durham Bulls baseball team in the Piedmont League, and thousands of fans saw him promenade about the diamond at old Doherty park in East Durham.

With his high-top beaver hat and fancy costume, never did a baseball team have a more staunch supporter. His antics on the field assured a good attendance.

Markham said that 30 years without sickness of any kind was the record of health he had to offer. His prescription for good health was plenty of exercise and lots of sleep, both coming at the accustomed time.

He seldom spoke ill of anyone, saying, "It will get you nothing but enemies."

Markham, who was coachman for Washington Duke for many years, in 1936 was taken to New York by Blll Lipscomb, a clothing store operator, and appeared on the "We the People" radio program, which was on a nationwide hookup.

When W. W. Fuller, general counsel for Liggett & Myers, announced that he was moving from Durham to New York, Markham was disappointed. He accompanied Fuller to Henderson to board the train to New York City, arguing with him virtually all the way to change his mind and remain in Durham. Markham said later that Fuller told him. "If you'll vote the straight Republican ticket from now on, I won't go." Markham wouldn't promise.

Although he said he never wanted a wife, Markham always sought a woman barber to shave him, saying, "A woman has more sense than a man." As to marriage, he said, "I'd rather have a cow. A cow doesn't talk back to you like a woman does."

Mrs. Margaret Noell Daily recalls that when she was only three her family moved into the old Blackwell house, the site of which is now occupied by Thalhimer's warehouse on Duke Street at the railroad crossing. "We children in the neighborhood used to have fun listening to Jerry talk," she said.

Mrs. Daily said that Markham, who lived only half a block from where she did, "wore bib overalls and stayed clean. He took care of all of us children. He did little cooking but lived high on the hog because people loved him and always wanted to give him something. Jerry had everybody's respect."

In 1937 his health broke and he was finally persuaded to enter the Durham County Home on Roxboro Road. Mrs. Pauline Yong Mangum, whose husband, the late E. T. Mangum, became superintendent of the institution in 1933, recalls that Markham let it be known early that he had bought and paid for his tombstone, burial plot, casket and funeral services.

"Uncle Jerry wanted to be buried as close to old Maplewood Cemetery as possible. He said that was where his old friends were buried or would be buried. So to be sure his wishes would be carried out, he had his big marker set up in Fitzgerald Cemetery, a small lot next to old Maplewood in the 800 block of Kent Street," Mrs. Mangum said.

When Markham died Nov. 11, 1940, at the age of 91, she said she contacted the marble works which had prepared Jerry's stone, and asked them to put an inscription and flowers on it.

"They told me that Uncle Jerry hadn't paid for the lettering, so I paid for it, knowing he would have liked this," Mrs. Mangum said. The monument, about five feet tall, obscured by brambles, weeds, leaves and debris, carries the following words: "At rest, Jerry Markham, died Nov. 11, 1940; an old slave and a friend to all; Markham."

"Scarbrough & Hargett handled the funeral services which were held at the grave site in an extremely heavy rainfall. The services were conducted by Father O'Brien, a Catholic priest, and the pallbearers were Lawyer Frank

Fuller, son of W. W. Fuller; Lawyer Percy Reade, county attorney; County Manager D. W. Newsom; county physician Dr. J. C. Holloway, County Home Supt. R. B. Nichols, and Lawyer Ludlow Rogers," Mrs. Mangum said. Despite the segregation and prejudice of the era, these whites attended the service.

Jerry Markham had no relatives, just friends.

Honor For Durham's Gen. Julian Carr

As Confederate Soldiers Gathered For 1922 Reunion

Gen. Julian Shakespeare Carr, Durham's beloved merchant genius and philanthropist, was reelected Commander-in-Chief of the United Confederate Veterans by popular acclaim back in the summer of 1922 in Richmond.

Thousands lined the sidewalks through the main streets of Virginia's capital city and cheered and wept as long lines of old veterans passed in review to stirring music of the old South.

The parade was a beautiful and colorful three-hour spectacle on a friendly, sunny day, and the Richmond *News Leader* said that "More soldiers of the Confederacy were in line than will ever again assemble on earth."

The newspaper's 2-inch-high headline read: "Hearts Throb As Army Passes."

Dressed in their many-hued frocks, the maids and sponsors waving the Confederate colors stood out in bold contrast against the gray uniforms and gold braid of the veterans.

Some of the old soldiers, determined not to break the tradition of many reunions, refused to ride in automobiles and trudged along with springy steps.

When the veterans passed under the shadows of the Confederate memorials on Monument Avenue, their enthusiasm knew no restraint.

There stood their great leaders—Davis, Lee, Jackson, Stuart—as they had seen them in life, and they saluted them with cheers and the "Rebel yell."

Gen. Carr was given a great ovation along the line. The crowds made frenzied yells for the commander, and, bowing first on the one side and then on the other in his automobile, he danced about like a lad and seemed to enjoy the occasion to the utmost.

Fifteen bands enlivened the march with music and happiness shown in the countenances of the veterans, and they moved along afoot and by vehicle.

Medals from Confederate Veterans Reunions; top medal shows an image of Gen. Carr; bottom is from 1922 gathering in Richmond, Virginia.

As the applause and cheers rang out from the sidelines, they bowed and waved flags and hats in response. Occasionally they could be heard singing *Dixie*. It was the zenith of reunion glory.

At every railroad station trains had poured forth excited visitors, and almost at dawn truckloads of visitors began arriving. Offices and businesses closed, and Richmond became the mecca of the greatest reunion of Gen. Robert E. Lee's men. The streets were crowded as never before. Pretty young women rode in the cars with the veterans.

Gen. Carr, who two days earlier had stated that he would like to stand aside and give some other veterans the chance to hold the high command, was the choice of his old comrades for the coveted post.

Carr, who had the magic touch in advertising and promoting the sale of his famous Bull Durham smoking tobacco and cotton products, rode in a large, chauffeur-driven machine in the unforgettable parade.

The night before, the Texas delegation of Confederate Veterans gave a dinner at the Jefferson Hotel to their commander and to Virginia Gov. and Mrs. E. Lee Trinkle, a native of Texas.

Breaking the monotony of the long procession of cars in the parade, several hundred members of the Forest Cavalry brought unexpected thrills as they came trudging on with slow but unfaltering steps.

Another thrill was given by Tennessee companies, wearing their field equipment and carrying "War Between the States" muskets and gleaming bayonets.

A touch of pathos was added by the sight of an aged and bent warrior in full field equipment including a blanket and musket, supported along the line by a young woman.

Some infantrymen, called the "Blues," wore blue-and-white uniforms with helmets topped by white plumes.

The fifteen bands were spirited and each nattily dressed, all varieties of uniforms represented. the blue and red of the Coast Artillery, the dark green of the Marine Corps, the white of the Navy, the gray of the Augusta Eagles, the cadet gray of the Oklahoma Military Academy, the white of Mississippi, and Confederate gray.

Spanish-American War veterans also were on hand, carrying once-familiar single-starred flags of the baby republic of Cuba.

Richmond gave its heart to the old soldiers for sure, seeing to it that every man had free room and board at hotels and homes. Pride was strong and enduring with the Virginians.

Benches were placed along the street for the veterans to rest and chat, and Richmond Kiwanians pitched their service tent where free tobacco products, soft drinks and stationery and souvenirs were ready.

There were interesting sidelights at the gathering of the some 7,000 of Lee's boys.

A group of old-time fiddlers, one with only one arm, gathered in one corner of the Coliseum where activities were centered, and while a grand ball was in progress, they held a grand ball of their own.

There was no fox-trotting, no jazz-stepping and no varsity hopping. The old soldiers took a backward step of 50 years and enjoyed the Virginia Reel, the Quadrille and the old-fashion "Square," all with vigorous foot-patting.

They put as much pep in their steps as if they were seventeen instead of in their four-score years. *Turkey in the Straw* and *Down Went McGinty to the Bottom of the Sea* contrasted sharply with the strident tunes of *Angel Child*.

The grand march, stretched out, would have extended a mile. A dainty old lady in the octogenarian class led the dance parade.

There were famous long-distance walkers who had taken a month to reach Richmond from their hometowns, cavalrymen, artillerymen, infantrymen, sailors, and the ladies. All came to be a part of the reunion, including the fashionable inside march.

Many of the women wore the dress of the antebellum days, with its hoop-skirt and its whatchername peeping discreetly from beneath, and many wore the gowns of grandma's day, with powdered hair of the early Victorian era.

Rebel yells were heard in the hall when Gen. Carr and Gov. and Mrs. Trinkle and their staffs appeared.

Howard Divinity, a 91-year-old black former slave of Mississippi, was on hand to recall the time he was wounded as he assisted his seriously wounded master during action on a battlefield.

N. C. Dalton and bride from the Jefferson Davis Soldier's Home at Beauvoir, Miss. were present at the reunion. The groom was 80, and his bride was 78 and the widow of a Confederate veteran.

Before leaving Beauvoir, the last home of Jefferson Davis, the home superintendent received a special invitation from President Warren G. Harding to have the entire wedding party visit him in Washington.

The invitation was accepted and 100 old soldiers, their wives and widows visited the president at the White House.

During the reunion word came from Fairview, Ky. that the Jefferson Davis monument under construction there, when completed, would be the second-highest memorial in the world; at 351 feet in height, it was topped only by the Washington Monument.

A Georgia congressman, in an address before the Sons of Confederate Veterans, faced Gov. Trinkle and paid him this tribute: "He is as handsome as Apollo, as eloquent as Demosthenes and, thank God, as 'dry as a bone.' "

The governor blushed amid the laughter and applause.

Gen. Carr issued a proclamation calling upon the people of the South and the Sons and Daughters of the Confederacy to contribute liberally to the fund to maintain the Manassas Battlefield Park.

One of the oldest persons at the reunion was 90-year-old Milton Homes of Clinton, N.C., a black veteran who was attending his first reunion. He had stories to tell.

Probably the oldest veteran on hand was "Wild Car" Carter, a full-blooded Cherokee Indian of Montgomery, Ala., who was a scout with Forest's cavalry.

He said he had a son, a Cherokee chief in Oklahoma, who was 70. Carter said that he knew Gen. Sam Houston well and that he fought in the war of Texas independence and in the Mexican war.

Several of the old soldiers in one automobile displayed "Memories of a Lost Cause," in the shape of two empty champagne bottles supported by staffs.

Smiling women of the auxiliary groups made an attractive appearance in the parade.

One old veteran from North Carolina was heard to call out: "I've made marches ten times as long as this. Come on Tarheels, let's walk!"

During the reunion the *News Leader* carried an editorial entitled "Why Do the Veterans Come?"

In part it read: "The youngsters among them are 75; the reverent seniors are high in the 80s. They have come, in many instances, unescorted; from the Gulf states, from Texas, not a few from the Pacific coast.

"Many are so deaf they can find no pleasure in public meeting. Others are so bowed by infirmities that pain must be their constant companion. None of them can stand for long, and few can relish the excitement of the dinners, dances, luncheons and motor trips that make a reunion a delight of a Southern girl's life.

"Yet the veterans are here—some with the consent of their families and some despite the protests of their children. They may lose interest in everything else; they retain it in their annual convention.

"Why is it? Why do they come to a reunion when they would find the same trip dangerously exhausting if undertaken for any other purpose?

"There come times when to meet an old comrade is to read in his face the shortness of time. It is that the reunion, in typifying the Confederacy, represents the greatest force that ever entered the lives of those old soldiers. . . . "

Days later an editorial, in part, read: "Will the inspiration we men of today have received from contact with those 'gentlemen unafraid' be transmitted onwards century by century, or will it slowly disappear?

"As some agonized thus on Monument Avenue this morning, perhaps they looked up and saw Lee in bronze. He was reviewing more of his soldiers than ever again will pass before him on earth.

"In the calm majesty of his attitude toward them, there was reassurance. He was as proud of them as they were of him. He knew, as none did, what his soldiers were and what they had achieved.

"As early as 1863 he wrote John B. Hood, 'There were never such men in an army before.' "

15

Personal Reflections

Living in the past? I'm one of the guilty. I cherish it.

I miss the days of circus parades, tobacco warehouse auctions, and gawking at the old train station and its fascinating operations.

There was Durham's deepest snow, in March 1927—18 inches and 3- and 4-foot drifts.

The Great Depression saw many of us depending on such delectables as liver pudding, streak-of-lean pork, white beans, greens, corn bread, biscuits, and blackstrap molasses. I still like that food.

Papa was paid in scrip. Despite a big family, mama was a playground supervisor and teacher, put on benefit plays for the North Durham School PTA, held taffy pulls, and made tea cakes and lemonade for neighborhood children.

Meeting people and enjoying interviews with those from far and wide, right in my own town, has been a truly great pursuit. I have shared friendship with people I'll never see again, and realize how refreshing it is to talk with polite young people.

The best of times? That would be moments spent in the company of my own family. Next would be enjoying the presence of regular friends.

Reporter Remembers

Sounds I'll never forget:

The raucous bellow of the Bull Durham tobacco factory's whistle which blew early in the morning to summon employees. It awakened everyone within earshot.

The click-click of the roller coaster at the old Lakewood Park Amusement Center.

My mother, Mollie, calling to William Cody (Buffalo Bill), who was impressive with his long, white hair and beard and western frontier garb. His stage coach was moving west on Chapel Hill Street in front of the Mangum home (now the site of the post office) as a feature of the Wild West Show in the Ringling Brothers & Barnum & Bailey Circus parade. Buffalo Bill was tossing out Zuzu ginger snaps as an advertisement of the product. When my mother yelled to him he smiled and hurled a box of the ginger snaps, which she caught and gave to me. I was a proud little boy, even prouder of her.

The hoofbeats of Lindsey Faucett's gray horse as it pulled Trinity College students' trunks and suitcases up the cobblestones of Church Street from the old Union Train Station.

The downtown traffic signals at each change of stop and go. A bell would ring. The town's old prize fighters, on hearing the bell, would immediately assume a fighting stance, as if the bell were directing the contestants to the middle of the ring at the end of a round.

John Philip Sousa's "Stars and Stripes Forever" on the Victrola record every day of my years in the old North Durham Graded School.

Fireworks early Christmas morning. That was long before the state banned such pyrotechnics.

The singing of spirituals by the black workers in the Liggett & Myers stemmery along West Main Street.

Walter "Sheep" Lambe, with megaphone and bombastic voice calling out "baseball today, 4 o'clock, El Toro Park," as he walked down Main Street.

Ash against leather as "Dusty" Cooke, Tom Wolfe, Jack Lindley, and Fred Tauby, Durham Bulls baseball players, connected with fast ones and propelled the sphere over the distant fence of El Toro Park.

The labored grunting of Durham policemen and firemen involved in a tug-of-war at the same ball park.

The chug-a-rum and tweeting of frogs and squabs at my North Street homeplace when my brother Cherry was raising these then popular delectables for the dining rooms of the Malbourne Hotel and the Washington Duke Hotel.

The relentless piano playing by an elderly man and the whirr of stationary bicycle pedaling by Durham's Charlie Rigsbee as each tried to outlast the other in a strange duel in a vacant store building at downtown Five points.

The Ohs and Ahs of the crowd watching the "Human Fly" climbing the First National Bank Building. He'd make as if he were falling, then call to a confederate in a window of the building who handed him an Orange Crush drink, which he sipped for advertised vitality.

Frank "Don't sell it, Frank" Barfield, auctioning land and tobacco.

The disastrous kerplunk of a first baseman's glove that landed in a huge pot of simmering brunswick stew at a land sale along Avondale Drive, after being dropped from a low-flying airplane as a prize to those attending the sale.

The calliope of a circus parade, the roar of hungry lions and tigers, the snarl of the black cats, and the trumpeting of restless elephants as the circus unloaded early mornings in East Durham.

The deep and mellow "ho, ho, ho!" of Battle Wheeler, playing Santa Claus at a Main Street store when he wasn't doing his "end man" stint as a minstrel and attending to his professional blood donor duties.

Charlie Walters musically slapping his feet against the pavement in his rapid gait downtown.

The metallic clatter of silver dollars in the pockets of those who had just been paid by the tobacco factories.

The many "Heavenly Lights," disciples of Father Divine, clad in white and walking rapidly down Main Street, repeating, "The spirit of the Lord has told me to tell the world, that Jesus is soon to come."

Oscar Matthews, peering into downtown business establishments, shouting homemade Bible verses of admonishment.

Pud Lucas, shuffling and "cutting a step" for a cigarette or a nickel.

Randolph "Nurmi" Shears' footbeats as he hurried to a Duke Power Co. bus, briefcase in hand and always bareheaded and grinning and glancing at his pocket watch.

Mayor W. F. Carr, dapper and smiling, and accompanied by a large dog, passing out "good mornings" to fellow pedestrians and loafing old cronies along Main Street.

Ma Gregory at the baseball park, constantly yelling encouragement to Durham baseball players: "You're better'n he are!"

The inimitable Jesse Crawford, he of small stature, rendering the Blue Danube waltz on organ in the huge amphitheater on the lagoon of Lake Michigan at the Chicago World's Fair in 1934.

A peculiar thrashing on the creek mud bank near "Fourth Trestle" as a king snake bested a big black snake in a fight to the death.

Socialist party leader Norman Thomas' persuasive talk at El Toro Park.

M. P. "Footsie" Knight's booming commands during the calisthenics in the old YMCA at the corner of Main and Roxboro streets.

The hearty "come in" of E. B. Bugg, operator of the Malborne Hotel, as he bowed in his dining room guests.

The buzzing of trapped insects on flypaper in most Durham homes during summer months of yesteryear.

The hoarse barking of partly devocalized dogs in the tower of Duke Medical School.

My mother's solos in Durham churches.

The cackling of chickens in coops at Sneed N. Bett's chicken and egg store in the Banner Warehouse on Morgan Street.

The singing of red-haired Lucille Brown at Durham High School, she who later became an opera house favorite, under the perhaps more glamourized stage name of "Lucille Browning."

Icemen with picks, chipping off hunks of ice in their rounds of Durham neighborhoods on horsedrawn wagons.

The spugging of tops (sharpening the metal points of tops to great sharpness and splitting the rival's top with accurate and forceful spins in unique duels).

Backyard horseshoes against metal stakes, mallets cracking wooden balls in frontyard croquet.

The slurping of soup by hungry patrons at old man Adcock's cafe on Parrish Street.

Violin and piano concerts in the spacious backyard of the Mangum home (now the site of the Olde House Restaurant) on Chapel Hill Street at the Lakewood Park area, where Japanese lanterns were strung and homemade ice cream served.

Colonel Hartman Bunn's singing and the chanting and moaning of the men and women who handled copperheads and rattlesnakes during his special services in the Zion Tabernacle on East Peabody Street.

The bleachers falling at Durham Athletic Park and my mother injuring her back during a Durham High School football game in which my brother Cherry and I participated.

The threats and cajoling of "old lady Rochelle," barefoot and defiant, as she marched her cows along unpaved North Mangum Street at Little Five Points.

Fiery outbursts of evangelists Ham and Ramsey, Cyclone Mack, and Gypsy Smith in Durham revivals.

The sharp and eerie train whistles of trainmen serenading their lady loves late at night and early in the morning.

A talking parrot, rasping "Polly wanna cracker?" and "Go to hell" as it pranced in a cage at a house on the corner of Mangum and Hunt streets.

Amens and "praise the Lords" at baptisms in the Eno River.

Duke University chapel bells and singing at Easter sunrise services outside the chapel. Dr. James Cleland's Scotch brogue and puns from the pulpit of the chapel.

Incessant chatter at bingo games in Beth-El Synagogue at the corner of Queen and Holloway streets.

Fire Chief Frank Bennett singing "She's the Lass for Me."

Frank Warner Jr. leading campfire songs at the YMCA's Camp Sacarusa on the Eno River.

Shorty Peeler's chuckle and E. S. "Doc" Swindell's high-pitched, musical laughter.

The one-man bands, piano players, and rag-slapping shoeshine boys at Ike Lindsey's City News Stand.

Male and female prisoners screaming from the windows of the Durham County jail on the fourth floor of the courthouse.

Concerts in Durham's downtown bandstands by the Durham orchestra of which my father was a member.

Shuffling feet of square dancers on the second floor of a Parrish Street building.

A. R. Wilson, judge of Recorder's Court, pounding his gavel, and court crier Howard Martin's sing-song voice. Solicitors Bill Murdock and Dan Edwards' speeches to juries.

Music maestro W. P. Twaddell slapping his baton against a music stand at Durham High School.

The VPI band playing Dixie. UNC's bells after victory.

Billy Arthur and Kay Kyser leading cheers at football games at UNC.

The tremendous ovation when Duke's Ace Parker galloped 105 yards against UNC, and when Duke's Dick Groat scored 48 points against UNC in his last basketball game; the tumultuous raving when UNC bested the Blue Devils 50 to 0, and topped the University of Texas after losing the year before.

The sobs of the Durham County school superintendent, Wilmer Jenkins, behind his office door upon learning that President Franklin D. Roosevelt was dead.

The celebration along Main Street when World War II ended.

Army Gen. Mark Clark's dedication speech at the Durham YMCA.

Superior Court Judge Henry L. Stevens' flagwaving tirade upon a college youth charged with distributing the Stockholm Petition.

The whirr of blades of overhead fans in Durham's old drug stores.

The ruffling of dresses when women wore several petticoats. The lapping of water by mules and horses at troughs in downtown Durham, the flutter of funeral home hand fans in steaming churches.

The muffled drums during the funeral procession for President John Kennedy.

Orson Welles' shocking series of alarming announcements on the radio program of H. G. Wells' "War of the Worlds," which terrified the nation.

Pleas to the jury by Willie Cates and Willie Benton, Durham painters whose argumentative eloquence in their own behalf swayed countless juries to render "not guiltys" despite evidence to the contrary.

Benny Cash's piano playing and Bennett Edwards' rich voice.

Press runs of our newspapers, and The Lord's Prayer delivered by Dr. Oswald Hoffman.

Some Things

Things I'll long remember:

Superior Court Judge John Burney chewing tobacco and eating peanuts at the same time.

Boarding houses along downtown Main Street.

"Buttermilk Crossing," an East Durham intersection so called because a horse shied, resulting in jars of buttermilk being thrown from a wagon onto the street.

Complaints about the bull's private parts being exposed on the huge Bull Durham smoking tobacco sign atop the American Tobacco Co. plant.

The office building of Liggett & Myers being moved from the south to the north side of Main Street on giant rollers while the office staff worked right on.

Lakewood Park, Erwin Park, Crystal Lake, Oak Grove Park, all in Durham.

The "Petrified Siberian Giant," on exhibition on a truck body at the southeast corner of Main and Roxboro streets.

The man "buried alive" at downtown Five Points in front of the old Central Lunch Cafe. It cost a dime to peer down through a hole to see him.

The pickled whale on exhibit along the railroad tracks near the Mangum Street crossing.

Old Jerry Markham, living in a white-washed railroad shack alongside the railroad tracks downtown; his aged white mule, cows, wagon, three dogs, and American and Confederate flags always flying making quite a sight.

Louis Blaylock, laboriously but enthusiastically playing beautiful old hymns on the chimes at Duke Memorial Methodist Church, lending a peaceful mid-day touch for miles around.

Big trucks hauling rock from the Nello Teer quarry on Denfield Street, and bounding along Roxboro Road, prompting a town wag to dub Roxboro Road "Nello Teer Boulevard."

Horse-drawn wagons hauling big steel cans filled with waste from the town privies, bringing yells from little boys holding their noses.

Fannie Hearst, author of "Back Street" and "Ice Palace," in an interview in the Bright Leaf Room of the Jack Tar Hotel, saying that while en route from Raleigh-Durham Airport to Durham she asked the airport taxi driver where her guests had booked her a room. "I thought he said Jack Paar Hotel. I told him I couldn't stand the s.o.b. Then he told me he had said the Jack Tar Hotel."

Being awarded a $2½ gold piece for making a talk on Durham High School art, at the Woman's Club at the corner of Buchanan Boulevard and Minerva Avenue.

Hitchhiking alone to the World's Fair in Chicago in 1934 in the hottest July in years, and going out to the Biograph Theater the day after Dillinger was killed by FBI Agent Melvin Purvis, and seeing a man selling, for 25 cents each, bits of white cloth, stained with the badman's blood on the walk.

My mother and sister Nell returning from a bus trip to New York and proudly showing their "best" souvenir, an autographed menu from Jack Dempsey's Restaurant.

Dr. Frank S. Hickman, dean of the Duke University Chapel, stopping every few yards on Main Street to chat, and his eloquent recitation of "Crossing the Bar" at the funeral of that beloved old lady, "Miss May" Hunter.

Victory S. Bryant's description of a buggy trip with his father to the railroad tracks in front of Trinity College, where President Teddy Roosevelt stretched a fifteen-minute stop to forty minutes as he warmed up to the cheering students.

Dr. Chancie D. Barclift, after his noteless, long prayer at the funeral services of Gov. William B. Umstead, repeating it word for word for the benefit of astonished newspapermen, including punctuation marks.

Metropolitan Opera tenor Jan Peerce giving a concert at the University of North Carolina where his son attended then returning the check to the school.

A nationally known radio commentator having his pocket picked as he dozed away at the bus station here.

Oldtimers telling me how much they enjoyed the barbecues cooked for big political rallies at the edge of town by my grandfather.

Our family washing locusts and persimmons and straw for the locust and persimmon beer my father made in the late fall or early winter. He used empty molasses barrels he obtained at a grocery store.

Schoolteacher R. N. Nycum's beehives at the rear of his home on west Markham Avenue.

My bicycle trips to Raleigh and elsewhere with Dan Edwards, Lyon Few, John Nycum and Conrad Plyler.

Lynn Few's luncheon speeches at Woman's College, substituting for his father, Trinity College President W. P. Few, Lynn was in high school.

Old man Dick Wright driving slowly along downtown streets in his Stanley Steamer car, which always looked as if it were going backward. Folks seeing him would invariably ask, "Is it true that he owns diamond mines in Kimberly, Africa?"

Crazy rumors that a nudist colony was being operated at Crystal Lake by the new owners, heirs-to-be of a fortune.

The time a well-known band leader, upon learning that an Air Corps colonel had leaped to his death from the "nerve" ward at Fitzsimons Hospital in Denver, jumped out the same window, breaking both legs but triumphantly bragging while he lay on the ground, "See, it didn't kill me."

Duke medical school Prof. George Eadie proving by scientific instruments what he already knew, that beer and ale are more cooling than ice water, tea, lemonade, and soft drinks.

A Raleigh woman arguing her own malpractice suit in Superior Court and falling dead before the bench of Judge Raymond B. Mallard, who earlier had said that just about everything had happened in his court except somebody dying.

Frank Toy, cook at the Oriental Restaurant, often added a teapot of Scotch when his friends ordered Chinese food.

Mrs. Der Wo, smiling sadly and giving away food, dishware, and cooking utensils when urban renewal forced her to vacate the Oriental on Parrish Street.

An amicable deaf mute minister, Roma Fortune, being greatly amused when pipe organ companies mailed him catalogs for his new church.

Catholic Father O'Brien, consoling, scolding, cheering and berating, praising and admonishing, but always the good shepherd and friend.

Sheriff "Cat" Belvin, holding aloft between two fingers a lighted cigarette, his gesture reminding one of a hunter sighting down a rifle.

A partly drunk man with blood and sweat trickling from deep scratches on his bald head, and holding by the tail a dead cat, going to the health department, telling Health Director J. H. Epperson that he thought the cat was rabid when it jumped on his head in his smokehouse and refused to let go. He choked it to death. "I hate to tell you, Doc, but it hurt so much I had to take a drink," he said. Epperson said he understood. The cat was found to be rabid so Epperson obtained the necessary serum for the appreciative victim.

Willis Holmes Jr., in a command performance, whistling the "Wabash Cannonball" in Recorder's Court before Judge Bus Borland.

Ladybird Johnson telling her daughter Lynda to quit chewing gum as the Ladybird Special train halted in Durham in early morning so she and Gov. Luther Hodges could make speeches in behalf of Lyndon Johnson.

Lord Franks of London, an executive officer of Burroughs-Wellcome, walking with a limp at the dedication of the firm's research headquarters in the Research Triangle Park, and saying, "Damn gout!" He didn't realize that his firm had produced a remedy, Zyloprium.

Papa George . . . An Unforgettable Man

I remember Papa. An unforgettably honest, witty, and kind fellow who never found time to complain.

At 15 he became an employee of Seeman Printery, and at 84 while in his 69th year there and the foreman of bookbindery, he died of a heart attack.

Papa was never an old man. His job was one of standing, not sitting, and he preferred walking. He never owned or wanted a car. When he left us in July he had already purchased his Duke football tickets for the 1955 season and was following professional baseball with a keen insight.

I was named after Papa George, just like he was after Grandpa George, who moved with his family in 1875 from Raleigh where he owned a tin shop. Grandpa made bullets for the Confederate Army during the Civil War.

The original homeplace in Durham was on the southwest corner of Church and Parrish Streets, right where Montaldo's was to locate later. The old well remains intact in the building, but is capped.

George E. Lougee II, father of the author.

Papa loved music, and a couple of years after joining Seeman's he became the youngest member of Durham's band and then the orchestra. He played the drums, bass and snare, and handled all of the sound effects gadgets, like the steamboat whistle, the siren, the train whistle, hoof beats, baby cries, etc.

Papa played for the road shows that came to the old Academy of Music, for silent movies and for dances, often at old Lakewood Park. I remember a marathon dance at Lakewood where for prizes the dancers would cling to each other for hour after hour until they fell asleep or fell exhausted.

Freeman Gosden, an endman for one of the minstral shows passing through, told Papa that he was looking to quit and form his own two-man blackface skit if he could find the right partner. Papa said that was a coincidence because a member of another minstral in town had said the same thing. Papa then introduced Gosden to Charles Correll of Chicago, and that was how the Amos and Andy team met. Papa said it was no big deal—anyone could have introduced them.

There were bandstands in Durham where the band gave concerts. They included stands at the mouth of Orange Street, at Chapel Hill Street, and back of the old city market (the site of the present Civic Center) at Morgan Street.

Papa was also a volunteer fireman in the old days and during the great fire of 1914 when most of Durham's business area burned, he suffered a badly cut hand. Papa had fireman's insurance and paid $1.10 every time a fireman died in North Carolina. An insurance official said that at the time of his death Papa had paid more money and longer into the fund than anyone else in the state.

Papa was 28 when he married Mollie Graham Malone, a telephone operator who was born in Danville.

I remember when Papa made the world's largest book which was placed on a Liggett & Myers hogshead truck and hauled along Main Street in a parade.

Papa loved martial music and more than once expressed regret that college bands had forsaken the marches of such dandies as John Philip Sousa when the bands performed during football games.

Papa was always a great Duke fan, but unlike me, never made excuses when the Blue Devils went down to defeat.

When Seeman Printery was on Corcoran Street near the railroad tracks, Papa knew a lot of trainmen and freight haulers. Now and then merchandise was damaged in shipment or highly perishable food had to be moved out in a hurry. So, sometimes Papa would come home with a bunch of bananas and smashed kegs of salt herring and raspberry jelly used in doughnuts.

We had a big family, but the neighbors had to help us eat the stuff.

People ate a big breakfast in those days and once Papa bought a farmer's entire wagonload of 30 chickens when the farmer became ill en route to town. Of course the chickens were complete with feathers and cackles, and for once we kids got enough fried chicken.

Papa was an artist with genuine leather and goldleaf, and some of the ledgers and other books he bound for the county remain in use.

In the old days baseball was the big sport, and Papa like a lot of other fans often went on train excursions to nearby towns to follow the Durham Bulls.

Papa knew Will Rogers, having met him when he performed on the stage. Rogers came to Durham occasionally and always visited the "rum room" at the American Tobacco Company where the Bull Durham tobacco was flavored. The humorist would hold up his head and sniff the air.

Papa once related that a nasty-tempered storekeeper in East Durham became so disagreeable that after he closed his grocery for the day, a few rowdies encircled the store with a big chain and hooked the chain to a west-bound freight train. The store building fell to pieces bit by bit.

In the winter Papa usually made a barrel or two of locust and persimmon beer on our back porch. He was given empty molasses barrels by friends, and the beer was free to anyone who cared to come by for it. Papa was a teetotaler except for a glass of the beer and an eggnog which Mama made on Christmas mornings.

As much as Papa liked fly fishing, he preferred a visit to the seashore to take in the sun, salt air, and salt water taffy. Once on such a visit Papa had a toothache, so he went to nearby Norfolk where he said he paid 50 cents to an advertised "painless dentist" to have the hurting tooth pulled out with pliers.

Papa once made us a large box kite in which he attached a kerosene oil lantern before sending the lantern aloft. He didn't light the lantern, explaining that "there are too many houses with wooden shingles now." That was the first and last box kite I ever saw. Papa used to tell us not to forget 1985, because that was when Halley's comet would return. He said it came every 75 years and that he and Mama wouldn't ever see it again.

Papa loved hard straw hats in the summer and those detachable shirt collars and gold cuff links. We were glad he didn't like spats and canes that some of the dudes twirled as they walked.

Papa liked the old-fashioned shaving mug and the cake of shaving soap, and witch hazel and bay rum aftershave. He was always clean-shaven and never was able to get Grandpa to cleave off all of his face foliage.

Papa had two brothers, Will and Virginius, and a sister, Nellie. They were a pretty tight-knit group as long as they lived. Uncle Virginius and Papa settled a lot of the world's problems sitting in porch chairs. I can hear them laughing now.

Before his first and last heart attack, Papa told me one day, that he wanted to go before Mama because he didn't want to die of a broken heart. Mama died nine weeks after Papa left us.

Sure, I remember Papa, and not just on Father's Day.

He Has Never Forgotten Mama; How Could He?

I remember Mama. Not only on Mother's Day, but every day I remember Mama.

Mollie Malone was orphaned at childhood when her young parents, Charles and Amanda Wilson Malone of Danville, Va., died of pneumonia. Friends sent Mollie to Baltimore where arrangements were made for her to be cared for and educated by the gentle sisters of a Catholic church. As a teenager Mollie trained as a telephone operator, and then came to Durham where job opportunities were more available.

Mollie Malone Lougee, mother of the author.

Papa, George Lougee Jr., who was a bookbinder at Seeman Printery, one day met and fell in love with the pretty, honey blonde telephone operator. He was 28 and she 19, when they married in Durham.

Their first child, William, died as a baby, and Mama always loved Lena Turner Borland for making a new dress for little William to be buried in.

Mama and Papa at first lived in his father's large home on Broadway Street, and later Papa built a one-story home on adjacent North Street, next door to that of Uncle Virginius Lougee and Aunt Mary.

Mama had four more sons: Edgar, Sam, Will ("Cherry"), and George III, before having her only daughter, Nell. Then came two more sons, Henry and Bobby.

Mama was expectant with Nell when she fell from a chair while adjusting a window curtain. The fall resulted in premature birth and injury to Nell, who as an incubator baby was so small she was fed from a medicine dropper and did not even fill a shoe box.

Doctors said Nell would never make it, but Mama knew better. She insisted that through love and care and God's help, Nell would survive. And so she did. She confounded the doctors by living more than 50 years.

When Grandma Lougee died, Grandpa, who years before in his tin shop and hardware at Raleigh made bullets for the Confederacy during the Civil War, moved in with us. Mama would have it no other way.

Meanwhile, our home had been renovated into a two-story house and Grandpa had his own room. Grandpa was hard of hearing and had poor sight, but Mama saw to it that he attended as long as he was able reunions of the old Confederate army boys when they were held at Lakewood Park here.

Mama always made a cake and had a little family party for Grandpa on his birthdays. He lived until 86, and everyone knew that it was Mama's loving care that gave him his longevity.

Mama entered Nell in a Durham Catholic school, never forgetting the kindness and dedication of the Catholic sisters to her in childhood.

Mama had a great sense of humor, and one day in a hurry to do some downtown shopping, she put her dress on wrongside out. She said later that everyone seemed to smile at her as she shopped. Then she realized it was her dress. "It didn't really bother me, it was so nice to see people smiling everywhere I went."

During the summers Mama would spread pallets on the floor for us children to take a nap. She'd offer a nickel for the first one going to sleep. It was good psychology, but of course there were differences of opinion as to the prize winner.

During school vacation days, Mama made pitchers of lemonade and those large, flat, delightful teacakes. Neighborhood children as well as others made themselves at home during such occasions. Neighbors jokingly said that Mama ran a rescue mission.

Mama also had a lot of black friends on nearby Corporation Street, and went to bat for them in times of need, like during the Great Depression.

While Bobby was a boy Mama wrote a series of stories, "Bobbie in Dreamland," after taking a correspondence course in writing.

Mama said she learned to cook from Grandma Lougee, and that at first Papa would go by Grandma's to get a snack. Grandma put a quick stop to that. Papa never complained, he bragged about Mama's cooking which kept getting better.

To help out with expenses Mama worked as a sales representative for such businesses as Durham Gas Co., Corley Music Store, and Larkin Products. Later she ran a nursery.

We didn't know how she did it, but she was also active in the PTA of North Durham Graded School, and staged minstrel shows, marionette shows, and even a womanless wedding, to raise money for the school.

As her children grew older, Mama took a job with the City Recreation Department as summer playground director, first undergoing first-aid training at the Red Cross.

On the playgrounds she taught the children sewing, basket weaving, clay art, catching and framing butterflies and flowers, how to make jumping jacks, and cut out a string of paper dolls.

Mama sometimes invited "her" playground children to our home where she'd make a big batch of taffy candy on a slab of marble and give each child a hunk to "pull."

On May Day the schools always had Maypole dances and children in the dances would wear varied and colorful crepe paper costumes. Mama made a redbird costume for me once, and while the citywide program was going on at Erwin Mills playground it began to rain. My costume began to run and it looked like I was bleeding. Mama said we needed the rain.

Mama and Nell once took a bus trip to New York City, and when they returned they said that what they had enjoyed most was visiting Jack Dempsey's Restaurant and having him sit down and chat with them. They were even proud of the menu he autographed.

Mama once took me to the State Fair, and at a sideshow a blindfolded man was calling out names and identifying objects. He spoke out and said in the crowded place: "There is a lady in a green dress holding the hand of a little boy. Is your name Lollie?" he asked. Mama answered "No." "Then it is Mollie," he said. Then he began to give the names and color of several objects in Mama's handbag.

This kind of shook up Mama. She later saw Wallace Lee, "the magician," in Durham, a family friend, but that couldn't satisfactorily explain how it was done.

Mama and Mrs. Hubert O'Briant, a neighbor, once went to Durham Athletic Park to see Durham High School play football. My brother "Cherry" and I were playing when the third-base bleachers at the park suddenly gave way from an enthusiastic, foot stomping throng of students and parents.

Mama suffered a severe back injury. Prior to that she was singing solos at Methodist churches of the city, but after the fall her voice was never the same. She had no trouble walking, however.

I loved the church songs that Mama sung, but I confess I enjoyed most her renditions of Irish ballads and *Won't you come home Bill Bailey?*

Mama would get me to pick out her library books. She said she liked them all, but I wonder.

Papa once bought two vacant lots in front of our home on North Street. The auctioneers of the property were the well-known Penny brothers, who wore tall, black, silk hats, and long spike-tail coats, and stood back to back as they gave their spiel.

Mama induced Papa to plant the lots with peanuts so that all of the neighborhood children could enjoy them.

Mama loved Trinity Methodist Church, and she had it arranged that if I were born on Sunday my name would be placed on the church's Cradle Roll. And so it was, when I was just 20 minutes old.

Mama saw to it that there were no favorites in our family, even though she had us to understand that Papa was the head of the house. Mama so loved the neighborhood children that we couldn't help but be jealous now and then.

Mama once won a lucky drawing at the Durham Merchants Association's Exposition held in a tobacco warehouse on Rigsbee Avenue. The prize, strangely, was a crate of Budweiser beer.

Now Papa drank only an eggnog on Christmas morning. The older sons had left home, and Henry and Bobby were young.

"What shall I do with this stuff?" Mama asked me. "Return it or will you give it away to someone?" I told her I'd give it to someone who liked beer. And I did, to some extent.

Papa was still working at 84 when he had a heart attack and died while preparing to go for a checkup by Dr. Joe MacCracken. Papa had told me sometime before that he wanted to die before Mama.

But I never considered him to be an old man. He always walked to and from work, stood on his feet while working, and always attended the home games of the Durham Bulls baseball team and the Duke football team.

Mama never fully recovered from Papa's death. Nine weeks after his funeral, she too was gone, just a few hours after I had left her side when she insisted with a smile that she was all right.

Forget Mama? Can you forget to breathe? Yes, I'll always remember Mama.

Early Durham Recalled from 'Pine Needles'

Mrs. Rosa Lyon Belvin, 89, the granddaughter of William J. "Billy" Duke, who founded Methodism in this area, remembers the first automobile and window screens in Durham.

She is the widow of Sheriff E. G. "Cat" Belvin, and lives at Pine Needles, her 38-year-old Colonial style home which nestles in a grove of pine trees on a 16-acre tract on Old Oxford Road at Catsburg.

"I named our home after my daughter Frances' school yearbook 'Pineneedles,' at Greensboro. My husband never did like the name. He said it sounded like a filling station," Mrs. Belvin said.

About a quarter of a mile to the east at the junction of Hamlin Road, is an old store-service station which for many years has carried a painting of a large cat on its front.

"My husband years ago built and operated the place. When he was a boy he was so small they called him 'Kitten,' but as he grew older he was given the name 'Cat,' " Mrs. Belvin said.

Sheriff Belvin loved baseball and about 40 years ago built a grandstand on a tract opposite his store in Catsburg. He had already laid out a diamond.

"He never charged a cent for anybody to play ball on the field, and since his death in 1963, the two-acre tract has been leased out to a recreation club for $1 a year. The club installed lights and they play baseball and football in daytime and at night," Mrs. Belvin said.

Asked about the name Catsburg, she laughed. "Lawyer Guthrie many years ago said that the store ought to be named after my husband, and that a cat should be painted on the front. There were few houses in the community so Mr. Guthrie said the area was Catsburg, and the community has always retained the title."

Mrs. Belvin was born on Duke Lane Road and the homeplace, which has been well preserved, still stands. "There were nine of us children and we inherited the farm from our mother. I later bought out the shares of the others, and now I am the sole member of my family still living," she said. "My grandfather was the oldest brother of Washington Duke."

Two of Mrs. Belvin's uncles, brothers of her mother, were killed in battle during the Civil War. One was a physician.

"I went to the two-room Duke Chapel School in the community. We always walked to school but on some bad weather days we'd ride the buggy," she said.

Mrs. Belvin has saved one of her report cards for the school term ending December, 1899, when she was 14. Her grades were: Grammar, 98; Geography, 97; History, 96; Lockwood's English, 92; Latin, 97; Composition, 90; Arithmetic, 95; Spelling, 99; Defining, 95; and Deportment, 100.

"I was too lazy to get anything but 100 on deportment," she laughed.

"All nine of us children but one were christened at infancy. Sometimes the preacher stayed overnight and the christening took place at home before going to church. To me, it was one of the most sacred of our rituals."

Mrs. Belvin remembers Duke's Chapel Church as far back as 1888. She said all Sunday School classes were held in the sanctuary.

"There were few attractions and the young folk looked to Sunday and the social life, when parlors would be crowded with boys and girls. The time was passed in singing around the organ and in conversation, this resulting in many neighborhood marriages," she said.

When the preacher went home with members of the church to spend the night, the best linens and silver, saved for the occasion, were brought out. Before going to bed, the family Bible was brought in and all the family called in for prayer. This was repeated the following morning before breakfast.

Mrs. Belvin recalls "Miss Bob Greene" who she said walked more miles to church than any other five persons in it. "She was stone deaf but a splendid lip reader," she said. "She read her Bible continuously and prayed without ceasing.

To walk from Durham to Duke's Chapel was all in the day's work to 'Miss Bob.' "

Chuckling, Mrs. Belvin recalled the Rev. Twilley who didn't mince words when it came to his salary from the church. "I shall never forget how red his face, extended up into his bald head, when he said, 'I can't live on it, God knows I can't.' He didn't stay with us long."

In 1910 Mrs. Belvin moved her membership to Trinity Methodist Church in town but she never lost contact with Duke's Chapel.

One year after returning from a children's day program in the rural church, she wrote B. N. Duke and told him that while the Dukes were giving vast sums of money to other churches, Duke's Chapel, the first church or public building to bear the Duke name, was being sadly neglected.

Duke later sent Prof. Robert Flowers out to Duke's Chapel to investigate, and that resulted in the present stone structure, "with the understanding that the church be used as a training center for Duke University ministerial students."

Mrs. Belvin recalls seeing the first bicycle when two of her cousins came out riding it. "One wheel was about four-foot tall and the other was real small."

Evangelists of wide fame came to Durham years ago and she remembers going to a meeting in a warehouse on Mangum Street. "There were two tiers of seats. People for miles around piled into buggies, wagons, and surreys to attend the services. Billy Graham had nothing on Sam Jones, and I believe his influence is still being felt," Mrs. Belvin said.

After she married Cat Belvin, they built a little home on Roxboro Road in Bragtown, which at the time was considered to be country settlement a long way from town. "When my husband went to work as a deputy sheriff under Sheriff John Harward, we moved into town and sold the house and two acres of land for $1,400," she said.

"This home was in front of what is now the Bragtown Post Office, and we had the first window screens in the entire community. We needed them, too, because there was a slaughter house in the area," Mrs. Belvin said. "Our home was also the first out there to have electric lights."

Mrs. Belvin recalls that she was attending Trinity College in 1902 when "there was quite a stir in the Woman's Building" when the first automobile came to Durham.

She said the "contraption" was built by Will Bryan and George Lyon, young Durham sportsmen, and everybody yelled to see the automobile travel around the school race track at the blinding speed of about 15 miles per hour.

"About this time too the electric trolley came to Durham and it was really a lifesaver because it was a means of introducing to Durham that never-to-be-forgotten Lakewood Park, often referred to as 'The Coney Island of the South,' " Mrs. Belvin said. "The park, whose sites is now that of Lakewood Shopping Center, had a dance pavillion, a skating rink, a roller coaster, a casino, bowling alley, swimming pool, and shooting gallery."

Mrs. Belvin said C. P. Howerton had a buggy shop on Mangum Street and Dick Howerton was the only undertaker in town. "He handled the services and also did the singing. His son by the same name was to handle the services and do the singing years later."

Mrs. Belvin said the first woman to own and drive a car in North Carolina was Miss Sallie Holloway, who later became Mrs. J. D. Patterson and lived in Greensboro.

"Miss Sallie was also the first woman to work in the Durham Post Office under civil service. Her home was located on the site now housing the Durham city and county school administrative offices. Chapel Hill Street was known then as Green Street," Mrs. Belvin said.

Mrs. Patterson's daughter Carmen, who was to become Mrs. Harold Bobo, was the first woman in North Carolina to pilot a plane, Mrs. Belvin said.

In the fall of 1905 the school at Mt. Hebron burned down and a new school was built farther out on Roxboro Road, in front of Cathelwood Farm, Mrs. Belvin said.

"I followed Miss Cora Malone and was the first and only teacher. I taught all the way from the first to the eighth grade and each class averaged 35 pupils," she said. "Don't ask me how."

Around this time prohibition was the hot political issue. It was hard fought but won out, and bootleggers quickly appeared on the scene, Mrs. Belvin said. "Morals can't be legislated, but can be instilled."

Also about 1905 Durham got its first health officer, Dr. Thomas Mann, whose first job was to eliminate the householders' practice of dumping their kitchen sink drainage into their backyards. He also banned pig pens from the town, she said.

"There were really loud howls about this, but Dr. Mann did it," she said. "Typhoid was rampant and vaccinations were given to fight it. Smallpox became prevalent and victims were required to go to 'pest houses,' " Mrs. Belvin said.

She recalled that a man named Mr. Brown, "a Yankee who had survived smallpox, was hired by the town to go ahead of those with the dreaded disease and to shout, 'Smallpox! Close your doors!' "

"In the early part of the century appendicitis made its appearance. Dr. N. M. Johnson was about the only surgeon in Durham and he often operated by lamplight on the kitchen table. Then Mr. George Watts came to Durham and built a hospital," Mrs. Belvin said.

At 89, She Can Drive and Has Her Memories

Ada Louise Yarbrough Leach went to the driver's license bureau Wednesday, on her birthday, apprehensive that she wouldn't pass the test. She thought it would take two or three tries at least to get a license to drive her secondhand Cadillac.

To her surprise and jubilation, she made it the first time, being cheered on by the examiner who was hard put to believe she was 89.

"I am restricted to driving during the daytime at just 40 miles an hour, but that's completely satisfactory to me," she beamed. "Fact is, I just drive to church, shopping occasionally, and once in a while to Chapel Hill or Raleigh where they have four-lanes."

Mrs. Leach, a widow for 25 years, lives in an apartment at Oldham Towers "where I have a good home and good friends."

She was born in Raleigh in 1884, and her father was head waiter at the old Yarbrough Hotel, a noted hostelry in those days.

"I was a little baby when my father and mother moved to Durham to work in the home of Washington Duke. The home was a mansion called Fairview and it was quite a place," she said.

She can remember when her mother would put irons in the big fireplace to heat, and then press Duke's high, stiff collars.

"Mr. Ben Duke, Mr. Washington's son, once gave my father a handsome Prince Albert suit and a tall beaver hat. My father cut a pretty fancy figure too and he was immediately recognized as the best-dressed man in the Calvary Baptist Church," she said.

Brodie Duke, a brother, lived in a spacious house on the site of the present Home Economics Cottage of Durham High School.

"I remember there was a little private lake with lots of goldfish at his home," said Mrs. Leach. "Little Mary and Angier, Ben Duke's children, and the Lyon children, they were all sweet people, liked to play about the grounds. One day we got into a boat at the lake and started paddling around when we saw what appeared to be a board floating in the water. Suddenly, the log opened its mouth and we saw a lot of mean-looking teeth. We got away from there in a hurry. Later, we learned that one of the Dukes had placed an alligator in the lake. I never did learn whether or not it was done for the purpose of keeping the children away."

Mrs. Leach said that as a child she attended Whitted School and then the Chatauqua, a school that later had its name changed to the National Religious Training School, a prep school. "I recall that Dr. James E. Shepard who headed this school, would have Gen. Julian S. Carr come and make talks. He was a very congenial, interesting man."

Later the state took over the school and the name was changed to North Carolina College for Negroes. Years later the name was altered to North Carolina College. And then about a score of years later it was changed to North Carolina Central University.

"It was through Dr. Shepard that I received my education, training which was to equip me to teach school," she said.

Asked how she met her husband, William, Mrs. Leach smiled. "We were both visiting at a Baptist church in Durham. At the time Will was an orderly at the old Watts Hospital at the corner of Main Street and Buchanan Boulevard. I was working and going to school.

Several months later the couple married. Mrs. Leach recalls every detail of the incident. "It was a rainy day. A man named Allen Green, a barber friend of Will's, came to my mother's home for us in a two-horse carriage. We rode to a private home for the ceremony and when we got out of the carriage the sun was shining and music was being played. That was in April 1905. And I remember that the house was decorated with lilacs, snowballs, and spirea."

She said she was only 17 and in order to get married her age had to be listed as 18 on the license. "Will was about 19 and they had to put 21 for him."

Will and Ada Leach had two children. Their son, William Jr., who lived in Washington, died of illness the day before President John F. Kennedy was assassinated. "I was there waiting for the funeral when the news came on television. I won't forget it," she said. "Will Jr. left two children."

A daughter, Sadie Ruth Leach, died when she was only 4.

Mrs. Leach's husband had 46 years of service with Durham Traction Co. and Duke Power Co. when he died while employed as an elevator operator.

"He was a kind, sweet person who loved red roses. That's why I have red roses by his picture," she said, nodding toward a corner of her small, neat apartment on the second floor of Oldham Towers.

Years after Will Leach died the urban renewal program bought the family's home on Fayetteville Street. "It was hard giving up our little home where we had worked, toiled, shed tears, and sacrificed to own it. We had won first prize in a garden show with our rose garden and of course, this had to be lost. But I asked the good Lord to help me accept the situation and He did," she said.

On Wednesday Mrs. Leach opened her door to a knock and in came fellow residents. Amid singing of "Happy Birthday" a neighbor presented a birthday cake with five candles she had baked.

Sunday at White Rock Baptist Church where Mrs. Leach is a member, a soloist sang in her honor, "Oh Divine Redeemer."

"I am happy all of the time, even when 'Arthur' visits me," she said. " 'Arthur' is arthritis. That's what we call it."

On Nov. 20, for the 4th anniversary of Oldham Towers, Mrs. Leach wrote a poem entitled "God Bless Oldham Towers." It is to the tune of God Bless America.

The poem goes like this: "Oh God, we thank Thee for Oldham Towers. Stand beside it and protect it with your love from the heavens above. Yes, Lord, we thank Thee for giving us this home and for the friend (Carvie Oldham) who designed it for the senior citizen." Chorus: "From the ground floor to the four walls, to the seventh floor, and every room, God bless Oldham Towers, Our home, sweet home. God bless Oldham Towers, Our home, sweet home."

She Recalls 'More Gracious' Durham a Long Time Ago

The elderly lady is retired. She feels that the use of her name would smack of notoriety; so she prefers to be anonymous.

But she likes to recall the Durham of yesterday, which she said was "more interesting and more gracious."

She recalls that an old Mr. Leathers owned the land now occupied by Central YMCA on West Trinity Avenue and used it as a peach orchard.

"At the turn of the 20th century I recall that as a little girl he always gave me fresh peaches in season. The grown folks had to pay for them."

Southgate Jones first lived on West Chapel Hill Street near where King's Business College is now, and his little cottage later was moved to the site of what is now Central Carolina Bank's operation center on Morris Street, she said.

Asked about horse-drawn streetcars, she laughed. "They were really something," she said. "The depot was located at the corner of Morgan and Morris streets, about where the Duke Power Co. bus depot is now located."

Before the Imperial Tobacco Co. building was built on Morris Street between Morgan Street and Fernway Avenue (now occupied by several business firms), Imperial had a small wooden building on this site. The building later burned.

Imperial's first machinist, a man named Ausley, was a friend of all the children in the neighborhood. He worked in the boiler room, but he often left his work to chat with the neighborhood children who entertained themselves romping about the adjacent pine woods.

In the backyard of Ben Duke's home, later to be known as Four Acres, at Chapel Hill and Duke streets between Willard and Jackson, there was a private school with about 10 children. The teacher was a Mrs. Sneed. From there the children went to nearby Morehead School, no longer in existence. The pupils rode to school in horse-drawn buggies.

Billy Crabtree, a stubby fat man who surprisingly could chase down thieves, was the chief of police. He was also employed at the Durham City Market, then located where the Union Train Station was built in 1905. Crabtree used a broom to discourage dogs from snatching at fresh meat, beef, pork, and game.

Orange Street, the narrow alley running between Chapel Hill and Parrish streets, obtained its name from a group of mock orange trees that grew in the immediate area.

Farmers bringing tobacco into Durham always watered their horses and mules at a huge trough at downtown Five Points, at Main and Morris streets.

Proctor's barroom was at the spot now occupied by Eckerd's on Main Street. Other saloons were scattered about the downtown area, with perhaps the most popular alcohol oasis, Happy Patty's Place, being located at 113 S. Mangum St.

A man named Pope built and operated the Waverly Ice Cream Co. on Holland Street. "Old Man" Baer from Baltimore established the Durham Ice Cream Co at Main and Duke Streets. His Rumkist ice cream, containing real rum, was a popular item until North Carolina law told him to concentrate on vanilla, chocolate, strawberry, and tutti-fruit, leaving out the alcohol. The City Ice Cream Co. at Five Points had the richest ice cream in town for years.

Jack and Herbert Barnett, little people often called dwarfs, gave Roxboro a place on the map when they joined the Ringling Brothers circus.

Loch Lilly, a popular water hole in Roxboro, was originally named Barnett's Pond.

Sam Jones, a great evangelist who today would rival Billy Graham, had an outstanding singing master named Green. He was given the initials XL, short for excellent. Jones, so it was said, was a penetrating fire-and-brimstone orator who could get at the roots of one's emotions.

In the old days women dipped snuff. Railroad Mills was the popular brand, and a lot of folks used a sprig from a sweetgum tree to convey the snuff to their jaws. Women didn't smoke cigarettes in public.

There was a graveyard right smack dab in the middle of East Main Street in the area now occupied by Oldham Towers.

Madame Elrado was Durham's first palmist, and she was popular because she could tell the women all about their secret thoughts.

Main Street downtown was first paved with cobblestones.

"Big Lou" ran a redlight district in East Durham. A handsome woman, she was about the most popular figure in town outside of the bartender, a blacksmith and the fellow who put on cockfights.

The Trinity Methodist Church steeple was the tallest point in the town.

When President Teddy Roosevelt came to Durham in 1908 and his private train stopped opposite old Trinity College on West Main Street, people from miles around came by buggy and wagon to hear the "Rough Rider" and "Trust Buster" speak.

The old freight station at Great Jones and Main streets, built in 1883, was first known as the Globe Warehouse and was operated by Lee Warren & Pope.

Covered wagons brought in tobacco to be weighed there. The old Fairbanks scales used was said to be as straight as a die.

Japanese or jack-o-lanterns were popular. Beautiful and very decorative, these collapsible illuminations were hung in backyard trees during watermelon slicings and lawn parties.

Box parties were also popular, usually held as benefits to raise money for churches. The gay blades always bought boxes from their sweethearts or girl whom they had a "crush on." These parties were extremely popular in Hillsborough and Roxboro.

Gilbert Kerner, of Kernersville, known as "Reuben Rink," became widely known when he painted the famous bull on the Bull Durham sign at American Tobacco Co.

The first time the old "Bull" whistle blew at the Bull Durham factory, the bellows frightened everybody within two miles.

At Christmas, American Tobacco Co. gave each of its male employees a jug of whisky and a turkey.

The wife of a prominent Durham businessman became outraged with her husband and advertised that she was going to throw her wedding ring into Eno River. And so she did.

The Fitzgeralds manufactured the first commercial brick in Durham; digging out and cooking the clay right where Wellons Village is located. A big sunken place near a parking lot at Wellons bears mute testimony to the bygone business.

Baptisms in creeks and rivers were popular, with singing groups on the banks and picnic lunches making the occasion quite an event.

Women kept diaries, jotting down their thoughts, rundowns on their courting ventures, records of funerals, and gossip. The diaries were usually hidden under the mattress, in an outhouse, a barn, or under a rock at the spring.

These, so my informer told me, were part of the good old days beyond recall.

Loves of Fab Page—Horse Races, Fairs

Fabius Haywood Page, 88, has three great loves: animals, horse races, and state fairs. Now, with failing eyesight and hearing, and with legs that threaten to give up the fight, the once rugged fellow consoles himself with memories and comradeship.

Better known as Fab, Page lives in a 53-year-old house on Page Road, "a short piece from the old homeplace" which rests on land his folks have owned for five generations. A widower—his wife Annie died four years ago—Page has a housekeeper and good neighbors, who see that he doesn't lack for company or anything else. And his needs are few.

The walls of the living room of his two-story, white frame house, are lined with photos and plaques of horses and mules.

About a mile from the rear of his home on a wooded hillside, is a cemetery where Page has buried six horses and four mules, old friends, indeed. At the graves are tall granite tombstones with eight having the inscriptions: "Ted, the fastest saddle horse. Had a white face. 1920-1945." "Kate, steel gray mule, very intelligent. 1902-1930." "Maud, brown mule, very gentle, 1906-1939." "Lulu, bay mule, very swift, 1902, age 28." "Dan, best of all 5-gaited saddle horses . . . erected by F. H. Page, owner of the animals he loved so well." "Bessie, driving mare, Brown, white face. 4 white feet, 1903-1937." "Starr, saddle and driving mare. Chestnut sorrel, white face, 1904-1939."

The graveyard is on land which the Raleigh-Durham Airport Authority has been looking at for its new runway.

At one time, Page said, he owned 334 acres, but Duke Power, Carolina Power and Light, and the City of Raleigh, took big hunks, leaving him with about 200 acres.

Page said that his great-grandfather, Obediah Page once owned "all the land from the Southern Railway to the airport. He distributed the property among his children." The Yankees, he said, "took everything but the land during the Civil War." Page said he deeded his cemetery property to his heirs in perpetuity so that it would be there after he is gone, unless destroyed by nature.

Asked why he decided to have a pet cemetery, Page said that when he was a boy of 9, he read a book called "Black Beauty," and it touched him. "I've always had great sympathy for horses and mules. We loved them so much. Our family used to trade them off when they got old, but I decided I was going to keep and bury my animals when they died."

Page was on hand in Louisville for 26 consecutive Kentucky Derbies, beginning in 1948. "I first started when the train was stopping at Nelson. Then they kept cutting off connections. I had to go anyway I could. The last time I caught the Seaboard in Raleigh. For about 20 years I made the trip alone, then I started taking my children and grandchildren." he said.

Shaking his head and frowning, Page said he never was "taken" by pickpockets until the last few years he went to the races, when he started walking with a cane.

"I remember once in Louisville I went into a store on Fourth Street to buy some of those detachable shirt collars," he said, "I think some crooks were watching me then. When I was getting on a bus to go to the races a fellow tripped up my legs. When I got to the race track and started to buy a ticket my wallet wasn't in my back pocket. He got the bulk of my money, all right, but I had some more cash in other pockets."

Page said this convinced him he should take travelers checks rather than money when he left home for the races.

"But those crooks are smart, they even got my travelers checks. But again, I had hidden some money in other pockets. Tickets didn't cost but $7 and $8 at first, but I have paid as high as $50 and $100 for a single ticket when I had to deal with scalpers," he said.

During the depression years things got real tough, and Page said he decided that transportation by horse was cheaper than buying gas for his Studebaker touring car.

"That was in 1931," he said. "I drove the car, it was a 1920 model, into a barn and it stayed there until 1965. Everybody came by and wanted to buy it. I'd knock them off by asking $500 for the car. One day a fellow came by and asked what I would take for the car. I told him $505. He said he had no money then but would come back."

"When he returned, he said his wife had the money but wouldn't let him have it. 'But I want it more than anything else in the world,' he insisted. He gave me $300 and a note for the balance. He let the car stay there for a long time before he came for it. Then he moved out of town. He was a college student, but I felt I could trust him. He paid me every penny and I was glad I took a chance with him."

Laughing, Page said he didn't start school until the fourth grade, because his mother was a school teacher and taught him at home.

Reminiscing, he said, "This ground was a big turnip patch before they built this house on it. I used to do quite a bit of fox hunting around here. I had all the good dogs I could get, about seven or eight blue ticks and black and tans, generally."

Retired Durham County game warden Marvin Ward who was sitting in, grinned. "He was also quite a squirrel and rabbit hunter, I recall," he said.

In the '20s Page went into the dairy business when he was 40. "We had 31 cows which were milked mostly by my wife, four daughters and one son," he said. "At first we hauled milk by horse and wagon to Nelson where it was picked up by Alamance truck and taken to Pine State in Raleigh. Then my brother, Hubert L. Page, who was also in the dairy business, hauled it in along with his milk."

Page said he had sold surplus grade A milk and hauled it to Nelson (where the train stopped) for as little as 8 cents a gallon. "It was a long ways to Raleigh because of the bad roads," he said. "When I drove into Durham and wanted to get there fast, I usually went by horse and buggy. Other times I went by wagon."

Asked what he did for excitement in his early days, Page chuckled, "I went to church. Well, I did like to go into town to see a silent movie. The shows at the Academy of Music were too high for me."

Page said he made pretty good money farming with tobacco and cotton, but that he had sold a crop of cotton for as low as 5 cents a pound and tobacco for as low as 3 cents a pound. "That was in the days of the depression," he said, "the time I parked the Studebaker. In 1935 I bought a Ford town sedan and drove it for 11 years before I sold it for $135," he said.

Page got out of the dairy business in 1963. His children were grown and gone, his wife had become ill, and good farm help was difficult to come by.

Asked when it was that he last drove a car, he grinned and said, "I've got a Chevrolet which is 27 years old and still runs like a top. I've also got a 1968 Cadillac. I believe I last drove about two years ago."

Back to the past, Page recalled that when he was a youth he was state fair happy, attending practically all day, every day the fair was on. Last year and this year were the first times he had missed going to the fair in 51 years. "I used to catch the train at Nelson at 2:50 a.m., go to Raleigh and stay all day, coming back home at 1 a.m. to shave and get fresh clothes and shine my shoes, so I could go back."

Smiling, Page said to the reporter, "I guess you're too young to have heard the old song, 'Too young for sleep, I've got no use for sleep.' That was me, too young and excited to think about sleep."

Then Page sang the song, giving his wife credit for teaching him how to sing. "She was a music teacher too," he said.

He said he used to spend most of the day in Durham when he came to see a picture show. "Then I caught the train to Nelson, at 2:50 a.m.," he said. "It was Train 22 and the trip cost 25 cents. During the depression the fare was cut to 14 cents."

Page said he remembered arguing with Capt. Coble, the train conductor, about wanting to ride the train from Durham to Brassfield. "He said, 'Do you mean I got to stop this train for just a 5-cent fare?' I told him I wanted to get there."

"And he did it after I promised to get him a real good watermelon," Page said.

"That was the time it cost a dime to ride to Bilboa. A lot of folks don't know where Brassfield and Bilboa are located."

Page said he looks at television but "can't keep up with it." He has difficulty reading the newspaper, even with a magnifying glass, which he says hurts his eyes. "I just turn up the radio," he said. His housekeeper, an amiable Mrs. Allen, smiled. "He wants it real loud," she said.

Page, who frets because of diabetes which he has had for 22 years, said, "I just don't like a hearing aid. Can't even find any shoes large enough for my feet. I weighed 265 pounds for 30 years when I worked hard. Now I'm down to 195 pounds."

Page still votes. He has been a member of Cedar Fork Baptist Church since 1901.

An Ex-Rounder Says Hooray for Old Days

There were two swimming pools in Durham—at the old YMCA on East Main Street, and at Lakewood Park, but Joseph Martin Cagle recalls that he swam in Ellerbee Creek and Strayhorn's Pond.

"Strayhorn's in North Durham was just a big spring in the side of a hill, concealed by a clump of trees. We swam in our birthday suits," he said recently.

Now 72 and retired after a career as a construction worker, horse trainer, sign painter, and export shipping clerk at the American Tobacco Co., Cagle says he doesn't like the changes in Durham.

"It makes you sad and mad, the things which have come about in a city which once had leadership and pride," he said. "I believe we have fallen behind other cities of the state which once were not even in our class."

Cagle was born in Durham on Dec. 28, 1904. "The doctor delivered me at home. That's the way a lot of us came along at the time."

Reminiscing, he said, "Claiborne Rochelle, one of the older boys in North Durham was a leader and my ideal. We were a gang of rounders, Claiborne, Reid Latta, Floyd 'Bulldog' Latta, Hick Riggs, Johnny "Bo" McCowan, Henry Deadman and myself."

Cagle said that an Italian operated City Ice Cream Co. at Five Points, North Durham, and sold ice cream cones for a penny. There was also Colcough Grocery Store, Spain's Meat Market, North Durham Drug Store operated by L. C. McDonald, a grocery operated by "old man Kadis," and a barber shop operated by a black man named Streeter.

"I remember as a boy seeing 'Bulldog' Latta with his head shaven during the summer," he said. "I went to the barbershop and told the barber that I wanted my hair cut just like 'Bulldog's.' When I got home my mother cried. It was Christmas Eve."

Laughing, Cagle recalled a preacher named Monk, who would get intoxicated and ramble up and down the street, wearing a long coat and mumbling. "He looked like an undertaker," he said. "None of us boys bothered him."

Rochelle, Cagle said, "was a regular Hercules, he was so strong. Many a time I saw him pick up the front of an automobile and turn it around so it would face the wrong way. The police learned that the drivers weren't parking illegally, just that Claiborne was around. His father, L. S. Rochelle, was a tough one too. They once declared his hands to be dangerous weapons."

Grinning, Cagle said that Claiborne's sister Wylanta married several times, once to Brodie Duke. "Brodie had a Thomas Flyer automobile when he was courting a woman. While he sat on the porch with her, his chauffeur, a man named Lucas, would take the kids in the neighborhood for a ride, sometimes to Eno River. He drove real fast on Mangum Street which was unpaved, leaving a plume of dust, and usually made it to the river 5½ miles away in 5 minutes."

Fire horses were pretty well trained in the days before trucks, and when the fire bell rang the horses stood still while the harnesses dropped down on them, Cagle said.

"There were only two fire stations at the time. One was on Mangum at the corner of Holloway Street, and the other was on West Main Street in a portion of Liggett & Myers Tobacco factory. One of my uncles was a fireman, and Dennis C. Christian was fire chief. He had a bell in his house and it would ring there at the same time an alarm sounded," Cagle said.

While living at 821 N. Mangum St., Cagle said he had "a great time" lighting the gas light atop the poles on the street before the gas company employee made his rounds for that purpose. "We boys had a lot of fun running behind the streetcars, jerking a rope which pulled the trolley wheel off the wire and stopped the car. It sure kept the conductor and motorman mad with the kids in North Durham."

Cagle remembers well old North Durham School on North Street. He said that one of his teachers, Mrs. C. C. Warren, lived in a house across the street from him. "She was plenty strict. I carried her books home from school a couple of times, but when I found this didn't improve my grades, I quit carrying the books. I figure she thought I would," he smiled.

"A man named Gwinn was the principal, and he was followed in this post by Miss Lilly Jones. I transferred to Fuller School on Cleveland Street, and Miss Maggie Holloway was my new principal."

Cagle said his father, Jim Cagle, was first a constable and then a policeman under Chief Freeland. "My father became sergeant, which made him next to the chief, really something in those days."

Taylor Cheek and Edgar Cheek, Saul "Sullie" Mason, and several other fellows had an orchestra which sometimes played at North Durham School, he said. "I think Miss Minor, the music teacher, played the piano for them at the school," Cagle said. " 'Sullie' later played and sang for Kay Kyser's band."

Cagle recalls the first airplane he saw. "I took a ride in it right away. It was a homemade biplane with a Ford T-Model engine. The pilot had flown for our country during World War 1. The landing field was a field off Roxboro Road."

Laughing, Cagle said the pilot was arrested after he had flown over the baseball park in East Durham, causing fans to jump and fall from the bleachers, and the players to hug the ground. "I remember there was a big sign with a painted bull on the park fence in the outfield. Anybody hitting a ball which hit the bull sign during a baseball game got $25," he said. "There weren't many players who did it. The team, you know, was called the Durham Bulls because Durham was famous for Bull Durham smoking tobacco and a bull was the emblem."

Cagle said the Durham YMCA basketball team was simply fabulous, beating college and semi-pro teams regularly. One of the victims was the fine team, the White Phantoms of the University of North Carolina.

"We played football right where the Brodie Duke premises had been on Duke Street at Durham High School. Basil Watkins later better known as an attorney, was the volunteer coach. We called Paul Sykes our '60-minute fullback,' " he said.

Cagle said that his math teacher, H. E. Nycum, loved to talk about the notorious Jesse James. He said they were friends and we liked to listen."

Grinning, he recalled that Claiborne Rochelle's mother raised chickens and cows in her backyard, and would walk her cows down Mangum Street, which was dirt, her bare feet kicking up dust and the cowbells ringing. "She also had a pig pen on Trinity Avenue, and Claiborne and I would pull a barrel of slops on a two-wheeled cart to the pen. One time he turned the barrel of slops on me. He said it was an accident and I couldn't argue with my hero, the strong man," Cagle said.

He remembers that when he was delivering meat for Spain's Market, he didn't relish going to the Wilson home on Mangum Street. "The Wilsons had a clothing store downtown, which was nice, but they also had a big, old goose which would chase me when I opened the gate to deliver the meat."

"Run-around swings" made of long strands of cotton from Pearl Cotton Mill and tied to trees were sources of fun, too. "They once made a movie of Durham. I wasn't in it but my goat was," Cagle laughed.

Policeman W. B. Burgess operated a street sprinkler owned by Durham Traction Co. (later succeeded by Duke Power Co.). "There was a big tank of water on the streetcar body which Burgess used to wash the streets," he said. "Four of us boys worked on this contraption, handling the levers. We often doused people when we saw they were not looking. It really soaked them. Burgess didn't like this, or so he said. He later became captain of the Durham Police Department's detective bureau."

As a boy he said he saw company D, an artillery company drilling along Mangum Street. "At the start of World War 1, Company M, infantry, was almost wiped out by Company D in France," Cagle said. "It was a mixup in orders. My cousin Charles Wills of Company D was the only man in his outfit not to come back home. He died of pneumonia."

He recalled that the night before the Durham boys left here to go to war they gathered at the Academy of Music. "A fellow named Pickard, one of the soldiers, danced a clog on a platform, and Jake Nurkin imitated Charlie Chaplin. They were good, and people threw money on the platform for them," Cagle said.

"As the train pulled out of the station, Barney Puryear, the bugler, stood on the rear car, playing his horn. It was quite a patriotic sendoff."

Cagle said he was painting signs for a contractor in Miami when a hurricane hit, making up his mind to move elsewhere. He left. That was in 1926. "I was rambling around in Columbus, Ohio when I got a job training horses. The fellow I worked for taught me the trade and I liked it," he said.

After similar jobs in several other states he returned to Durham in time to join his brother and several other friends for a trip to New York to see the Jack Dempsey-Georges Carpentier fight.

He later worked for Frank Barfield, auctioneer, painted signs and assisted in real estate sales. Then he was employed at the American Tobacco Co. where he remained until retirement.

While working for Barfield, Cagle was lead singer in a quartet, composed of himself, Charlie Cash, tenor; Charlie Barfield, baritone, and Plez Pickard, who played a bass horn instead of singing bass.

He married Thelma Watson in 1929, and they have three children: Mrs. Carolyn C. Cox of Durham, Mrs. Betty Jo Griffin of Jacksonville, Fla., and Charles N. Cagle, who recently returned to Durham from Saudi Arabia, where he was superintendent on a job for J. E. Jones Construction Co., of Charlotte. The Joseph Cagles have 10 grandchildren.

She Cherishes Past and Watches Present

Mrs. Lyda Moore Merrick cherishes the past, but she is attuned to the present and the changing world whets her curiosity. She says that when you get beyond 80 "it begins to make you shiver," so her age is a private matter.

She is the daughter of the late Dr. A. M. Moore. She says he and her father-in-law, the late John Merrick, were good friends and both men died at the age of 59. "They were in the prime of life and if they had had all the medicines and scientific know-how available now, perhaps they would have lived longer."

"My father was the first black medical doctor in Durham and was the second in his class to graduate from the Leonard Medical College of Shaw University in Raleigh," Mrs. Merrick said.

She said that in the late 1880s he "tried to get things started in Durham where there was next to nothing. He was a farm boy from Columbus County and my mother, Sarah McCotter Dancy Moore of Tarboro, was a school teacher."

Mrs. Merrick, the widow of Ed R. Merrick, said that his father, who owned three barber shops in Durham, recommended that Moore come here to cast his lot. "They were as close as brothers."

Dr. Moore and John Merrick founded the North Carolina Mutual Life Insurance Co., the Stanford-Warren Library, and several other institutions. Merrick-Moore School was named after them.

"Mr. Washington Duke loved John and took him on several trips. John would shampoo the Duke women's hair," Mrs. Merrick said. "My husband Ed as a boy would play with Ben, Buck, and Angier, Wash's sons."

Mrs. Merrick went to Whitted School, which at the time had nine grades. Then she attended Scotia Seminary in Concord. It's now called Barber-Scotia. Next she was a student at Fisk University in Nashville, Tenn. "Back in Durham I taught music for five years, and in 1916 married Ed in White Rock Baptist Church, right next door," Mrs. Merrick said.

Laughing, she said, "I remember that in 1911 Papa bought a T-model Ford. It was really something."

She said, "We always had a lot of company in my parents' home. C. C. Spaulding (the late Charles Spaulding, a Durham bank executive), my father's nephew, lived with us for a while. His first job was that of a bus boy at the old Carrolina Hotel. Papa had sent for him to come here and help with the insurance company which papa and John Merrick were setting up in papa's office on the site of the present courthouse. The location then was called Kemper's Corner, the corner of Main and Church streets."

Mrs. Merrick said she still has some of the company's early day stationery. "I didn't ask papa many questions. In those days children were supposed to be seen but not heard. Papa was gone most of the time because he was an old fashioned family doctor who made night calls," she said.

Mrs. Merrick said her father-in-law-to-be started building a house for her and his son Ed as soon as they became engaged. "So, after the ceremony we moved in at 906 Fayetteville St. There was no honeymoon. Papa and mama lived at 606 Fayetteville St., and John Merrick lived at 506 Fayetteville St.," she said.

Ed and Lyda Merrick had two daughters, Constance (Mrs. Charles Watts) of Durham, and Vivian (Mrs. J. J. Sansom), whose husband is a banker and lawyer, lives in Raleigh.

"My husband died in 1967. We have four grandchildren," Mrs. Merrick said.

Recalling the old days, she said that when she was a girl, Fayetteville Street was unpaved, "a horse street," and Durham was "just a hick town."

Mrs. Merrick said lamp lighters came around every day to light the street lamps, and most everybody's children had to pump water and get wood for cook stoves and fireplaces.

"When I was born the county line ran through our house. Papa had a farm right where the Stanford Warren Library is now located. The Fitzgerald brickyard was right across the street from our home," she said.

"I can see Richard Fitzgerald, with his four sons on a wagon, going to work. He educated his five daughters, but not his sons," she said. "Robert was blind, but a smart man who had been a school teacher and a lecturer. He is the grandfather of Paula Murray, who wrote 'Proud Shoes.' She is a good friend of mine and was here from New York this summer. She is also a top lawyer and recently studied for the ministry, although now 67."

Mrs. Merrick said her father and John Merrick were instrumental in getting Duke to build Lincoln Hospital, and her father started the library in Durham in the basement of White Rock Baptist.

"Papa in the old days did surgery on the porch. He sewed up wounds and pulled teeth and handled about anything that came along," she said. "They called him 'Daddy Moore.' "

Remembering the old nurses at Lincoln, Mrs. Merrick said, "Julia Latta and Miss Cotter gave their lives to the hospital. They were that dedicated."

She said that her father would take his children by buggy on his Sunday rounds, some of them into the slum areas, where he pointed out that some people had to live poor. "We enjoyed going to the Fitzgeralds' home place which occupied an entire block in the Chapel Hill-Duke Street area. They had an estate, but we loved most of all his grape arbors. Durham is so cut up now it's not easy to place exactly where the house was located."

"We were't rich, but we had plenty to eat. Mama stayed home to raise the family and to help those who found a place under our roof. One was Dan White, related to Congressman White, way back in the Reconstruction days."

Mrs. Merrick said she had a happy homelife as a girl and young woman, and was always busy in school.

"After marriage Ed wouldn't let me keep my music pupils, telling me that he could support me. But I hated to give up my pupils. I had one of the first music classes in Durham. I also played the organ in White Rock Baptist and at St. Joseph AME I played the violin, and in my early years was a member of an orchestra."

"My daddy had the biggest Sunday School in Durham. He always said, 'Wash your feet and come on to Sunday School.' He was the first superintendent of Sunday School at White Rock."

Mrs. Merrick said her father owned an organ when he was married and her mother learned how to play it without an instructor. "Then he bought a piano. Mama had a good voice, too. They still have a class at White Rock named after papa. At first it was the 'Dr. Moore class,' but following his death they named it the 'Moore-Kennedy' Class, because W. J. Kennedy took over the class."

Besides being a musician, Mrs. Merrick is an artist. She has given most of her works away, but some of her pictures remain in her home. The latest is that of Jimmy Carter, complete with a peanut.

She is reluctant to discuss her many achievements, but it was she who devised the first braille publication for blacks in the world. It was first published in June 1952. It is printed quarterly and is a 78-page magazine which is free to the blind. It is called the Negro Braille Magazine.

"I would get material anywhere I could," Mrs. Merrick said. "I'd try to use what I thought would be interesting to me if I were blind. I've written about outstanding black people, such as Martin Luther King, and I once dedicated an issue to Mrs. Eleanor Roosevelt."

She said the emphasis is on black history, and there are excerpts from such periodicals as Ebony, Jet, and Essence. "I was responsible for the operating costs of the magazine. Clubs put on drives for needed money to publish, and in my younger days I did so many things to get operating expenses. The Federation of Women's Clubs in North Carolina adopted us as one of their projects, giving us $500 a year. Ed would often dip into his own pocket to help. I would say, 'Ed, we owe this to the Lord. We have been a healthy family and we are saved to serve.' I feel that our people could help. The blacks sought to support the project. There are several black millionaires, but I haven't been successful in getting their help."

The present subscription list numbers about 400. "We have a board and Josephine Clement is chairman, but I still do what I can for it. John Washington has added a feature to the magazine, 'The Reader's Right.' He is an assistant editor, because we can't read braille."

Washington, now about 55, and blind, has three children and a blind grandson. His wife also blind, is a teacher.

Mrs. Merrick said Washington was the blind infant who was abandoned at Lincoln Hospital 55 years ago.

"Nobody wanted him, but everybody at the hospital loved him, and so did we and several others. The late John Scarborough named him John, after him, and the baby's middle name, Cotter, came from head nurse Pattie Cotter. Later, Washington was added."

"There was a fire at the hospital and we took the baby into our home. After going to several foster homes he entered the school for the blind at Raleigh, and later took a masseur course in Chicago. Now he is a professional masseur at the Durham YMCA. He has always been smart. His wife Ruth is very skilled. I tell her, 'Ruth, you have an eye in every finger.' "

"I became interested in starting the magazine because I have a great deal of respect for the blind. They don't call it a handicap, just an inconvenience."

Mrs. Merrick has been a member of St. Joseph AME Church for 55 to 60 years.

She uses a magnifying glass to read, listens to radio and television, and "keeps up with things."

Halloween Once a Mad Mardi Gras

Shove off Christopher Lee, Boris Karloff, Bela Lugosi, Mr. Hyde, and Frankenstein's monster. Transylvania is off limits today.

The headless horseman, ghosts, witches, bats, black cats, hobgobins, and evil pumpkins are back for their annual frenzy.

T'is Halloween, come shades of night with spooky moans from the grave and satanic screams from Halloween past.

Halloween, the old folks used to warn, "is a time to stay home with your shades drawn and with cotton in your ears and sit in your porch chairs and swing inside the house."

An occasion christendom inherited from the pagans, Halloween is shortened from All-hallows-eveo." It is the night of all witches which the church transformed into the "Eve of all saints."

Way back when this writer was a wee lad and attending a Halloween carnival at old North Durham Grade School, bobbing for apples floating in a big wash tub of water was exciting and challenging.

A little boy almost choked trying with his forehead to wedge an apple against the side of the galvanized tub so he could sink his teeth into the fruit and extract the prize. Then he persuaded his father to try it.

A crowd gathered. The papa reluctantly removed his coat, got down on his knees and leaned over the tub. His head submerged, he went for an apple.

Alas! When he attempted to bite into the peeling his false teeth fell out and clunked mockingly against the bottom of the tub.

Sputtering, dripping, and highly embarrassed, he rescued his teeth with one hand and grabbed the elusive apple with the other. I can hear the crowd laughing, even today.

Years ago, in the 1930s, Halloween was a devilish if not hellacious time in Durham town. Stores were decorated in orange and black and in some windows were large painted cardboard witches stirring up a fiendish concoction in big black cast iron pots. Menacing bats and spider webs, glaring jack-o-lanterns, black cats, gruesome pumpkin heads, corn stalks, and weird sounds that sent shivers through young passersby made everyone aware of the day.

Wagon wheels over uneven street pavement conjured up thoughts of an approaching headless horseman or a skeleton.

Main street from Roxboro Street to Five Points (Muirhead Plaza), was blocked off when darkness came. Avalanches of humanity descended on downtown Durham. Costumes and masks and makeup of every description, and worn by young and old, created a colorful conglomeration.

The sounds were musical, deafening, and almost frightening. The city's anti-noise ordinance took a bad beating. There were cowbells, sirens, trumpets, whistles, drums, washboards, and even forbidden fireworks. It was bedlam which came every October 31, and the furor stirred up was enough to drive a self-respecting goblin, ghost, or witch back into his or her habitat.

Store windows and car windows were scrawled with soap, chewing gum was stuck on car door handles, car horns and door bells were primed, and garbage cans were overturned, dragged along the street and abandoned. The Bull City's mad Mardi Gras took over.

Many years there were queen and king contests and costume judgings and prizes awarded. This all came after the romping, pushing, shoving, and patting came to a conclusion on the main drag.

Manning Place adjacent to the Durham Auditorium (Carolina Theater), which had been swept clean and sometimes slickened-up by cheap talcum powder or flour, became the scene of street dancing to live music.

The scene was repeated on Pettigrew Street from McMannen and Corcoran Streets.

The downtown street celebration was welcomed by police who figured the hell-raising would be so isolated that neighborhood mayhem would lessen and complaints to headquarters decrease. But that wasn't altogether the case.

There were still mischief-makers who wreaked havoc in most all sectors of town. They prowled around thinking up new ways to do it while continuing the old play of exchanging chairs and garbage cans, some of which they placed atop trees and posts. Gates were taken from their hinges, door bells rung incessantly, dead cats gift wrapped and left on porches, pet dogs and cats painted, buckets of water placed over doors, outhouses overturned, and messages and pictures chalked or painted on sidewalks.

There were many false fire alarms and police calls, flying sacks of water, powder, and homemade confetti.

For the more sophisticated there were charity balls at the Washington Duke Hotel and the Malbourne Hotel. Of course there were spook movies. The Duke University band or orchestra often played on the courthouse steps or at El Toro Park (Durham Athletic Park) where the mayor crowned the queen and king of Halloween.

On more than one occasion hairdressers and store clerks came to work dressed for the Halloween flavor.

Trick or treat finally arrived here and the "small fry" took over the play. World War II calmed things down on the home front and the special street programs went out, much to the approval of the police.

The Church Overflows as Her Friends Say Farewell

It was the kind of a funeral service only the very good could anticipate. Union Baptist Church on N. Roxboro Street was overflowing. The tributes were beautiful, the music inspiring.

Mrs. Josephine Omega James Knox, 71, who died last week, was described by the Rev. Dr. Grady D. Davis as "a most unique combination of faith and work."

He said she was "the manifestation of the Book of James which illustrates very vividly that in order to be saved you must demonstrate faith and work. I believe Sister Josephine Knox was the personification of both."

Known simply and affectionately as Jo, Mrs. Knox had been cook and governess for more than 40 years in the home of the E. M. Camerons in Hope Valley.

Cameron, who for about 47 years at Duke University was coach of basketball and football and athletic director, said, "She was a dedicated, lovable, and gracious person who had a way of making people happy."

In the Cameron home, Jo cooked for the greats of the sports world, well-known entertainers, political figures, and countless friends at Duke University and Duke Hospital.

But more than that, Cameron said, she was "an inspiration to everyone who ever knew her." Dr. Lenox D. Baker, who in the early days was trainer for the Duke football team, said Sunday, "She was Durham's ambassador of goodwill."

Union Baptist was overflowing. Those on hand included the Cameron family and friends from Charlotte, Burlington, Kinston, and Morehead City.

Dr. Davis said that "so many people were so deeply influenced by Sister Knox. You can even see something, feel something, by her presence in the casket in the aisle. I want the family to take courage and share together something in the legacy of this great woman."

Dr. James T. Cleland, dean emeritus of Duke University Chapel, speaking in behalf of the Cameron family, said, "It seems like I've been their private chaplain since Christmas, 1945. That's when I met this wonderful woman, Josephine Knox."

"What I remember most about Josephine was that she hugged you so tight in her greeting that it nearly cracked your ribs. I was glad she taught me that tremendous affection," he said.

Dr. Cleland said the Camerons remembered her "not as a cook, but as the pulse, the conscience of the family, who loved them and the church.

"Mrs. Cameron said her last note from Josephine was to thank her for a new

Bible. Already she may be teaching cooking in that celestial place. Josephine was so unique, God broke the mold when He made her."

Deacon Jake Sowell, "a pillar" of Union Baptist, spoke of Mrs. Knox's work in the church. "When she first came to the church many, many years ago, she said she wanted to buy a broom and start helping out. She put up money for floor and wall tile, bought a rug for a dedication room, saying she didn't want her name mentioned. She gave often for various projects, always telling me, 'you know how to fix it.' "

Dr. Davis said Mrs. Cameron had asked him for help in establishing a memorial in the memory of Mrs. Knox.

"She said Jo was a real, intimate part of the family—saw the children born. It's no secret that when a Christian lives a life like that it means something," the minister said.

Mrs. Lucille Fuller was called on to sing a song in Jo's memory, and as the sweet words to "When the Gates Swing Open Let Me In" filled the sanctuary, sobs were heard.

Testimonials from Frank Alston, principal of Hillside High School, and from Dr. Davis in behalf of his congregation were read and "Amens" resounded.

The choir sang softly "Over My Head," and fresh tears fell. It was hot in the church and women used programs to fan themselves and to stifle moans while men mopped wet foreheads with their handkerchiefs and dabbed their eyes.

"I am touched by this service," Dr. Davis said. "I now have a stronger feeling about death."

At that moment a loud clap of thunder muffled his words. Lightning flashed sharply and rain began falling heavily.

Dr. Davis said he had seen the partially handicapped Jo "pulling herself along with two canes as she made her way down an aisle. I'd say, 'Let me help you.' She'd smile and shake her head. 'No, I can make it,' she'd say. If I had been in her condition I think I would have stayed at home. Not her, she had faith and kept working."

The outside storm grew louder. "Don't worry about it," Dr. Davis said, "We're in the hands of God."

Turning to the casket, he said, "Thank you sister in that aisle. You did a lot of good, touched a lot of people. God called you to come up, to come up, that you'd done enough down here."

Dr. Davis told his audience that he would give the final services in the church and that they would not have to accompany the casket to Beechwood Cemetery in the rain.

However, before the body was laid to rest, the sun burst through as if on schedule and gave Jo a triumphant departure with bright shafts of gold that lighted up the sky.